GAMBLING
FOR LIFE

*"Harry Findlay has lived a gambling life like
no other – full of wild highs and desolate lows.
He and Neil Harman have done justice to this
rollercoaster life with a book as unflinching
and honest as it is gripping and entertaining"*

– **Donald McRae, The Guardian**

HARRY FINDLAY
GAMBLING FOR LIFE

WRITTEN BY NEIL HARMAN

Sport Media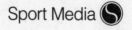

*"You're born, you take shit.
Get out in the world, you take more shit.
Climb a little higher, take less shit, 'til one
day you're up in the rarefied atmosphere and
you've forgotten what shit even looks like.
Welcome to the layer cake, son."*

– Michael Gambon as Eddie Temple in *Layer Cake* (2004)

I dedicate this book to the 2014 Australian NRL Premiership-winning South Sydney Rabbitohs:

Kirisome Auva'a, George Burgess, Luke Burgess, Sam Burgess, Tom Burgess, Beau Champion, Jason Clark, Bryson Goodwin, Greg Inglis, Alex Johnston, Luke Keary, Apisai Koroisau, Ben Lowe, Isaac Luke, Cameron McInnes, Chris McQueen, Nathan Merritt, Nathaniel Neil, Joe Picker, Joel Reddy, Adam Reynolds, John Sutton, Ben Te'o, Lote Tuqiri, Kyle Turner, Dave Tyrrell, Dylan Walker and coach Michael 'Madge' Maguire.

Other great teams and sportsmen have made, changed or shaped my life, but this group of men saved it.

Sport Media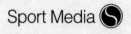

Copyright © Harry Findlay & Neil Harman

The right of Harry Findlay and Neil Harman to be identified as the owners
of this work has been asserted in accordance with the Copyright, Designs
and Patents Act, 1988.

Written by Neil Harman.

Paperback edition first published in Great Britain and Ireland in 2018 by
Trinity Mirror Sport Media, PO Box 48, Old Hall Street, Liverpool, L69 3EB.

www.tmsportmedia.com
@SportMediaTM

Trinity Mirror Sport Media is a part of Trinity Mirror plc.
One Canada Square, Canary Wharf, London, E15 5AP.

1

Hardback ISBN: 978-1-910335-60-4
eBook ISBN: 978-1-911613-01-5
Paperback ISBN: 978-1-910335-88-8

Photographic acknowledgements:
Harry Findlay personal collection, Tony Woolliscroft, Mirrorpix,
PA Images, Getty Images, Adrian Sherratt, Mark Cranham/Racing Post Photos.

Editing & Production: Adam Oldfield
Jacket design: Rick Cooke

Printed and bound by CPI Group (UK) Ltd, Croydon, CR0 4YY.

Contents

i.	*Acknowledgements*	9
ii.	*Introduction: The Alchemist*	15
1.	The All Blacks	27
2.	The Young Philosopher	42
3.	Taking The Wrong Card	61
4.	Doing Bird	78
5.	Starting Over	99
6.	Las Vegas Or Bust!	126
7.	A Fellow Traveller	137
8.	Big Fella Thanks	145
9.	The 13th Man	180
10.	You Win Some…	194
11.	Horses For Courses	213
12.	Asian Handicap	248
13.	Warning Off	267
14.	The Trying Game	289
15.	You Couldn't Make It Up	312

Harry's Reflections: The sports stars that made a difference 343

i. Acknowledgements

I have written about professional sport since I was 16 years old. It is safe to say that in decades of newspaper work, able to brush shoulders with so many personalities and indulge in adventures, stories, scrapes, staggering emotional highs and lows, meeting triumph and disaster, I haven't come across anyone quite like Harry Findlay.

He was first in my company when, on a fake pass, he gatecrashed a tennis press conference at the 1986 Pretty Polly Classic at the Brighton Arena, sat in the front row next to his mum and asked a question of a very young Steffi Graf.

Subsequently, I would see Harry at tennis events – Monte Carlo on quarter-final day with a glass of champagne in his hand springs to mind – and wonder who the hell he was. Amid physically honed athletes, he did look a little incongruous.

HARRY FINDLAY

One day in Melbourne in 2007, we talked at length and discovered we had something much in common, a fixation with so many sports – I wrote about them; he bet on them.

It wasn't easy to persuade Harry to engage in this enterprise. He has told me a hundred stories – many of which I initially thought were too far-fetched – but as the months went by, I realised that for him to have done all that he had in his life, a total and utter adherence to the truth was vital.

When I first discussed the project with him, Harry was suffering, and in that respect, we were brothers. He had spent his last brass farthing trying to resurrect British greyhounds and I had lost a job that was a consuming passion. We were both in a bit of a tailspin. This has been a cathartic venture for the pair of us.

The fact that Harry has been with Kay for almost three decades speaks volumes for her remarkable patience. And devotion. People who gamble to Harry's extent don't usually have – or keep – a partner. To Kay and his daughters, Jade and Ella, a tip of the hat for being so nice and normal.

To Harry's mum, Margaret – who is a remarkable character – and younger brother, Gordon, special thanks for their time and reminiscences.

When we set out, we didn't know how many people would participate, but the response was overwhelmingly positive. A debt of gratitude is owed to Will Beedles and Paul Dove at publishers Trinity Mirror Sport Media for believing in us. It has been an interesting ride as I'm sure they will agree! To Adam Oldfield, also, for his meticulous editing and revision.

Harry has an incredible network of friends and acquaintances. The loyalty of Glen Gill, Jim O'Rourke, Frank Harvey, Grant Devonish, 'Fat' Barry Pennery, Bradley Montague, Julian

ACKNOWLEDGEMENTS

Snow and Alex Williamson is without equivocation. Julian Richards and Alan Farthing told some lovely stories of Harry in his youth. Claude Thompson has to be the most gracious ex-armed robber I'm ever likely to meet. Thanks as well to Bob Webb, general manager of Coventry dogs, for his valuable contribution.

Eamonn Willmott, an old friend of both Harry and mine for many years, spoke eloquently, as did the redoubtable Philip Davies, the Conservative MP for Shipley, who I was delighted to see returned to Parliament this year. Andrew 'Chubby' Chandler was his usual effusive self. Thanks, Chubby.

I've twice been to Clonmel, Co. Tipperary, for the Irish National Coursing Meeting, and met a load of remarkable people, especially the O'Driscoll family from Skibbereen – Curley; Denis; dad, Noel; and mum, Nora – who took me under their wing and fed me from their table. Thanks also to Denise Lyons for her translation skills, 'Fierce' Pierce Connolly for his company, and to all at the Jeremiah Moynihan pub.

Eddie Donnelly and his brother, Terry, gave me a fascinating insight into the betting world, and their sandwiches! To Pat Morris at the Brighton House, Clonmel, grateful thanks for the terrific hospitality and especially the white puddings. Hope to see you all again in 2018!

From the world of horse racing, there was nothing other than warm hearts and warmer expressions. To Paul and Marianne Barber, Anthony and Angela Fortescue-Thomas, Clare Balding, Brough Scott, Brian Meehan, Sir Mark Prescott, Sam and Guy Sangster, Tim Vaughan, Barney Curley, Mick Channon and his sons – Michael and Jack – Claude Charlet, the *Daily Mail's* Marcus Townend and Lydia Hislop, a heartfelt thank you. I sat down with the legendary jockey Sir AP McCoy and met the equally legendary Denman. That doesn't happen very often.

I appreciate the fact that Tony Bloom gave up some of his time, and his acknowledgement regarding the Asian Handicap chapter.

If there are a couple of regrets they are that I didn't get to meet Big Fella Thanks. He was clearly an incredible beast. Veterinary surgeon Andrew Chivers spoke movingly about the dog's final moments.

And I truly wish that Alan Lee, a longtime colleague from *The Times*, who was a wonderful man and fabulous writer, especially on horse racing, was still with us to have seen this project come to life. He was a staunch supporter of Harry's and believed a real injustice was done with his warning off. Alan would have been more than a little rib-tickled at the thought of Harry and I in collaboration.

Harry had a decent relationship with many in the racing media. Among Alan Lee's colleagues, we are especially indebted to the quality of the work of Greg Wood of *The Guardian*, Chris McGrath of *The Independent* and Peter Thomas of the *Racing Post*. Donald McRae of *The Guardian* writes beautifully on anything. Matt Chapman, now ITV Racing's betting expert, and Jeff Stelling, such an outstanding stalwart on Sky Sports, offered their unequivocal support.

In the past few years, I've seen Harry on high highs and at low lows. My wife, Maureen, and I were once invited to his box at Royal Ascot and were stunned at his generosity and fervour – though I'm not sure Maureen ever forgave him for taking our frugal winnings and 'investing' them on some donkey at Kelso that barely broke into a canter.

ACKNOWLEDGEMENTS

I tried to come to terms with the complex world of gambling, though I rarely indulge myself and won't start now that we have completed this stage of the journey.

Of course, this book couldn't have been written unless Harry engaged fully, and there were times he doubted he could. But as the winning line approached, he finally got the bit between his teeth and his only regret was not being able to mention two unbeaten equine superstars, namely Frankel and Black Caviar. When 16-time world darts champion Phil Taylor was told about this venture, he exclaimed: "I'd better be in it, I saved his life twice!"

That's not far from the truth, but even 'The Power' didn't make Harry's Reflections at the back of book. It only goes to show that, as I realised halfway through this journey, Harry has enough material to fill three books. Probably half a dozen.

NEIL HARMAN,
AUGUST 2017

"And what if I had lost heart then?
What if I had dared not to risk it?
Tomorrow, tomorrow, it will all be over!"

– Fyodor Dostoyevsky, *The Gambler*,
originally published in 1867

i. Introduction

THE ALCHEMIST

Harry Findlay was 16 years old when he looked down at the betting slip in his hand, ran it through his fingers and never wanted to be parted from the sensation. He said it was as if he had been handed a free pass to the Magic Kingdom. He has been in the costly thrall of that magic ever since.

The allure of a simple piece of paper would open for Harry an absurd, compelling, one-off, once-in-a-blue-moon lifestyle. He rubbed shoulders with princes and sheikhs, lords and ladies, bookmakers and kingmakers, and connected in a telepathic way with sporting stars on whom he gambled sums large, small, and more times than he cared to count, life-changing.

Harry was never one to worry about a rainy day – "Otherwise, what do you do when there's a monsoon?" he said. He had a wonderful time spending his money and does not expect to be pitied because he indulged it. He chose the life. "All I used to get told as a kid was: 'Never a borrower or lender be' – do me a favour," he said. "Fifteen minutes later, the same people would go to the bank and borrow £120,000 over 25 years to pay for a £23,000 house!

"When you're traveling around the world, you're winning; when you can't afford a decent bottle of wine, you're losing. When gambling goes wrong, it's a terrible thing, but a gambling man's word is worth ten times the word of any so-called businessman. In business, if you do a bad deal, you move on and do more bad deals; but if you're a gambler, it's such a small world, everyone knows if you're a wrong 'un. Gambling is full exposure, there's nowhere to hide."

Harry was baptised into the thrill of the gamble at the John Hampden Grammar School in High Wycombe, Buckinghamshire, by Eamonn Willmott, a fellow pupil, who was a bit of a playground legend. He was the best there was at 'pennies against a wall'. Harry watched in awe and couldn't wait to have his turn. The pair have remained friends from those days of adolescent adventure. Willmott said: "Harry's an alchemist. The force you picked up from him was his absolute love and passion for every element of gambling. There is no one in the world quite like him."

Harry Findlay has lived entirely on his own extraordinary wits, an innate ability to spot a champion and to back those instincts with hard cash. He has run with the hare and been chased by the hounds. In the early years it cost him his freedom, more recently his integrity, and when the crisis was at its worst, almost his sanity.

THE ALCHEMIST

Now is the time to tell his tale. It is not one without blemish. He has not pleased everyone. He knows he has not always been a saint. Telling it from the extremes of his point of view did not sit well, especially when he entered the gentrified arena of horse racing. But Harry's moral compass has sustained him through the rough and the smooth. He is honest, opinionated and very plain-speaking. He could not have gambled the way he has without being straight with himself and the many people – punters and non-punters alike – whose paths he has crossed in four astonishing decades.

"When I was bang under pressure as a gambler between 16 and 19, driving my Mum and Dad mad for readies and then robbing Peter to pay Paul in order to have a bet, Sundays were always a day for reflection," he said. "Thirty-five years ago on the Sabbath, there was nothing to bet on, and all you had for teatime TV was Harry Secombe on *Songs of Praise*.

"One Sunday evening, all I was wishing for was that by the time Harry was back on the following week, I wouldn't have to, nor would I, tell any more lies. Sure, I wanted to have more money and still be in the game, but most of all, no more lies. Once you tell one, you've got to tell another one. It was a catastrophe for your brain, and as a gambler, you can't have any brain damage. I'd told enough lies before I was 20 to last a lifetime."

The stories that unfold here are all told with the self-deprecating sincerity that is Harry's hallmark. Even when he was winning fortunes, he never took himself too seriously, though if his good name was impugned, he would challenge those who did it without reservation or a backward step.

Ask those who have spent most time in Harry's company for

a single word to describe him and if the first one they use is almost always 'loud', the second is invariably 'generous'.

***

In these pages, you will read how Harry fell in love with greyhound racing on his first night at Slough dog track; the credit card fraud for which he was imprisoned; how he turned his life around winning the lion's share of £2 million betting on the newly-formed Asian Handicaps through the 1998 World Cup; took the Irish hare-coursing world by storm; became a member of the Australian cricket team; wagered and lost £2 million on a single rugby tournament; co-owned one of the greatest of Cheltenham Gold Cup winners; fought for his good name after an unwarranted warning off from horse racing; tried in vain to preserve the British greyhound industry with his own money; and how a simple, signed Rugby League shirt saved him.

Barely a waking moment in his adult life has gone by without Harry thinking about where he would next score. Gambling is an addiction – a dangerous one. You don't have to tell him that. He has never been a follower of convention, just his own conviction. He knows the odds as well as anyone, has worked them out as well as anyone, and in the billion-pound frenzied competition of today's computerised betting world, he has trusted to his own remarkable judgment.

He always knew he had the nerve, the patter, the instinct and the nous for picking more winners than losers, and backed that with his own (and other people's) money in the absolute belief that he knew the true odds.

THE ALCHEMIST

This book is for all of those who have entered a bookmakers' premises, heart going pit-a-pat, shuffled nervously towards the counter and pushed a scrawled note and a fiver across the desk, trying not to make eye contact with the person behind it for fear they had recognised a mug punter who wouldn't know odds-on from Sod's law.

It is for those who have spent hours poring over newspapers pinned to the wall, been captivated by the commentaries from the rows of TVs, and clung to the belief that the next bet was the certainty of which they dreamed.

It is for those who thought that they can handle the pressures and discovered – often at an awful cost – that they couldn't. Harry's life has been an exception, because he did what he did and survived. For many more people than we care to imagine, gambling cost them all that they had. There are many tragic cases where individuals lost so much money they couldn't live with themselves any more.

The next race or the next match could make or break, and they came every half an hour of every day, every week, every month of every year. Imagine your life depending on that? Harry's did, and still does. And while this book will chart and challenge the extremes of his lifestyle, he tries to use it to educate the 'ordinary' punter as to how best to play the odds.

For anyone who has ever made a bet, has lost a bet. Harry certainly has. But there are not that many who bet as much as Harry, as often as Harry, as emphatically certain of himself as Harry, as indulgently as Harry.

In his youth, he mucked out kennels and hired out tools, he worked part-time for City Index and talked himself into a newspaper column on greyhounds and a stint as a Sky TV commentator, but he never had a real day job. These were time-fillers. As a kid needing ready cash because there was a dog he had to back, he once persuaded a potential employer that he was a dab hand at hod carrying. After five minutes in agony, he realised he couldn't even raise the bricks off the ground, let alone over his shoulder and up three flights of stairs.

He quit there and then. "I got the biggest bollocking of my life that day, on a building site in the middle of nowhere." Harry's life was not meant to be one spent in physical labour.

In so many ways, he is larger than life. He will swear like a trooper one minute and the next indulge in the most sincere acts of generosity, which hardly befits the recurring image of the gambler as someone who thinks only of themselves. He has loved nothing more than for others to share in whatever good fortune has come his way.

Many of the stories he relates will seem too far-fetched to be real but are readily endorsed by his friends and sportspeople – some of whom tell more outrageous tales about Harry than he can remember about himself.

It has taken a lot of strength for him to engage in this enterprise – an uncharacteristic show of restraint brought on by the decision of the British Horseracing Authority in 2010 to disqualify him for six months on the charge that he had – in layman's parlance – backed horses in which he had a personal stake, not to win. "They ruined me, they took my life away," he said.

He will go to his grave believing the inquiry was nothing more than a trap designed to bring down a personality who had grown too noisy for the high society patrons in the upper echelons of the Sport of Kings. But he has been able to bounce back, starting from the bottom and building once more on nerve and gut instinct.

A lot of people who play sport have taken Harry under their wing, told him their troubles, their weaknesses, their foibles, though as tales of match-fixing have taken stronger root in recent years, so professional athletes under constant forensic scrutiny have been less inclined to want to be seen in the company of someone who they know will have wagered money on them.

Harry called it the 'Hansie Cronje Effect'. Before the late former South African cricket captain was implicated in match-fixing allegations and subsequently banned for life from the sport, a number of sportsmen Harry had befriended were more than happy to let him mingle with them and share their secrets. It has become very different these days, less open and far less fun, much like the world of gambling.

To bet significant sums now is not just a matter of using one's instinct – the distinction that has marked Harry out so decisively across a range of sports – but by following carefully manufactured algorithms designed by companies who employ computer geeks hunting in packs, where every sport is televised. And when the action stops, the screens are flooded with advertisements which have (very successfully) made gamblers appear like people you would like to share an afternoon with. They are almost to be admired.

Tap. Tap. Boom! There goes your life, son.

Harry speaks of his devotion – personally and financially – to Roger Federer, Tiger Woods, Martina Navratilova, Lester Piggott, Jimmy 'The Whirlwind' White, Frankie Dettori, South Sydney Rabbitohs from the Australian Rugby League, the

New Zealand All Blacks, Big Fella Thanks (Ireland's celebrated coursing greyhound), Denman (the legendary Gold Cup winner from 2008) and many more.

To have got to know and bet on these stars were the moments when he was truly free, bigger than life, and in his very special element.

When the BHA's decision robbed him of that freedom, he was crushed. He would resolutely turn his back on horse racing, a sport in which he was beloved by many but sneered at by the hierarchy. A lot of them wanted rid of him, and they got their way.

He has always been unmistakable has Harry Findlay. In recent years, he has dispensed with the youthful trappings of grandeur. The loud, lairy coats and the hat subtlety tipped at an angle of his teenage years have been replaced by a polo shirt habitually hanging loose outside a pair of shorts and open-topped sandals. He will climb into the passenger seat (he has never driven a car in his life) and you become immersed in the day's ups and downs.

There never seemed to be enough air in his lungs for Harry to complete a sentence, for the words spilled out like ketchup from the nozzle when you have turned the bottle upside down and tapped on its base.

It is not easy to keep up with Harry once he gets started. A big, effusive man with plenty to say and never, it seems, with quite enough hours in the day to tell you all his stories. He will start on one and then a memory is stirred and he'll go off at a hurtling tangent about a horse's colours he's suddenly recalled, or a specific dog on a specific night at a specific track over a specific distance.

The stories will flow and he will be amazed at his own

powers of recollection. He rarely requires recourse to a fact-checker. They come out in a jumble – the odds, the weather, the opposition, the journeys, the rises and the falls.

When he did break the law, he had a lot of fun doing it. But in the end, he couldn't wait to get caught. The stories that unfold about his time at Her Majesty's convenience at three of this country's prisons are riveting, haunting and often amusing. If you had told him when he was sent to HMP Brixton in October 1983 that, within three decades, he would be in the executive box at Royal Ascot next to The Queen's and would own two winners at the meeting, he would have dismissed the notion as entirely too fanciful, even for someone with his imagination.

Today's Harry Findlay has had to eschew the five-star lifestyle he once enjoyed. He knew it would not last forever, nothing does in the perilous, surrealist world he's inhabited. The days of being lauded for owning a great racehorse, a feted greyhound, for knowing how to play and exploit the Asian Handicap as well as anyone alive may be gone, but he is not yet out of the game.

He said: "I live in a modest home now, but I'm still winning. I'm surprised. Two years ago, part of the reason I was so depressed when I lost everything and thought there was no moves left was I didn't think I could still win.

"Johnny 'Lights' Herndall, a great gambling philosopher, said when you get over 40, you automatically start to lose your arsehole. It's a lot harder now the computers are taking over. But I still win. Even if I run out of money, I sell something else and I start winning again.

"I don't want to sound flash, because I'm going to take great joy in this book telling people how many times I've been skint. It's not being skint through gambling. Yes, short term I might have a terrible weekend, a terrible week and sometimes a terrible month at the most. One of my sayings is that when you're doing well and winning, you're never as good as you think you are; but when you're on the floor, you can't pay the rent, you're starving, you think you're a complete arsehole, you're not; you're a lot better than you think you are.

"Just because you've won a few million over a period of time, doesn't necessarily mean you've always got loads of money, especially when you're buying horses or lending people stuff all the time. I've made a lot of mistakes but my philosophy has always been that you can't have it back.

"Even as a young lad I used to read the obituaries in *The Telegraph* and go to the bit about how much money they'd made. Surely it would have been more interesting telling us how much they'd spent. When Warren Buffett dies, he'll be worth over $80 billion, but he's spent less than $2 million. I'll have 80 pence in my will and have spent £20 million. Who do you think got the maths right?

"I'm 55, my missus is 48, and sure I'd like to get some more security for Kay and my two daughters in case I keel over. We've done so much travelling and so many things, we don't need tons of money. If I had all the money in the world now, I wouldn't own a horse or a racing greyhound again, I've never driven a car and I don't want to live in a big house, so all I really want money for is to turn left on the plane and carry on fine dining. Everything is relative, and that's the great thing about being a gambler.

"When you're used to an exuberant lifestyle, you can't change completely. I spend a lot, lot less than I did, but I still want to have Eggs Benedict three times a week. I still want to go and do what I do and, touch wood, that's never changed. I'm now an absolute expert on Riojas at under a tenner, and Macon has always been the best value Chardonnay in the world anyway, so I haven't suffered too much!

"But if people are going to open this book and be happy that I've gone skint, forget it. I've never been able not to do what I wanted to do and no one is better at juggling money than me. I ought to be in the fucking circus."

Exactly 150 years on from the publication of Dostoyevsky's novel, which the Russian wrote to a strict deadline in order to pay off his gambling debts, it is time to enter the mind of another man who always dared to risk it all.

1

THE ALL BLACKS

No one knew what to say. Most couldn't speak anyway. The drinking had long since stopped. Half-empty glasses stacked up. Harry Findlay was too busy screaming for the All Blacks to go for a last-ditch drop goal to notice exactly what his pals in the corporate box at the Millennium Stadium were doing.

Nearing the bitter end of the 2007 Rugby World Cup quarter-final in Cardiff between New Zealand (upon whom Harry doted) and France (not the opposition he had been expecting to see at that stage), it was clear that the £2.5 million he had wagered on the All Blacks had gone.

Paul Barber, a Somerset dairy farmer, co-owner with Harry of a very special horse called Denman and one of the invitees for the night, had seen a lot in his life but struggled to relate to the atmosphere in the glass-fronted area that isolated the Findlay party from the rest of the world.

"For months before the match, all we heard about was this great gamble of Harry's. As the match wore on, you could just tell the French were going to beat them," Barber said. "I'd never seen a sight like it – grown men so distraught. Some of them were crying! We dispersed very quickly at the end. I couldn't take it any longer."

The final shocking score was France 20, New Zealand 18. Harry had done his bollocks and, as a consequence, had brought a lot of people down with him. "It was the sort of atmosphere you had to escape from," he admitted. "If I'd been an innocent bystander, I'd have wanted no part of it either."

Harry, as usual, felt more for all those he had persuaded to part with their cash on the All Blacks than he did for himself. Everyone in the company had sacrificed a lot of money – the shock was palpable. But Harry's loss absolutely dwarfed anyone else's.

His whole life had been shaped by the need to bet, and here he was, at 45 years of age, knowing that the largest sum he had placed on the outcome of a single sporting event was in someone else's pocket rather than his. More than half of his entire worth had been obliterated.

Regardless of the manner by which the mighty New Zealanders had fallen foul of the flaky French (the conclusive try was shaped by an illegal forward pass), Harry was suffering. How could anyone, even someone as unrelentingly positive as Harry Findlay, possibly recover from such a catastrophic blow?

"I was asked dozens of times in the aftermath what was it

like to lose £2 million on a rugby match," Harry said, "but it was difficult to explain. I remembered many times when defeat was harder from both a mental and personal finance point of view. This was a different kind of pain, and with it the general numbing realisation that I'd cost a lot of other people money as well."

***

A gambler attracted polar opposite characters, with very little fudging in the margins. Harry knew them as 'the funkers' and 'the begrudgers'. "The funkers wanted you to win; the begrudgers hoped you'd lose. A or B, simple as that," he said. "Charlie, who helped look after our garden when we lived in Bath, was a funker."

Charlie the gardener – Harry never did know his surname – tended the sprawling Rowas Lodge landscape a couple of times a month, trimming the lawn and shaping the trees before popping into Harry's office for a cup of tea and the latest gambling gossip.

Invariably, talk would turn to the bets of the moment, and if the discussion centred on a horse, Charlie said he would follow it with interest, though mostly with support more moral than financial.

"Now and again I said: 'Charlie, this is a nap, have £20 or £30 on,' and he would, but in general he was happy enough just cheering them on for me," Harry said. "Bath is one of the few towns in England where a pub is more likely to show rugby union rather than football, and like most men in the area, Charlie knew his rugby union.

"When I kept harping on about what absolute moral certainties the All Blacks were to win the 2007 World Cup, he didn't disagree, and, like me, he was a fully paid-up member of the Dan Carter fan club. Carter was the best fly-half in the world – we all knew it.

"About a week before the tournament began, Charlie asked what were the best odds available on the All Blacks. I said that the Corals price of 4/7 was the way to go. I thought no more of it until I walked into my office the following morning and found a big frozen ice-cream tub on my desk.

"There was no mint choc chip inside, just £28,000 in ice-cold cash. After my missus, Kay, drove me into town as quick as she could, I swapped it for a betting slip, which was Charlie's voucher for his £28,000 to win £16,000 on the unbeatable All Blacks."

***

Eamonn Willmott woke on the day of the match and was gripped by a sensation of nausea. "I was going to go to Cardiff but I had a weird feeling about the day – as if something not good was going to happen," said the man who first introduced a 13-year-old Harry to the rudiments of gambling. "I decided to pull out of the trip. All of Harry's winnings over the past year had just been doubled up. He'd win 50 grand on a horse, then another, and it would go straight on the All Blacks."

On the train from Bath to Cardiff, Harry was doing what he did every day, on his mobile betting the horses as the journey unfolded. There was nothing different in his demeanour, he was the usual upbeat, confident Harry.

New Zealand were rugby union's unstoppable force in 2007.

Every reliable signpost acknowledged the likelihood of a black-shirted romp through the World Cup. They possessed in Carter the world's pre-eminent player, a fly-half of consummate handling skills who had radar in his boots, especially when it came to kicking goals.

Very few punters were backing against New Zealand taking the cup home, but when it came to supporting them with hard cash, no one was more convinced of their tournament-winning potential nor endorsing that judgment as extravagantly as Harry.

"In 2003, I had a hefty bet on them to win the tournament, but I was far from all-in," he said. "I was a bit of a Carlos Spencer fan, the fly-half before Carter. He was brilliant, an extrovert performer. If the All Blacks were winning, he'd do his tricks – kick a ball over the other geezer's head, run around him and catch it. He was a showboat. But if you wanted to win World Cups, he was a liability.

"I likened him to Titus Bramble, the old Newcastle United centre-half. He was a decent player was Titus, but whenever you watched him defend, you knew it was only a matter of time before he'd commit some reckless act. Spencer was the same, an improviser.

"It was 0-0 in the 2003 semi-final against Australia, he had the ball and wanted to do something clever, so he threw an arrow pass crossfield on his own 20-metre line. With New Zealand on top in the early stages, you couldn't have had imagined a worse time to take such a liberty.

"Stirling Mortlock made the easiest of interceptions and suddenly the Aussies were 7-0 up. It quite simply changed the tempo of the game, put the All Blacks on the back foot and the Aussies ran out winners, 22-10."

The first time Harry set eyes on Dan Carter was when he made his debut against Wales in June 2003. The kid scored 20 points and was a real revelation.

"He played a bit in the 2003 World Cup, but by the time the 2007 event came around, he was like the rest of the team, just about unplayable," Harry said. "The fly-half position seemed even more pivotal in those days. He was the kicker and hardly ever missed.

"I watched a lovely documentary with his modest father, Neville, stood next to the goalposts he'd erected in the garden of the family home in Southbridge. He said that wherever he placed the ball, Dan would make the kick, and talked about just how much his son had practised over the years.

"In the two years leading up to the 2007 finals themselves, I thought the All Blacks were brilliant and timing their challenge to perfection. I also knew their coach Graham Henry wouldn't leave a stone unturned in his quest for the Holy Grail.

"Over that period of time, I effectively used the All Blacks via Betfair as a high-profit bank account. They may have been 4/7 when the competition started, but I'd managed to have £2.5 million at the average price of 1.78 [just under 4/5]. It was the bet of a lifetime and, for sure, financially it would have put me in a very strong position. To be honest, as much as for the money, I was looking forward to the buzz of cheering them home."

What Harry – and the legion of friends he told to back the All Blacks with as much as they could lay their hands on – had not bargained for was that their opposition in the last eight would be the tournament hosts, France. He had expected it to be Argentina, but the South Americans exceeded expectations by topping their qualifying group which meant that France, runners-up to them, would play New Zealand, the runaway winners of Pool C.

It was the one element of the day that kept nagging at him. New Zealand against Argentina was a nap; the French could throw a giant spanner in the works.

Even then, as stories of a niggling injury to Carter began to surface, it was hard to find many in the Millennium Stadium who could see any other result than an All Blacks victory. They had romped through their group, scoring 309 points and conceding a mere 35. Their play radiated confidence and the team looked buoyant to the point of being unstoppable.

"It did start to go wrong a bit when Argentina beat France in the opening match of the tournament. I thought: 'Aye, aye, this is a bit naughty,' but the Argentinians played really well and won 17-12," Harry recalled. "Maybe then, yes, I should have by rights have cut it [his stake] down by five or six-hundred grand, which I didn't – although I made up for it at half-time in Cardiff."

That the quarter-final would not kick off until 9pm, served only to extend the nervous anticipation which gripped the group throughout the day. Harry's box at the Millennium was at one end of the stadium, slightly to one side, giving the throng inside an expansive, diagonal view across the Cardiff pitch. Each of the friends Harry had invited were treated to a welcome bag as they arrived, inside which one of the gifts was a clock in the shape of a rugby ball, to have as a keepsake.

Charlie the gardener was in the company, as were Barber and Paul Nicholls – Denman's trainer, who was in the throes of preparing the chestnut gelding for a massive tilt at the Cheltenham Gold Cup the following March.

Harry's friends and betting buddies Jim O'Rourke, Glen Gill and Alex Williamson, and a few other mates from around the country, were stuffed inside, eager to participate in the extended celebration that would follow a New Zealand victory. In the early stages of the match, the All Blacks were dominant. Champagne reinforcements were being sent for.

"They should have been 14-0 up at half-time, but at 13-3, the enigmatic French had a squeak," Harry said. "I was still smarting from them playing France instead of Argentina, and at half-time I had to go for a Smokey Joe. What made me more nervous was that none of the phones were working in the box."

As he stood outside the stadium, puffing away, seeing that his mobile had some reception and having a doubt or two about the outcome, Harry made a smart call. He laid £600,000 on New Zealand at 1.03 to win the match (which would have cost him only £18,000 had New Zealand won the game) – an investment that would end up reducing his overall loss to £1.9 million from the original £2.5 million.

Carter limped off midway through the second half leaving the New Zealanders in a tactical quandary and the patrons of the Findlay box increasingly overcome by a sense of foreboding. "The thing about France was, even if they were shit, they still had enough ability to put in a good performance. From 1 to 15, they had bits of talent all over the place," Harry said.

"Carter was off, his replacement – Nick Evans – was injured, and no one was prepared to go for the three points. Alex and I worked closely together at the time on all things sporting and we were pleading for the All Blacks to go for the drop goal. We knew the maths, and the probability factor favoured that option, but they seemed compelled to go for the try.

"We were behind one of the goals, not directly, but even from almost head-on you could see the forward pass for the French try. I wasn't even bothered when they scored, I knew it would be brought back."

But it wasn't brought back. The try was awarded. The French were suddenly on their toes, fluent and confident. They had become the immovable object.

In their match report the following morning, *The Daily Telegraph* reflected on the despair and disbelief engulfing so many in the ground, unaware of how much those inside one corporate box were particularly hurting.

"New Zealand regathered themselves. [Richie] McCaw decided to keep it tight. Rodney So'oialo plunged over, but McAlister pushed the conversion right, 18-13. The All Blacks remained on the offensive but could not capitalise. The suspicion increased that Wayne Barnes, the English referee, was not on their side. Then came a burst by Damien Traille.

"His pass to Frederic Michalak appeared forward but was not called by the officials as Jauzion scored with 10 minutes to go. Panic was slowly rising as Jean-Baptiste Elissalde prepared for the conversion that put France 20-18 ahead, ultimately the winning scoreline.

"Fear fuelled the All Blacks as they hammered through the phases inside the French half. McCaw remained wedded to the idea of the pick-and-go tactic that brought So'oialo's try, but the French wall would not be breached. McCaw later confirmed that 'a drop kick was never part of our plan,' particularly since Evans had also been forced from the field. It was plan A or nothing."

Jauzion's improbable (and legally flawed) try brought the pall down on Findlay's company. They knew that was that.

"I should have been a tad more professional in the first place, but I booked the box in advance thinking that New Zealand would have been playing Argentina and it would be a great night," Harry said.

"If Argentina had been the opposition, the All Blacks would have been 1/11 or 1/12, but because it was France, they were five-and-a-half to win one [2/11]. That was a big difference. It was so much about Carter, and he was the best in the business by a fucking country mile. Even now people try to tell me that backing them wasn't the right thing to do. But they were wrong, and there is nothing worse in gambling than the aftertime merchants!"

McCaw criticised tournament organisers in his book *The Open Side*, writing: "I don't blame Barnes, but I do blame the people who appointed the most inexperienced referee on the roster to a World Cup quarter-final between the hosts [Wales staged four matches in the competition] and the favourites.

"My beef wasn't with Barnes so much as with his inexperience. This was his biggest game by far. On the big stage, an inexperienced referee is likely to become so afraid of making a mistake that he stops making any decisions at all. By the end of it, I thought he was frozen with fear and wouldn't make any big calls."

Henry, the All Blacks coach, devoted a chapter – *Train Crash at Cardiff* – in his autobiography to the grievous experience. He went so far as to wonder if an element of match-fixing had been involved, highlighting the fact that in the last hour, his side was not awarded a single penalty.

Anton Oliver, the New Zealand hooker and a student of World War I history, evoked scenes from rather more bloody battlefields. "The feeling in the shed [dressing room] is like no-man's land," he said. "There's a sort of desolate decay and – I don't want to dramatise it – the smell of death."

For Harry it was a familiar odour. "I'd have been happy to die in there with them," he said. "I wouldn't have said a word, and I'm sure it was the same for all of them. I know what it meant to the coach. It probably affected him the most.

"After the match, I was on the train home in a carriage crammed full of cheering Frenchmen. I was in a sort of surreal world. A part of me was thinking about all those London black cab drivers I'd been telling for the previous two years that the All Blacks were a certainty. I must have wiped out half the rank."

Jim O'Rourke was with Harry on that journey, as he had been on so many sporting expeditions down the years. "Harry loved sport, loved it all with a passion," he said. "If you love what you do, you take the winning and losing. If you get one wrong, you've got to get the next one right.

"The All Blacks bet was a long-term project. We knew they were unplayable, we knew they had Carter and we knew they'd win. In those days, it was largely about the kicker. And Carter never missed. We were Dan Carter before we were the All Blacks. He went off injured and then the match was a dogfight. It was like a kind of death at the end. The train ride back was horrible.

"But Harry got up the next morning and said: 'Let's go again.' His mum, Margaret, once said to me that it was never about the money for Harry. Money was a chip and the more chips you had, the better you could play life with.

"The definition is: if you have – and lose – £2.5 million on the All Blacks, you don't wake up the next day wanting £300k on the next thing; you go back to being a professional. If there were two horse bets – one was £200 and the other £300 – that was how he'd stake. It was irrelevant that he lost £2.5 million on the All Blacks. He warranted every race on its merits. He never over-staked."

Four years later and still in thrall of the All Blacks, Harry's wager on a New Zealand victory to win the 2011 World Cup was £230,000 – more than 60% of his wealth at the time – to win £210,000. For the last half hour, as they clung on against the nemesis French in the final, Harry could hardly bring himself to watch. "I was shitting myself," he said. New Zealand won 8-7. Talk about fine margins!

A few days after the match, Harry shared a beer with Steve Hansen, the All Blacks assistant coach who rose to become their esteemed head coach. "I couldn't resist asking him about the last 25 minutes as France continually piled on the pressure, with all of the play happening inside the All Blacks half where the concession of a penalty could well have been fatal," Harry said.

"Steve's answer blew my head off. He said some of the team were laid low with a flu-type virus in the days leading up to the game, nobody more so than Richie McCaw. Steve described Richie's performance as truly heroic and said he had collapsed in his arms after the game as he escorted him across the pitch to the press conference. What a man."

By 2015, Harry did not bet on the outright winner of the World Cup until New Zealand roundly trounced the French 62-13 in the quarter-finals – the largest winning margin in a knockout stage in the competition's history.

"I wasn't blown away by them in the build up to the competition, and to be honest, before they played France, the thing that impressed me most about them was the black boots they all wore," he said. "Even the adidas stripes were blacked out and they looked like an army from the get-go. But they were sensational against their great enemy, and straight after the game, I had almost all I could afford at the time – £11,500 to win £10,000 – on them for the tournament.

"The next day, after reading Matthew Syed in *The Times* comparing their performance with a first-class rendition from a philharmonic orchestra, I had another £3,000, meaning the bet was £14,500 to win £12,500.

"If you'd seen the missus and me dancing around in our tiny front room when Ma'a Nonu powered clear for the try that put the title beyond doubt [the All Blacks beat Australia 34-17 in the final], you'd have thought I'd had another £2.5 million on them.

"But when it was the only £14,500 you had, and you were cheering on one of your favourite teams, that's exactly what it felt like anyway. And I had a small fund to build on again."

Over the years, many people asked Harry why he supported the All Blacks so fervently, rather than one of the home nations. "Most of the time it was because they tended to be in great form or were nigh-on unplayable," he said. But with New Zealand, Harry's devotion went deeper.

"It was all about their humility as people," he said. "A story that encapsulates that happened during the 2015 World Cup, when they had booked into a hotel in Swansea to prepare for their quarter-final against the French.

"They'd played Tonga the night before in Newcastle and phoned ahead to ask the hotel in Swansea two things: that they brought their own slab of beer – as each player was allowed one beer per evening – and they didn't want their own dining room or preferential treatment, but wanted to eat with the other hotel guests."

According to a friend of Harry's who was staying in the

hotel, the All Blacks arrived fatigued after a long journey (their flight was delayed a couple of hours) and the players headed to their rooms. As their luggage arrived in two trucks, the hotel porters were sent to unpack them, only to be turned back by coach Hansen. Within two minutes, the entire squad was back downstairs unloading the lorries, not only carrying their individual kits, but everything else on them as well, before taking their personal bags back upstairs.

"It summed up everything I love about them," Harry said.

***

The tale of the bet to end all bets had always been the one that garnered the headlines, took people's breath away and provoked suggestions that Harry had been reckless – stupid, even. All he had done was recognise a team of all the talents and backed it with as much as he could afford. It didn't bankrupt him.

Willmott, whose early-morning sense of dread was well justified, said: "No one born could do £2 million on a couple of bad calls on a rugby match and not be slightly off-tilt. You have to be at your very best to get back, and you ain't going to be. You just can't do it. You can't trade fearful – you have to be brave."

Harry admitted that recovering from this one would not be easy. "In my lifetime, I've known gamblers take real blows, and this was heavy duty," he said. "Alex Williamson was crying for the last ten minutes of the match. Charlie the gardener had his rack on the match and took defeat like a real man, that's an understatement. He knew his rugby, he knew all about it, he was there, he believed in it.

"Truthfully, part of the reason I had so much money on the

All Blacks was that I was going to slow down a bit if they won," he said. "I had that in my head. Not because of the finance, but the philosophy. I was thinking of my age, my weight; there's a lot of stress involved in this life and I didn't want to keel over. I wanted to look after my health a bit, and that's why I was so annoyed at what happened."

Memories of that night were branded on the minds of the occupants. Alex Williamson, hurting as much as many financially, recalled that, ten minutes after he had left the box, Paul Nicholls suddenly reappeared, looking for the freebie clock he'd left on the table in the middle of the room. "I just remember thinking, given all that was going on, how funny that was," he said.

Harry's partner, Kay, hadn't joined the group in Cardiff, she was used to watching big sporting events on her own and preferred to see the game tucked up in bed with her then seven-year-old daughter, Ella.

"When it started to go pear-shaped, I was really nervous, but at the end of the game, the first thing that came to my mind was Charlie," she said. "Seriously, I just couldn't believe it. He'd worked all his life as a gardener. He came in one day with ice-cream boxes that had been stashed in his freezer with all that money in them.

"I thought: 'Oh my God, that man's life savings have gone.' Then Harry rang and he was just the usual Harry. 'Oh, It'll be all right, we'll survive, we'll come through.'"

2

THE YOUNG PHILOSOPHER

Henry Panther, the Head of Mathematics at John Hampden Grammar School in High Wycombe, was used to getting his own way. Mr Panther's favoured form of corporal punishment against simpering scholars who stepped out of line was liberal use of his T-square against the soft cheeks of their backsides.

As the teacher doled out the weekend homework one Friday afternoon, Harry Findlay spoke up. Young Harry didn't think logarithms should be taught as part of the maths curriculum. "Excuse me, sir. What do we need these for? Surely arithmetic and algebra are separate subjects," said the 13-year-old. It was his *Oliver!* moment.

A hush descended on the classroom, but Mr Panther – "a

Winston Churchill lookalike who drove a big old-fashioned, fat Saab and frightened us out of our wits," according to Harry – resisted the urge to brandish his emblem of torture this time. Perhaps he saw the algebraic logic in his pupil's logarithm argument. Maybe it was because he had a grudging admiration for the boy.

Mr Panther had caned Harry on his first day at senior school, when the teacher walked into the classroom just as a satchel was aimed at Alan Farthing, a former junior schoolmate who happened to be sitting next to him as the desks were occupied in alphabetical order.

"I knew I was going to be whacked," Harry said. "He was standing at the door looking like the Fat Controller in *Thomas the Tank Engine*. Henry Panther enjoyed the fact that he could do it, and if he had the hump, he could really hurt you."

Alan Farthing would go on to become a highly successful businessman. Harry knew that would happen. "His dad took Alan and me to see *Bambi* at the cinema, and Alan had a real go after because I was in bits, crying at the story. I knew he'd end up getting chunks. He was a bit of an animal. If I picked one bloke in our class to succeed, it was Alan Farthing."

Maybe if Harry had listened more intently in commerce lessons he could have earned a regular income in a manner less taxing than the one he ultimately required to make ends meet. The commerce teacher was also happy to administer leather to skin if pupils didn't do what he expected of them. "He used to say at the start of every lesson: 'Findlay, Tapping and Westland, and anyone else who hasn't done their homework, step to the front of the class,'" Harry said. "He had this real hard shoe. I guarantee all three of us got it before every single lesson."

His teachers never knew quite what to make of Harry. Kids with a streak of independent thought tended to have that effect. In his first set of monthly exams, Harry finished seventh in his class. The next month he was 22nd and realised he was not going to be a scholar. 'Let them have it,' he thought of those kids who took their education terribly seriously. Harry would be in category '3D', the lowest stream, along with Tapping and Westland. He never completed a single piece of homework. He never actually started one.

From the age of 13 and his first clash with Henry Panther, it was clear Harry could not be a slave to formality. "I was a bit of a philosopher even then," he said. "Maybe a little early to fully appreciate the meaning of life, but I kept a diary from then until I was 16. I wanted to write everything down. The entries were personal and honest, and at the end of every day I would give that day marks out of ten.

"In my third year, Wednesday was maths, German, maths, double physics, followed by French. We had double games at the end of the day to look forward to, and if that was rained-off – and it always seemed to rain on a bloody Wednesday – the evening was shit TV and listening to Radio Luxemburg. That was a definite zero out of ten."

The nine-and-a-half out of ten days were usually Saturdays, when Harry scored for Hithercroft Colts in the morning before sneaking off to Stamford Bridge to watch Chelsea, or walking to Loakes Park for a Wycombe Wanderers home game and was back in time to take a girl to the pictures or the disco. Though he was a regular at Chelsea matches, Harry never paid the fare to get there, nor the entrance fee into the raucous Shed End.

There was one particular bolshie inspector who worked the

line from Buckinghamshire into the West End, but as soon as he was spotted, Harry would leap off at the next stop and wait for the following train. "Most of the inspectors ignored 14-year-olds, but not this old bugger," he said. "Nowadays you try to go through a barrier without a ticket and fucking alarms go off everywhere. I think back now and wonder: 'How did we get away with it?'"

From High Wycombe via Marylebone to Fulham Broadway, then a short walk to the ground, Harry mingled with the crowd, saw a friendly face, asked if they minded if he came in with them and squeezed through the rusting, heavy metal turnstiles not parting with a penny. "Everyone did it," he said. "Not once did the geezer on the gate say I couldn't go in. I saw Ray Wilkins make his debut against Norwich – I was 11. All that long hair he used to have. Everyone thought he was a God."

The first and only time Harry was robbed was in the adrenalin-soaked forward rush of humanity when Chelsea scored five times against Hereford United at the Bridge in 1977. After one of the goals, Harry went to reach for his wallet and realised he'd been buzzed. From that day to this, he carried his money in his front right trouser pocket and vowed never to own a wallet.

His local team, Wycombe Wanderers, were a long way off their current Football League status in the 1970s. The first time Alf Findlay took his son to a match under lights against Enfield in the 1968/69 season was an incredible experience. An Isthmian League club back then, Wanderers were eligible for the old FA Amateur Cup, and in 1974, were drawn away to Evenwood Town (now Spennymoor Town) from County Durham. A cavalcade of five coaches left the gasworks 50 yards from the ground at 5pm the night before the match and reached their destination at 9am the following day. Harry was 11 years old and travelling alone. He was lost in the magic of it all.

"I needed permission from my parents to go, and I had to graft my balls off to get it. I was only 11, but they knew how much it meant to me," he said. "There were all these older blokes around me talking football and nothing else, seasoned Wycombe fans who'd been to all the away grounds.

"Time just flew by, and before I knew it, we were at a motorway café at 3am having a full English breakfast. It was so exciting. We arrived in County Durham just as the shops were opening and all chipped in threepence each to buy one of those old orange Wembley footballs.

"The coach parked under an aqueduct and we played a match – a small five-a-side competition in a field where a bunch cows were grazing – and I was convinced I was the happiest boy in the world. Wycombe won the tie 3-0 and the whole experience had a marked effect on me. We got back to the gas station around 3am. Two older guys were supposed to take me home to Downley but I woke up on the coach on my own and had to walk home. Forty minutes later, I saw a silhouette of my dad outside the house smoking one of his roll-ups. He gave me a right bollocking, but I didn't care. I knew I wanted to be around live sport forever.

"I was proper football crazy. I used to read *Billy's Boots* in *Scorcher* and dreamt of the day I'd have a pair of magic boots. I soon worked out I needed them! If *Shoot* magazine didn't land on the front mat before 9am on a Saturday, I'd go into meltdown. I went on the train at 10 years old on my own to watch Chelsea play Everton. My mate Graham Bullpet was an Everton nut – he loved Alan Ball. He didn't believe that I'd been to the match, so I showed him the programme. I might as well have shown him a million pounds, his eyes were popping out of his head. Chelsea won 4-0, but he just wanted to know what it was like. He said: 'Can I come next time – but my mum will kill me!'

"I couldn't understand why there was no football on TV on a Saturday afternoon. This old fellow in a pork pie hat called John Rickman came on talking about horses and I used to hate him. I said to Dad: 'Can't we get this old sod off? Why's there no football on?' The whole week at school, to me, was about waiting for 3pm on a Saturday to come around. The four walls of my bedroom were plastered with memorabilia. I used to draw football pylons and stanchions on my general workbook at school."

Harry never wanted for anything that wasn't connected with football. He didn't want Scrabble, Monopoly, or jigsaw puzzles. His idea of heaven was his parents buying him the Manchester City away kit of red and black stripes, or Birmingham City's blue shirt with the white panel down the middle. "If I was in charge of Birmingham now, I'd bring that kit right back," he said. "What's the point of being plain blue like everyone else? I was freakish about my football kits and totally freakish about football.

"The only thing I saved for in my life was the fare for the coach trips to watch Wycombe away. I had a little piggy bank and would put pennies into it all the time. I went to Dulwich Hamlet and Walthamstow Avenue, Runcorn and Bishop Auckland, I watched Wycombe in the semi-final of the Amateur Cup against Hendon at Griffin Park where they lost 2-1 and were robbed by the most blatantly bad refereeing decision of all time. Hendon's first goal was two yards offside. I watched more live football than anyone else I knew. Football was everything to me.

"I knew I'd probably never play the game when, during the first week at school, waiting outside Class 9, I saw a kid called Joe Blochel[1] play keepy-uppy for five minutes with a fucking tangerine. From that moment, I assessed that my chances of being even a semi-pro footballer were about eight-million-to-one."

If football had been Harry's obsession since he was five, it was watching two sporting legends from another world that he was mesmerised beyond even his own vivid imagination. "Think of being an 11-year-old and seeing gymnasts Olga Korbut and Nellie Kim working their magic on the beam right under your nose," he said.

"Our school got tickets for the Wembley complex. I walked out after the performance with all these girls and I thought about all my mates, the mugs, at home watching *Nationwide*, *Z Cars*, or some other crap, and I'd been to see Olga and Nellie. They were incredible."

***

Harry – christened Henry McDonald Findlay – was born in Glasgow on January 20, 1962, and his first memories were being taken on the handlebars of his father's push bike to stand and gawp at the planes as they landed and took off from Prestwick

---

[1] *Blochel would sign associate schoolboy forms for Southampton but never made the first-team and had a brief, unfulfilled loan spell at Wimbledon.*

Airport, and staring in wonder at the fire engines as they roared through the streets of the city, the fireman on the steps at the front ringing the bell. Then there was the blue Mallard steam train his dad took him to see at the central station. "It was guaranteed to have been Salvador Dali's favourite train," Harry said.

The Findlay family – father, Alf; mother, Margaret; and younger brother, Gordon – relocated to South Ockendon in Essex when Harry was five. Alf and Margaret were both nurses, Margaret having been one of the youngest people in Scotland to qualify as a matron, while Alf specialised in helping anyone with mental health disorders.

From Essex, the Findlays moved to Micklefield in High Wycombe before settling into a former nursing home in the village of Downley. The wages of two nurses were not going to afford the family a luxury lifestyle, but they never wanted for anything. Alf worked with local children, a lot of whom had Down's Syndrome and who became regular visitors to the Findlay home. "They didn't have negatives, and I learned plenty from being around them," Harry said. "Every Christmas my dad's presents from them would be the same – over a dozen two-ounce tins of Golden Virginia, all piled up next to the tree."

Every summer, Alf and Margaret would make sure they took their sons to the coast for a summer holiday, be it to Tenby, Bournemouth or Yarmouth, where Harry fell in love with the bingo. "I hated the games," his mum said, "but Harry kept winning at it and bringing stuff back to the chalet – frying pans, vases, painting sets… Then he started to enter and win a lot of competitions – bikes for him and his brother and a Roberts radio for his dad. But he didn't win the one he really wanted."

From the moment England lost in the 1970 World Cup in Mexico, Alf and Harry had been saving up to try to raise the money to travel to the '74 Finals in West Germany under their own steam, but worked out it was a thankless task. The only way they would make it was to win something. Harry spotted that the *Radio Times* was offering two sets of tickets and an all-expenses-paid trip to the Finals. He told his dad he'd win, and entered.

"When I got the letter from the competition people, I tore it open, thinking: 'I've won, I've won,' but it was for the third prize – a set of red suitcases. I was 11, right on it, and distraught. Mum kept saying: 'Och, Harry, they're lovely, they're lovely.' She must have kept the fucking things for 20 years."

***

In his first year at John Hampden, at every break between lessons and at lunchtimes, Harry played 'football fives' against the school wall at a penny a boy with his mates. The winner would usually take away around 7p or 8p. By end of the first year, the lads had moved on to 'pitch and toss'.

Eamonn Willmott was in the year above Harry and introduced him to playground poker dice, and it wasn't long before he was in the regular three-card brag school. Harry started to team up with a pal of Eamonn's – Terry Nicholls, a Jack the Lad who was punting mad and knew a fair bit about the horses. Not only that, Terry's father owned the best dog at Slough – Black Fortune. It wasn't long before Harry and Terry would regularly sprint down to the bookies in their lunch hour to place a few bets with whatever cash they could lay their hands on.

Inevitably, the hum from the mother's network reached Margaret Findlay's ears. "I phoned all the bookies in town and told them they were not to serve Harry Findlay – 'You'll know him, he's wearing a John Hampden blazer.' One of them said: 'You don't think he comes in with his blazer on, do you missus?'

"At one point there was a bookie in Marlow chasing him for money because they allowed him to have credit, which they should never have done to a schoolboy. I went over and tore them off a strip. It didn't change anything. Harry had already begun to hitchhike to the dogs in the evenings."

"Mum didn't want me to do any of this kind of stuff," Harry said. "There was never any gambling on her side of the family, they weren't even allowed to play cards on a Sunday at home. Her dad wouldn't have it. She didn't know where it came from with me."

Harry was 15 when he heard that a group of lads from the local Licensed Victuallers' School were going to Newbury races, and they were happy if he came along for the ride. "I didn't know the difference between hurdles and fences, flat or the jumps," Harry said, but he arrived at the course with six pounds in his pocket and ended the day's racing with ten. At the back of the old stand after the meeting, through a haze of cigarette smoke, the boys concocted a plan to go to the Slough dog track that night. Harry tagged along.

"I'd never heard of greyhounds and genuinely thought the lads were mucking around talking about watching dogs race," he said. "We went into the cheap area and I was right at the trackside on the third bend for the first race when the dogs went past. They blew my head off."

Two nights later, Harry snuck on a train from High Wycombe

to Wembley Stadium – "a doddle" – he said, and was there an hour before the doors opened. The thrill of it all was too much. Within a few days, he went from not knowing what the sport was, to finding any way he could to get to as many tracks as possible, six nights a week.

***

Margaret Findlay soon got to hear what her son was up to and vowed to put an end to his latest all-consuming passion. She determined that the only way to persuade Harry that gambling was a mug's game was to take him to a meeting – at the old White City track in West London – in the hope that he would lose all his money and, at the same time, all his interest.

The night it went wrong for her started promisingly enough when Harry lost his entire £4 kitty on the first three races, on which he bet £1, £2 and £1. Harry asked for a loan from his mum. Margaret relented thinking it was the chance to teach him a lesson about not getting into debt. It turned out to be the worst thing she could have done. He turned £2 into £6 before having his last £2 bet of the night on Lordsbury Pride at 11/2.

"He was a massive fawn dog, Trap 5, in a graded S5 race [six bends]," Harry said. "He did the business and made sure I left the track with £17. But the dog that really did the damage to the rest of my life was Balliniska Band. I had four quid at evens to win the highlight race of the night, and to this day I can't remember having seen a dog go faster to the first bend."

Less than 48 hours later, armed with his new-found wealth, Harry placed £2 on Balliniska Band at 20/1 to win the holy grail of greyhound racing – the Derby at White City. He followed that up with another £3 at odds of 14/1 the following week.

In his commentary for the BBC on the Derby final, Harry Carpenter was surprised how poorly Balliniska Band broke from Trap 5. It mattered not, because with his sensational early pace, he still managed to grab a crucial first-bend lead from Saucy Buck and went on to win in a time of 29.16 seconds, equalling Glen Rock's track record. Harry had £85 to bank. "I knew I was a genius from that moment," he said. "And in essence, I was fucked!

"I'll say this, if you take a youngster gambling for the first time and he does his bollocks [loses everything or almost everything], he'll probably walk away forever; but if he wins, you're in trouble. The moral is, if you take a youngster gambling, make sure he does his bollocks."

Alan Farthing, Harry's old schoolmate, did his bollocks on his first night at the dogs and never bet again. He was saving the money he earned working part-time at the local Woolworths and putting enough aside to pay the HP on a moped he wanted. From his £6-a-week earnings, £20 a month went straight into an account for the motor. Then Harry enticed him to Wembley dogs one evening. "Harry guaranteed he'd make me a load of money. The £20 was all I had in the world, and after eight races, it had all gone. I didn't remember Harry having a penny on himself," Alan said. "It was the last bet I ever had."

As tales of Harry's gambling exploits circulated, his notoriety was on the rise. Julian Richards was a year older and decided he had to find out for himself what the buzz was all about. "I heard that this kid was scoring a lot of goals for Hithercroft Colts, and when I went to see him play, he scored a couple of times and claimed a third which hardly touched him as it flew in," Julian said. "He had plenty of front but was no more than a clever – but average – slow goal-poacher.

"Then, one evening, I was at the Wimpy next to the railway station, chatting up a few girls, thinking I was cool. In walked Harry, this kid from the under-16 football team wearing a cowboy hat and boots. I said: 'Findlay, where are you going?' trying to take the mickey out of him. He was off to the reopening of the Rainbow Theatre in Finsbury Park to see Lynyrd Skynyrd. Harry was going to see the biggest rock band in the world and there was me thinking I was cool."

Harry remembered that concert vividly, and not just for the music. "When Lynyrd Skynyrd started to play *Free Bird* and *Sweet Home Alabama*, the place erupted, and behind us there was a great group of 30-year-old birds who all stripped off their tops and got their tits out," he said. "Everybody else was looking at the boys in the band, but I was 15. I couldn't take my eyes off the girls. I don't think Julian ever forgave me for going to that concert, and most of the group, including the lead singer Ronnie Van Zant, were killed in a plane crash just a few months later."

The friendship between Julian and Harry began to evolve. "When he left school, he started to come to the pub and mingle with the older guys, and that's when we really became friendly," Julian said. "He was probably drawn to me more because I had three sisters [Harry went out with two of them], but also I wasn't into gambling at all. At 15, the other guys would flock round him saying: 'Harry, who's going to win the National, who's going to win the Gold Cup?' and if his tips didn't come up, they'd start to have a go at him. As for me, I preferred to talk about music, football, women and beer.

"In the village, some kids thought he was arrogant and loudmouthed. I just saw him as confident, intelligent, interesting, funny and great to be with. A lot of guys in the village didn't want to do anything apart from stay around there. We all played football, cricket, went to the local pub; it was a good life, but Harry always wanted to go to London, Windsor, or there'd be a band in Oxford he had to see. He was always gambling, usually successfully. One time, on his winnings, we stayed away four nights in a row at posh hotels in Windsor, Slough and High Wycombe. After the third night away, I just wanted to go home. But Harry didn't.

"I was doing pretty well at work and was promoted to a junior manager's role. Harry rocked up in a cab one afternoon to tell me he was going to Slough dogs. They called up from reception to say: 'There's a Harry Findlay to see you.' I worked in a nice office, had a big swivel chair and he couldn't believe it. But I was dressed a bit scruffily. The next day he came round to my house with a pair of new shoes and three silk ties. He said: 'If you're the boss, you've got to dress like the fucking boss.'"

***

Harry Findlay and steady employment was a non-starter. He left school at 16 with O Levels in Art and English Language, and his first 'job' was as a kennel hand for Rod Markwell in nearby Marlow for the princely sum of £15 a week. He would only take home one wage packet.

Margaret had to drive her elder son for the 6am start on his first day of real work. Harry, in a tracksuit and wellington boots, popped into the newsagents to buy the *Sporting Life* and bumped into Terry Venables, then the manager of Crystal Palace FC. "He looked a million dollars, sun tan, black pinstripe suit, bright tie, the full works, and he couldn't have been friendlier or classier, so I went to my first day cleaning up puppy shit in a really good mood," he said.

That inner joy did not persist. "Markwell had a dog called UbeTrue – white and black, massive he was, the biggest dog I'd seen in my life," Harry said. "Rod's dad was 80-odd and he used to put a really tight muzzle on the dog at night. Markwell flew at me the next morning and said: 'Why did you put that muzzle on that dog?' I said: 'Look here, Rod. The chances of me putting a tight muzzle on a dog are about the same as me eating that table – I don't want to put a muzzle on any dog.' But I got the blame for it.

"Then I was grooming a pup in the paddock and heard one of Rod's owners talking about a dog he had at Hackney called Telegraph Hill, saying how incredible it was that he had never won a race there. He said he was a right ponce. I piped up and said he won at Hackney in a 683-metre inter-track race against Crayford and beat Blue Angel by a short head. I was there. He normally ran over 523 metres.

"The next day I brought the racecards in and thought Rod was going to tell me what a good lad I was. Instead he turned on me and said: 'You little bastard, you've lost me an owner.'"

It didn't help that the next conversation between Harry and Markwell became another, and ultimately, final argument. Markwell had paid £5,000 for a dog named Joe's Paddy which had won at Harringay, but Harry believed the dog to be no good. He was a 'screw' (likely to turn his head). He told Markwell the dog would definitely let him down. The trainer bristled.

THE YOUNG PHILOSOPHER

The first time Harry went to Oxford greyhounds, where Markwell was a graded trainer, Joe's Paddy went from 6/4 to 4/6 in the market, but Harry backed the second favourite that won. He had a £20 bet to win £50. As he was collecting his winnings, Markwell spotted him, queried his bet and sacked him on the spot.

"What happened to me in one week in the kennels was typical of my life – unbelievable. Mum said Markwell told her he got rid of me because I was only interested in betting and telling him what dogs he should be betting on and that I wasn't interested in clearing up their shit."

***

From a brief spell mucking out the kennels, the next stop was Reldans, a warehouse on the Cressex industrial estate. Their business was woman's clothing, and for Harry it was the best job in the world to try to pull birds. The first time the 16-year-old Harry was summoned to head office, he talked one of the secretaries – a 23-year-old cracker called Sue Parke – into a night at Wembley dogs to bet a certainty in a marathon race.

Eternal Mist was the bitch's name and she was running in the last race. Sue Parke had never been to the dogs before. Eternal Mist was 10/11. Harry bet £22 to win £20 and he persuaded Sue to wager a fiver, but she had to put the money on herself with the bookie.

Arnold Varlet was a stalwart of the trade at Wembley. He always stood at the back of the pitch wearing a pair of cotton gloves with the fingers cut out, akin to those trademarked by Wilfrid Brambell as Albert Steptoe in the hit BBC comedy classic of the era *Steptoe and Son*.

Varlet was in charge of the readies and paying out to the winning punters. His bagman knew the bitch Sue was looking to back and laid her an even fiver. With a typical last to first performance, Eternal Mist duly obliged and the stands erupted. Sue couldn't have been more excited as she stood in line to collect her winnings. Arnold flicked his fingers through a pack of crisp, brand-new £1 notes. "They look lovely," Sue said. "I know," he replied, "I always like to give a good-looking bird clean nickers."

Sue Parke roared like a lion, and a few hours later it wasn't only the readies in his right-hand pocket that Harry had Eternal Mist and old Arnie to be thankful for.

***

Reldans didn't hold Harry's attention for long and the next employment stop was a local mattress factory, Hypnos Limited. Harry couldn't stand the place the minute he walked in. "I was working with all these clapped-out 35-year-olds," he said. "All they did all day was play cards and talk about the latest episode of *Coronation Street*. I found it so depressing.

"When you're 16 years old you're thinking: 'If I have this job for 20 years, I'm going to be sitting here playing cards and talking about fucking *Coronation Street*.' Mum forced me to take the job and I've still not forgiven her. I wanted to be at the dogs. They used to put the beds on a slide from the delivery van and I decided to use it for myself, slid down, ran into High Wycombe and home. I said: 'Never again, I can't have a job like that.'"

Harry's fourth attempt at full-time employment lasted a little longer, the best part of four months. He worked in a tool hire shop where the money they took over the counter as deposits were too much to resist for a kid who had only one thought on his mind – how he could turn whatever he had into a little more.

"The shop would lend out big tools – hammers, cement mixers. These Jack the Lad builders came in and they had to leave a deposit," Harry said. "In those days it was almost always cash, so they'd give you the money that would go into a brown envelope in the till until they returned the tools.

"Martina Navratilova was playing Chris Evert in the Wimbledon final that year. The bookies were going 10/11 one and 10/11 the other, and at that price, I knew Martina was a must bet, so I took £140 out of one envelope and £80 out of another and had it on.

"I was listening to the radio, Martina was up by a set and a break of serve in the second, and anyone betting straight sets obviously wanted her to get it done quickly. The commentator was saying how she would love to get it wrapped up in straight sets, but not as much as me. I was looking out of the front window at the same time to make sure neither of the guys whose deposit I'd used was returning their cement mixer or kango hammer and wanting their money back.

"I won the money on Martina, put it back in the envelopes and no one knew anything about it. I did it a few more times, but I had to come unstuck. It happened the day a dog called Ahtis was running at Manchester White City. I had £140 to win £80. The dog ran just after 3pm and won, but someone came in at 2.20pm to return their tools and I was found out.

"Terry, the assistant manager, didn't grass me up to the boss, to be fair, but said: 'Harry, what have you done? I've gone to give the geezer his £100 back and there's half a dozen sheets of fucking toilet paper in the envelope.'

"I said to myself: 'Harry, make sure that never happens again.'"

It wouldn't. Two days later, he was sacked.

***

Harry's entire life until the age of 15 had been football, football, football. The first time he had a real bet on a horse race was the 1977 Grand National. Until 1976, he didn't know the race existed. "One Saturday, we were at Loakes Park, behind the goal. I was screaming for Wycombe and everyone else seemed to be listening to a horse race on the radio and had all had a bet," Harry said. "The winner was Rag Trade.

"The next year, I was getting into the horses. I backed Andy Pandy to win and was also on Boom Docker, who was 100 lengths clear going into the second circuit and pulled up. Andy Pandy would have bolted up but fell at Becher's second time around. Red Rum won it, his third National."

By now, Harry was finding new places to get to and avoiding the fare. "At 16, I marched into Grooms restaurant on Ascot High Street with my pal Willie Roberts one Wednesday lunchtime, when everybody in the real world was working. We had a lovely starter, a sliced duck breast with cranberry sauce and a fine dessert.

"We came out about 1.30pm, walked across the road to the National Hunt meeting, and as clear as a bell, I remembered thinking: 'This is going to be the rest of my life. I don't want a job, all I want to do is go racing, watch live sport and bet on it.'"

3

TAKING THE WRONG CARD

In the early 1980s, the staff at several Ladbrokes shops in and around London and Buckinghamshire arrived on Saturday morning to open up for the busiest business day of the week, only to be confronted with a recurring problem. They couldn't get in.

As such, there was a regular pattern of calls to local locksmiths who weren't inclined to drop everything at the weekend. It would invariably take a couple of hours for them to arrive and change the locks. Ladbrokes lost a lot of vital trade and the company was furious.

The reason for this massive inconvenience was always the same – the locks had been jammed with superglue. Why was this happening and who was responsible? No one ever found out.

HARRY FINDLAY

***

It was a typical Friday night in the Bricklayers Arms in Downley, High Wycombe, where the 19-year-old Harry Findlay and his mates would enjoy a few pints of lager before heading off for a curry in the town. One such evening, they decided to move on to the Le De Spencers Arms on the common before going for their Indian.

Harry had been at Hackney Wick dogs the previous week and was convinced there was a good thing in a 523-metre graded BAGS (Bookmakers' Afternoon Greyhound Service) race at the East London track the next morning. The fact that the event was on the BAGS service meant that the race was transmitted to all licensed betting shops.

Harry's mates in the 'Brickies' were on his tips as usual, and this time, hearing the lads' animated conversation about the dog in question, several patrons of the Le De Spencers decided to have a few quid on as well.

"My best pal at the time was Dylan Westland, who lived in Marlow Bottom," Harry said. "We were Saturday morning regulars at Sam Cowan's bookmakers in Marlow. We'd heard that Ladbrokes had taken over the shop during the week and didn't envisage having any problem getting on with the biggest bookmaker in the world."

Harry wasn't going great at the time, the £65 he had in his right trouser pocket was all he had to play with, and it was all going on. The bet was bolstered by support from the locals at both the Bricklayers and the Le De Spencers Arms, which meant Harry had a total of £200 to put on the dog.

He was expecting a decent price, and when the dog opened at

TAKING THE WRONG CARD

3/1, he was at the head of the queue at the counter. "£200 at 3/1 on Trap 1, please," he said to the woman behind the desk. "She took the ticket to the back of the office and got straight on the phone," Harry said. "Nearly two minutes later, as the dogs were going into the traps, she walked back to the desk and said: 'We're not taking the bet. We don't know you and don't want to take it.'

"I was in a blind panic. I said to her: 'How can you know me or anyone else, you've only been open four days?' But she wouldn't even let me have a fiver on."

It was audio commentary only in the betting shops in those days, but to make matters worse for Harry, on this occasion there was a fault on the line. 'Telephonic interruptions' was the reason for the radio silence. "It felt like I was waiting for the guillotine to fall," Harry said. "Then it came: 'Trap 1 the winner.' My legs buckled. I felt physically sick. Instead of £260 in my hand, I had £65 that felt like 65p. I had a dose of major brain damage, the like of which I never knew existed.

"Two hours later, two days later, two weeks later, it only got worse. It was and always will be my worst-ever gambling experience. The repercussions were all bad. I hated Ladbrokes ever since."

***

For Harry Findlay's mother, Margaret, thrift was in-bred. The fact that her eldest son couldn't resist gambling with whatever money he laid his hands on was always likely to provoke a confrontation. It didn't help Harry's cause that his younger brother, Gordon, couldn't wait to get home from his first job and give all the money he'd earned to his mum.

Margaret believed she was entitled to rent from Harry, but it was disappearing into the hands of those whose disposition didn't involve giving it back unless they had to – the bookies. "I didn't have it to give her most of the time, and her patience gave out," Harry said. "She tossed me out on my ear."

There were times when he had the cash, but even then life for Harry was never straightforward. In the early hours of one Sunday morning, when Harry was 16, the phone rang at the Findlay home. On the other end of the line was an officer from Gerrards Cross police station.

That night, Harry and his pal Graham Bullpet had turned the £30 they took to London's White City Stadium into more than £200 before the two dogs they had gone specifically to back had even gone into the traps. The pair then had £100 on Inside Straight at 7/2, and when he won, they loaded £220 on White Mercedes – "a beautiful white and fawn dog," Harry said – at 10/11. He shit in. The boys had £750 between them and felt like millionaires.

On the train home from West Ruislip to High Wycombe, as they approached Gerrards Cross, Harry had a brainwave. "Fuck it, let's stay at the Bull Hotel," he said. The pair got off to walk the mile from the station, arrived at the five-star hotel around midnight, approached reception and asked for a twin room. Harry handed over £50 from the bundle of tenners. "I don't think they liked us much straight away, but acted as if there was no problem at all," Harry said.

Harry and Graham were waiting in reception, believing their room was being prepared. Harry was dreaming of the five-course breakfast he'd be enjoying in a few hours when the front doors flew open and two coppers walked in demanding to know where the lads had got their money. Harry opened his White City racecard and was going through the bets race by race when one of the coppers laughed and said: 'Okay, you two, come with us.'

They were taken to the station where they sat until 3.30am, when Graham's dad arrived to get them out. Margaret simply shook her head when she heard the tale. The fact that her son had half of £750 to his name softened the rent problems for a while, but it was only a matter of time before he was hit by a couple of losses and money was tight again. Unless his share was paid, Harry would have to find somewhere else to stay.

"Sometimes, I was away for weeks on end," he said. "Dad would go mad. He used to be my biggest fan and he was worried about me. He would say: 'The lad's probably freezing somewhere,' but Mum was granite. That's the way it went.

"I'd been homeless in London plenty of times after the dogs, you either went onto a bus or to the train station. There were heat panels and you could lie against those and get a bit of warmth. The cops would come around every couple of hours and wake me up. I couldn't understand that and it really pissed me off. I'd say I'd missed the last train home and didn't have anywhere to sleep. Invariably, I'd be pretty smartly dressed. I didn't look like a down-and-out.

"One morning, I was woken by a fella at Victoria station who said: 'D'you want to come and tidy out a kids' cinema?' The place was like a bombsite. I swept it from 6am 'til 9am, but at least that meant I had enough for a bet at Hackney after tea and a bacon sandwich. I permed a couple of winners together, turning it into £70 by the end of the day, and that seemed like an absolute fortune then. I had a Chinese dinner and felt like a king for a day, but it didn't last long. That's what gambling could do for you."

Margaret Findlay remained unrepentant. "I was taught that you worked and gave your parents the weekly housekeeping; I suppose it was a Scottish thing," she said. "I didn't relent. I was determined. But many a night I cried myself to sleep."

It didn't help matters when creditors came knocking on the Findlay's front door. Brian Moore of Derbywise bookmakers in Marlow had allowed Harry to run up a £1,400 credit bill despite him only being 16 years of age, and thus all his bets were illegal. Harry begged his mum to tell Moore to "fuck off," but when a wreath was delivered to the Findlay home, she'd had enough and got a loan to repay the debt. "Brian Moore was a snake," Harry said.

It was a view he had of many bookmakers. Apart from helping out impresario Barry Hearn at the last minute and being the odds-layer for a day at *Fish 'O' Mania I* – the biggest angling event of its kind (where Harry lost over £3,500) – the first time he tried his hand at bookmaking was not only a disaster, but one of the biggest regrets of his life.

Harry had known the Bowler family in High Wycombe since he was 10 years old. Ian Bowler was the Hithercroft Colts' goalkeeper from the under-11s to the under-16s, and Harry was also mates with Ian's older brother, Neil. "He leant me the £400 I needed to buy Kerry Head at the Tralee sales on my first trip to Ireland at 19. I'd never owned a greyhound before; I had less than £20 in my pocket at the sales, but I saw the dog and couldn't resist him. Neil stumped up the money," Harry said.

"The Bowlers were really good people. Their mum died young and the new partner of their father, Joe, was an old family friend called June, an ex-gambler and real character. I thought she was amazing; she helped get me back in the game on many occasions, once ringing me on a Thursday afternoon telling me to come round and pick up a cheque I could take to the butchers to cash so I could go to Slough dogs that night. We'd go 50/50 on any profits. I turned £40 into over £550 in three days. But it didn't always work out like that.

"The big mistake we made was buying the betting shop in town. At 19 years of age, I was far too young and far too eager to back a winner instead of laying a loser. The first day the shop opened, an Irishman called John Kennedy walked in after a hard day's graft as a bodger at a local factory.

"He had sawdust in his eyes, up his nose and coming out of his ears, everywhere. He had £20 with us on a dog at Manchester White City, and as I was listening to the race commentary, I realised I wanted the dog to win. I had no chance of being a bookie!

"The con men soon opened up accounts with us; we paid when they won and got left over when they lost. We wouldn't have lasted as long as we did if Grittar hadn't got us out of trouble when I backed him to win the 1982 Grand National with £200 at 10/1. But it wasn't long before we went under. I disappeared in shame and never showed my face for a while. I don't feel I ever let anyone down a tenth as much as I did the Bowlers."

Harry didn't just leave High Wycombe – he disappeared from the country. No one knew where he was for days until Julian Richards, his old school chum, received a phone call. "Harry was speaking in furtive tones and said he'd been to Yugoslavia," Julian said. "God knows how he got there.

"He said he was at Heathrow airport, but I couldn't tell anyone where he was, I just had to come and pick him up. I was renting a place as my dad had just kicked me out. Harry wanted me to put him up for a few nights, but I couldn't tell anyone he was back. Those few days turned into six weeks. I went to work and he got into my bed and slept during the day. When I needed the bed, he slept on the floor."

Harry's less than complimentary view of bookies, and his desire to beat them any time he could, was formed in those years of teenage hardship and angst. He knew he was good at what he did, but the bookies either couldn't see it or didn't want to know.

"I was a lad who had a talent for picking winners, and a swagger to match, but never once in all those early years did a single bookie take me under his wing or offer me any advice," he said. "They were all so fucking blinkered, they only ever thought of the next race or the next hour. None of them saw the bigger picture. How much realistically could they win off me? Where did they think I got my money from?"

Another local kid prepared to back his own and Harry's opinions with hard cash was Graham Moore. Harry told him about a dog named Dene's Mutt who was running in his first marathon at Shawfield in Glasgow. He'd fallen in love with the Pam Heasman-trained dog after his first race in A8 grade at Wembley, tracked him ever since, and couldn't wait to see his debut over eight bends.

The favourite in the papers was Jane The Nailer, a pace-less Irish stayer who Harry told everyone Dene's Mutt would lap. He said: "Graham Moore and I were walking on Downley Common at lunchtime on the day of the race without a dollar between us when he suddenly said: 'Fuck it, let's sell my car and have it on!' We were at Heathrow less than three hours later and on our way to Scotland. We told the whole track to lump on, and they duly did."

Jane The Nailer smashed out in front while Dene's Mutt missed the break and was behind early. The boys' cash looked in serious trouble until, coming out of the second bend, their dog took off like a rocket and quickly powered clear of his rival to win by four lengths.

It wasn't the only time Graham Moore stepped up to the plate. The pair went to Sheffield for the 1983 World Snooker Championship together, and it was Graham who pulled up much more than the lion's share of the cash in the lads' quest to be able to survive solely on the punt.

It was Graham's mother-in-law Anne who had been keeping Harry in the game on a daily basis anyway. "As Don Cuddy would have said: 'She had a heart as big as a watermelon,' but not only that, she was head cashier at Corals in town," Harry said. "Anne was the best I ever knew for a back price [i.e. getting 7/4 about a horse or greyhound when the show had just gone 6/4]. Whatever Corals shop that Anne was working in was where you'd find me every afternoon."

On the first night at the Crucible, they were on a very young Mike Hallett at 5/2 to beat John Spencer, a former champion. Spencer won 10-7, the money was lost, but Harry had been further smitten by snooker and the characters who played it. "The atmosphere there was unreal. All everybody wanted to talk about was sport and betting. I was in my element," he said.

"We only just survived at the Crucible, despite our nap Steve

Davis doing the business, and then moved on to Leicester. When in Sheffield, it hadn't taken long for us to team up with Willie Thorne – the professional player and gambler – and his team. We found out Willie's best friend was Gary Lineker, and after only three hours at Willie's club in the Midlands, Gary had taken £60 off Graham at snooker.

"Gary was nearly as good on the green baize as he was on the football pitch. He played Graham with a copy of *Shoot* magazine sticking out the back pocket of his Farah trousers. His picture was on the front page, despite being only 22. I quickly learned that Willie was the greatest practice snooker player of all time, and over 20 years later, when Stephen Hendry was unplayable at the Crucible, Willie still spanked his arse in money matches at the matchroom table at Handsworth Snooker Club in Sheffield."

From Leicester, the lads headed to Pontins holiday camp in Prestatyn, North Wales, for the Pro-Am competition staged annually a week after the World Championships. It was a knockout event anyone could enter, and all amateurs got a 25-point start in every frame from the pros.

Harry and Graham's money would be on Willie Thorne. They watched the early rounds upstairs on the public tables where the talk was of a really promising Scouse talent with a distinct haircut named John Parrott. Harry saw the kid win his first-round match 3-1 but admitted he wasn't overly impressed.

Willie Thorne told the lads: "It's all very well these amateurs playing on public tables with cloths like lightning, but when they get through to the last 16, they've got to play on the matchroom tables down here. Then it's very different."

Three days later, Parrott was through to the last eight where his opponent would be – Willie.

TAKING THE WRONG CARD

Warren King, the best player to emerge from Australia since the revered Eddie Charlton, assured the lads that Parrott had no chance. At the same time, Harry was throwing all his money at Dunbeath, a horse ridden by Lester Piggott in the Mecca Dante Stakes in preparation for the summer's Epsom Derby. Dunbeath looked a certainty, but got turned over at York, heaping even more pressure on an increasingly fraught and fidgety Harry as Thorne stepped up to face Parrott.

"I never got pissed, but before that match I'd had a few treble vodka and oranges. I didn't fancy it at all," Harry said. "There were brown wicker partitions between temporary seating, and I kept sneaking a look through at the table. The first two frames were really scrappy. Parrott won a prolonged first frame that took over 40 minutes, and came from behind to win the next. He was 2-0 ahead.

"Everyone knows I loved a frontrunner more than anyone else, so I thought I was done. I was at the bar with Warren King and he was talking like a complete non-gambler. He said: 'Don't worry about it, Willie will go bish, bash, bosh; it'll be all over in an hour, he'll beat him 4-2.' I wanted to strangle him. All I'd heard for three days was about the thin cloth and what was going to happen when he came down to play on a real table, and now, an hour into the match, I was 2-0 down. Willie may have been a great, but he wasn't the best player from behind.

"I had another drink and looked through the wicker fence, praying Willie was at the table. I could see his lovely smart waistcoat, so he was obviously potting balls, and I could hear he was on breaks of 48, 55, 56 etc, so I went back to the bar thinking it was 2-1. When I looked at the scoreboard, I realised it was already 2-1, so it was going to be 2-2. A few minutes later it was 4-2 to Willie, just as Warren King had said.

"That night was the drunkest I'd been in my life. Willie had such a great night with us that he ended up sharing our chalet. When we woke up, he said: 'Fucking hell, I'm playing in half an hour.' He jumped in the shower and I legged it out of the chalet straight to Corals. I managed to have £200 on Terry Griffiths at 1/2. He beat Willie 4-0."

***

The bookmakers of Buckinghamshire and London either didn't possess the imagination to see the earning potential from employing Harry's special mix of cockiness, youthful charm and appreciation of a good bet, or they were simply blind to it. But there was a group of people around the Slough dog track who did have their eyes on him.

Harry was always smartly dressed and had the gift of the gab that made him a target for the credit card con men who, at the time, were concentrating on buying whisky and cigarettes to sell on. It was not a liaison that enthused Harry in the slightest. He got off on the thrill of the race, the tingling sensation of a bet, but the small-time gangsters had a persuasive manner when they made a beeline for the kid with the chat. It seemed to be a decent way to have more readies in the pocket for the next race. And Harry being Harry, he was soon far better at it than those who had taught him how to earn a few bob from a stolen credit card.

"It was murder buying Scotch and fags because, nine times out of ten, no matter how good you were, the staff at off-licences would know what you were up to and you had to be really good," Harry said. "I was the best at it, but at least twice a day I'd end up running out of places, or losing the cards.

"It wasn't for me to be running down Wembley High Street like Allan Wells or being anyone's Joey for very long. I decided to go on my own. Once you had the connections, it wasn't difficult to buy the stolen cards. It cost more for the ones with easier signatures to copy, but I wanted the most difficult ones. There wasn't a signature that I couldn't replicate exactly in minutes."

By this time, Harry was trying to watch as much live sport as possible. The European Open golf tournament was staged at the prestigious Sunningdale course in Berkshire; Harry had first gone there on the opening day as a 20-year-old. He hadn't been on site for 15 minutes and was heading for the practice putting green when Greg Norman, the great Australian player, walked past, and with a big smile, said: "G'day, mate."

"Forget about Rock Hudson or Clark Gable, Greg Norman looked like a real film star," Harry said. "Seeing him stride down the fairway was something else. I was fascinated by the whole day. I loved the huge manually operated scoreboards, the beautiful course, everything about it. The thought of being a caddy seemed like a great idea. Could it be possible to travel around the world working alongside these great golfers and actually get paid for it?"

Harry made sure he was at Wentworth on each of the four days of the World Match Play, a hugely prestigious event in the 1980s. Long before the advent of Sky Sports, and with limited live TV coverage, the tournament was one of sport's biggest turnover betting markets. "The action was unreal, with so many punters turning up to watch it live," Harry said. "Selling

£140 Cashmere sweaters for £70 to punters at the scoreboard was a lot easier than trying to buy bottles of Johnnie Walker."

Dogs were always Harry's No.1 port of call, and more often than not he was racing six nights a week. He also enjoyed going to watch the big one-day cricket matches at Lord's, Hove, Worcester and Chelmsford. They were real gamble-fests. "So many of the same gambling faces would turn up at the same events," he said. But it was at the golf where he could really cash in, selling top-quality merchandise.

The daily bet was still the obsession, and it would only be at those times when the punting was unsuccessful that Harry would resort to using the cards. "I only considered it was something to fall back on when I wasn't going well," he said. "There were no qualms – I hated banks ever since my mum explained how mortgages worked when I was 14 and I worked out how much it was costing her to buy a £14,000 house. I knew that what I was doing would only cost the big banks and never the individual cardholder. You really couldn't believe how easy it was in those days.

"I remember one night going out for dinner at least ten-handed, where everyone insisted on paying their share in cash. I managed to put the entire bill on my card without anyone smelling what I was up to, least of all the maître d'. Leaving the restaurant, I realised I'd just been paid over £500 to eat and drink the best food and wine I'd had in my life."

Harry's passion for golf was growing, as were his horizons. He wasn't limiting himself to UK tournaments but was hopping on a plane and heading off to as many venues in Europe as he could reach, whenever he had the funds.

One of the sport's emerging stars at the time was English

teenager Paul Way, who won his first European Tour event – the Dutch Open – in August 1982 aged 19, and was being tipped as a potential Ryder Cup selection for the following year. Harry found himself sitting next to the exuberant Way en route to a European tournament and was amazed that the golfer's passport was three times thicker than anyone's he had ever seen.

"Harry grabbed it off me and couldn't believe all the places I'd been to, he was flicking through all the stamps," Way said. "I realised then he had a thirst to travel as far and as wide as he could to watch sport. He had a massive enthusiasm for life."

Harry knew he'd never have the talent to be a golfer. "Everyone realised how shit I was with a club in my hand, but it didn't stop me teeing off with some of the finest talent in Europe on practice days before tournaments," he said. "The players gave me a one-and-a-half shot start on the par threes. I played Ronan Rafferty on an impossible long-distance downhill par 3 and smashed a three-wood to within three foot of the pin. Everyone on the tee almost died laughing. I enjoyed those days even more than the tournament itself."

There was something about the character, the charm and the colour of golf professionals that Harry felt instantly at ease with. He bumped into Rafferty's fellow Irishman, John O'Leary, on his first day at Sunningdale, as the golfer purchased his evening paper on his way out of the course. "He treated the newspaper seller with so much respect, telling him to keep the change, but in such a classy way. A few weeks later, I was drinking with him and his pals – Sam Torrance and Nigel Birch. They were terrific guys with loads of charisma and living an incredible lifestyle, and it was great just to be a part of it.

"Sam did to me in the snooker room in the member's bar at St Mellion course in Cornwall exactly what Gary Lineker had done to Graham Moore in Leicester. But it was for a lot more money!

"I was a massive fan of the young golfer Mike McLean and I used to bet on him against other players over 18 holes. Sam had his winnings from the snooker victory on somebody to beat Mike, and by the time I got to the course to go around with Mike, Sam's man was already five over par. I'm sure he only wanted to teach me a snooker lesson and not take my money, so played up his profit on somebody he already knew had little chance of winning."

The last tournament Harry attended outside the UK before the credit card net finally closed in was in September 1983, at one of the tour's most idyllic locations – Crans-sur-Sierre in Switzerland, where the two top players in the field were British stars Nick Faldo and Sandy Lyle.

Paul Way had introduced Harry to Faldo in the car park at Fulford golf course, near York, a few months earlier, and his first impression of the Hertfordshire lad who was about to burst into the game's firmament was how intimidatingly huge he was. Harry was clambering from the passenger seat of Way's car as Faldo pulled up alongside. "We got out at the same time and I thought I was stood next to the jolly green giant," Harry said. "He was a monster of a man."

Faldo against Lyle in the closing stages of the Swiss Open was a captivating duel. "I thought to myself: 'All those silly bastards in England working all day long and here I am watching Faldo and Lyle, ten and 11 under par, playing stunning golf,'" said Harry. "I was out on the 8th, 9th 10th holes, there were about

30 people around, and that was where I wanted to be – watching golfers having a ding-dong on a beautiful course. But I had a sense that it wouldn't be long before I had my collar felt.

"That night, we had dinner in the clubhouse. When Paul Way's asparagus arrived, he sent it back because it was cold! The pressure with the credit cards was starting to tell for me and I snapped. 'It's supposed to be cold, you fucking idiot,' I said to him. 'This time last year you'd have been ordering a prawn cocktail and a well-done steak, so don't worry about it.'"

Way didn't mind the admonition one bit: "I was always a confident bastard, but being in Harry's company was never a bad thing. He exuded confidence on a daily basis and was great company. None of us worked out what he was up to until just before he got nicked."

The end of the line would come at the World Match Play a month later. Harry had been to the opening two days of the championship – when most of the betting action took place – and had no reason to expect a tap on the shoulder in the relative sanctuary of the Wentworth members' bar at 5.30pm on Saturday evening.

"I turned round and the second I spotted the crimplene blazer, I knew I was nicked," Harry said. "What did surprise me was after admitting who I was and what I'd done, we walked out of the clubhouse and there were two police cars and four motorbikes all with flashing lights in the car park. I felt like Al Capone."

Paul Way was in America when he learned of Harry's arrest. "I couldn't help but laugh when I found out he'd been stood at the bar next to Nick Faldo and Greg Norman when they nicked him."

4

DOING BIRD

The exercise yard at Brixton prison was hardly Kew Gardens, but for one hour in 24, there was a scent of freedom as inmates stretched their legs and sucked in some fresh air. Harry Findlay was ready to join the daily trudge one day when one of the warders said: "Nah, it's raining."

Only a drop or two of rain was falling, but if the screws decided it was too wet, the rules dictated that the prisoners remained in their cells. "This was after 23 straight hours solid banged up," Harry said. "I just lost it for half a second."

Harry grabbed the screw by the lapels, screaming: "It ain't fucking raining," and quickly loosened his grip. "I just wanted to be outside for a while," said Harry. "The screw didn't do anything at the time and I thought: 'That's handy, I got away with it.'

"Nothing happened the next couple of nights and I forgot all about it. But the night after, at about four in the morning, there was a bang on the door. Knock. Knock. Knock. My cellmate, Steve Wheeler, was lying in bed, so I got up, went to the door and the screw said: 'Where's Findlay, 288059?' Like a complete mug, I didn't know what was coming or going on. I thought my mum had died or something.

"I walked out of the cell and 'boof' – the first punch landed straight in the guts. I got a right going over, no headshots, but a barrage of body blows."

Harry thought one fellow inmate would be sympathetic. Claude Thompson, who had befriended Harry from day one inside and was the hardest nut in the nick, listened to the story.

At first Claude laughed, but with an edge to his voice Harry hadn't heard before, he said: "Did you really think you were fucking going to get away with that, Harry? This is Brixton, you c***."

***

When Brixton prison was opened in 1891, the overwhelming majority of the early intake placed 'in custody of the Keeper of the House of Correction' were what the prison's records noted as 'the idle, disorderly, rogues and vagabonds.'

Those like Henry Durrant, accused of 'feloniously stealing a greatcoat, the property of William Streater, in the county of Surrey,' and Daniel Reardon, arrested for 'unlawfully hawking and exposing for sale a quantity of spirituous liquors, called rum and brandy, for which offence he is convicted for the sum of ten pounds, which he hath refused to pay.' Poor Reardon was sentenced to two months' hard labour.

HARRY FINDLAY

A new name was added to the felon's list in October 1983 for what he described as 'taking the piss with multiple credit cards over a prolonged period' – a 21-year-old Harry Findlay.

After his arrest at Wentworth Golf Club, Harry was taken to Egham police station, where the cops tried every trick in the book to attempt to extract more information from him. Had there been a middle man involved? Who had he been selling the top-end gear to? And was there anyone else they should – or could – nick?

"They'd wake me up at three in the morning, telling me my dad wouldn't want to know me, anything to try and get me down," Harry said. "The next moment they'd take the opposite route and want to be my best mate. In the end, they gave up. Credit card fraud was all about 'front' and being good at the signatures. They soon worked out that it was just as well I was a mad gambler and got too attached to the golf, otherwise I could have milked the system for a very long time."

Harry went to court and was refused bail – though he didn't even know what the word meant – but because of overcrowding in the prisons, he was sent back to the cells at Egham station, where life was frankly, pretty tolerable.

In the evening, his pal Dylan Westland could bring him a chicken dhansak from the local Indian takeaway, there were nice plates to eat from and he was allowed to wear his own clothes. Within a couple of days, he even had the coppers bringing him in the *Sporting Life*. The cells were clean and the beds weren't too hard.

But the relative niceties of police custody were not to last for long. After nine days, he was placed into the back of a Black Maria and driven the 30 or so miles to Brixton.

DOING BIRD

***

What would prison life be like? Harry recalled the nights spent as a child with a vivid imagination sitting entranced with his dad as Jack Hedley, Robert Wagner and Edward Hardwicke starred in the BBC series *Colditz*, losing himself in the stories of allied POWs and their attempts to escape from the notorious Nazi prison.

The film *McVicar* had only been out for 15 months, and he had already seen it twice! So he fancied he knew what to expect from a spell of confinement. "One thing's for sure," Harry would say. "Unlike life itself, prison is the only place where everything is almost exactly as it is in the movies."

Harry was given his number, prison gear and taken to a Victorian-style bathhouse, stripped to the bare essentials and sprayed from head to toe in lice powder. He was told to take a bath (the plug was a big wooden stake), and it was while lying in three-and-a-half inches of shallow water and looking up at the ceiling, he realised life had changed forever.

"The windows were like the height of the Eiffel Tower, it was frightening how high up they were," he said. "And even they were covered in bars. That was the moment it all really dawned on me – shit happens."

Harry would be on remand for five-and-a-half months before he was officially tried for his fraudulent use of credit cards. It was a torrid existence, time spent almost equally between Brixton, Pentonville and Wandsworth. He didn't complete the Big Four of London's prisons. "They never sent me to Wormwood Scrubs, so I missed out on my own personal Grand Slam," he said.

During the time at Wandsworth, he met two fellow remand prisoners who were waiting for their Crown Court date regarding a major heroin case and didn't fancy their chances. "One of them was a good-looking version of Mick Hucknall, the Simply Red lead singer, and the other had the face of a young Toni Nadal, Rafael Nadal's uncle and coach," Harry said. The two men also had an encyclopaedic insight into motor racing and especially two characters Harry had not heard of – an Irish driver named Tommy Byrne and a young Brazilian, Ayrton Senna.

The conversations would start in the exercise yard. Harry learned that Byrne had the potential to be the best driver Ireland had ever produced, but he was a complete loose cannon. They told great tales of Byrne's errant behaviour and total lack of respect for the haughty bigwigs that ran the sport, and couldn't believe some of the things he'd got up to. They thought he was a legend.

Harry also found out all there was to know about Senna's prodigious talent, his religious convictions, personal life, pedigree, the intensity of his focus and that he had the potential to be a Formula One world champion one day. It was obvious to Harry that his exercise partners were closely involved with the Van Diemen team for whom both Byrne and Senna raced in the early eighties before, in 1983, the Brazilian went on to win the British Formula Three Championship representing West Surrey Racing.

"The lads knew so much about Senna and explained why Terry Fullerton had stuck with go-karts and not moved on to cars," Harry said. "Terry was the best anyway, and his experience had made him virtually unbeatable in the go-karts, but this kid

Ayrton toppled him. Despite our dubious surroundings, you could just tell these two guys were the real deal."

***

His Honour John Ellison QC savoured his reputation as the scourge of the bench in the Royal Borough of Kingston-upon-Thames. Ellison's 2000 obituary in *The Daily Telegraph* referred to a case where one defendant – with sentence passed and judge's admonition ringing in his ears – proffered a 'V' sign from the dock. Ellison promptly returned the gesture.

When dealing with a habitual drunkard standing (just) before him, Ellison instructed the man to return to his home town in the north of England – 'a far better place for alcoholics than Reading.'

"Everybody told me I was in trouble with this judge, but my legal aid solicitor reckoned I was a cert to be released – credit card fraud with no previous convictions and the fact that, at 21, I'd spent six months in three of the hardest prisons in the country, he was convinced I'd be home that night," Harry said.

The judge's summing up was brutal – describing Harry as the worst type of criminal, the black sheep, the biggest thief in history and how bad he felt for his mum, who was in the public gallery. But Harry still believed he was about to be released. "I just didn't see how he could slag me off so badly and then send me down on top of it," he said. "I was looking at my shoes, thinking: 'Don't smile, don't laugh.' I thought I was a moral to be going home. Then he said: 'Two years.'

"I was looking forward to betting on Scotland in the rugby that weekend and watching it with my dad, but instead they took me down to this cell. About ten minutes later, there was a knock on the door and a guard was standing there with a paper plate with one of those bloody super mousses and a potato croquette on it. I couldn't even think about eating. He said: 'You've got a visit from your mum.' There was a small glass partition with bars across it and I just remember crying. She said: 'There's nothing I can do for you, son.'

"That night, I was back in Brixton, banged up with two Asian fellas and a piss pot. The first rule of prison was that you didn't shit in the cell overnight, you waited 'til the morning, but they'd already crapped. I had leg cramps all night and didn't sleep a wink. I couldn't stop thinking: 'This is what it might be like for the next two fucking years.'"

***

Around teatime the following day, Harry was allocated to the prison's C Wing. Something that might make life tolerable inside was a decent cellmate. Harry was shown into a cell that was 'like a room in a two-star hotel.' There was a nice piece of carpet on the floor, a sideboard with a big radio on top playing *Radio Gaga* by Queen, and he shook hands with Steve Wheeler, a convicted armed robber.

"I could tell Steve was a proper geezer straight away, and after a few hours chatting with him, I felt almost human again," Harry said.

The next morning, Harry was sent to the light industries factory and introduced to the daily toil of sewing mailbags on a 'shitty old' machine. Harry was minding his own business in the back row, trying to take in as much as his distracted mind could.

Steve, his cellmate, was working in the cutting room with Claude Thompson, recognised by fellow inmates as the guv'nor on C Wing, and told him about the new kid who talked a lot about sport, especially snooker. Claude decided to find out more.

Harry saw this big figure walking towards him, drawn instantly to the only pair of dungarees he had seen on anyone in the nick, and a giant brown comb jutting from the front pocket that was obviously required to contend with the man's wild Afro hairstyle. "What's all this about you and snooker?" Claude said.

"I was a Jack the Lad with a bit of a reputation. I was in for six months for burglary that time," Claude said. "Harry said he knew Jimmy White, and I was amazed because I used to go wherever the best players were in South London. Jimmy White and Tony Meo were kids with talent. I played snooker for money all the time.

"They were quite a bit younger than me. I was the main money player – a grand a frame in the 1970s. These lads were in their early teens, they were good, but didn't have much experience. I won loads of Pro-Ams, and I represented London with Jimmy, Tony and Neal Foulds. It was probably my fault Jimmy turned into an alcoholic. I used to buy the beers and sneak them out to the toilet for him. He was drinking pints at 13-14 years of age."

So good a player was Claude at the time he was locked up, that Jeff Foulds – Neal's father – wanted Claude banned from playing his son because the quality of his snooker was really doing Neal's head in. Neal remembered Claude as a 'charming lad, a left-hander who could really play.' It was as the two were in the middle of a frame at a hall in South London one day that someone walked in and Claude pulled up, mid-shot. "I don't like the look of him," he said. The next thing Neal Foulds knew, his opponent was being escorted from the hall and shoved into a police van.

Harry also knew the South London snooker scene pretty well. He'd met Jimmy White a few times and was good mates with Foulds, not only through snooker, but because they were both mad for Wembley dogs. The fact that he had such a bond with a prisoner of Claude's influence was manna for Harry. In turn, Claude felt protective towards the new kid on the wing.

"He'd tell his stories and we'd play backgammon," Claude said. "I'd played that for money too, and though Harry hadn't played before, he still wanted to gamble that he'd win. I said I'd teach him the rules, but he wouldn't listen – he wanted to work out for himself how to play because that was his attitude. I admired that, but it cost him a few quid.

"Harry had this infectious personality that not everyone liked at first, but after a while, you couldn't help but take to him. The cells were open during the morning, and when it came to the screws' lunch break, they'd lock us up and last thing you'd hear was: 'Where's Findlay! Where's Findlay!' Harry would be out collecting the bets he'd had on for the blokes.

"He made the screws' life a misery because they'd want to eat and instead had to spend time trying to find him. But even they started to like him so much they'd bring him the racing results. In the end, they just let him get on with it. I can't think of another prisoner who had that effect on screws, who were real tough nuts, all of them.

"And Harry was the only con on the wing to go to Art History classes, and he clearly knew more about Salvador Dali than the teacher! She obviously fell for his charms. Neither Harry nor I smoked, but he'd always come back from the lessons with three or four classy cigarettes she'd given him and pass them on to the lads."

In prison, challenges between inmates were ten a penny. Everyone wanted to get one over on someone else, often with loads of side bets taken on the outcome. Not only was Claude a very decent snooker player, but he had boxed to a decent level and was one of the best athletes in a place where being able to run faster, jump higher and especially hit harder than anyone else, placed you in a position of privilege. So when the gauntlet of a race with Harry was thrown down, he knew what the outcome would be.

"Harry wasn't as big as he is now, but he wasn't keeping fit like me, and I was convinced that his 20-yard start wasn't enough," Claude said.

The race – over 100 yards and with the wager of an ounce of Old Holborn tobacco to the winner – was to be run between the cells and the light industry factory. These things didn't just happen by accident in a prison. The screws had to be consulted and permission granted. The race would take place as the inmates made their way to work. A screw was stationed every 20 yards down the course to make sure there were no shenanigans.

The concrete space was jammed, resembling the quad scene from *Chariots of Fire* for the Great Court Run at Trinity College, Cambridge, where Harold Abrahams (Ben Cross) broke the record when racing Lord Lindsay (Nigel Havers). There was little such finesse about Thompson v Findlay in Brixton's barren prison yard.

Harry was caught a few strides from the finishing line, and as Claude was about to pass him – "he was taking the piss from three yards behind," Harry said – he stumbled, fell and landed in a ditch, splitting his head and grazing his arms and legs. A stunned and mortified Harry was greeted with roars of laughter as the blood trickled down his cheeks. "There must have been fifty of them looking into the ditch, all pissing themselves," he said.

Claude said that the whole scene was nothing like he'd seen in all his many years of bird. Screws and inmates laughing together, lost in the hilarity of it all. The only person who wasn't laughing was Harry, who ached all over, and for once, actually felt a bit sorry for himself.

***

With only one shower a week and the temperature outside starting to rise as summer approached, Harry's long hair was already getting on his nerves. A cut head on top of that only made matters worse. The following morning, as the inmates arrived for more work on the mailbags, he went straight to the shearing table and treated himself to a full buzz-saw cut.

What Harry had no idea about was that such a dramatic, new hairstyle would constitute 'a radical change of appearance.' One of the rules of prison life was that when an inmate was released, he should look the same as he had in the picture taken on his first day inside. A group of screws saw the 'new' Harry and announced: "You're nicked." He then heard Claude scream: "You fucking idiot, what have you done!"

This radical change would be small beer when measured alongside the next incident to befall Harry. The ingredients this time were a knob of butter, a metal tray and his cellmate, Steve Wheeler.

Harry said: "I was a single fella without a girlfriend and Steve had a young family, he was a year or two older than me, married with a two-year-old daughter. Steve would get really nervous about his wife coming to see him for the monthly visit. For a couple of days before, he was on edge; then after the visit, when he'd seen his missus and nipper, I left him alone with his thoughts for a while because it really used to shake him up. I only had my dad who came to see me once a month, and that was it. I remember thinking: 'Never have a kid and end up in prison.'"

Claude's connections in the right places had helped Steve find a cushy kitchen job, and with it, a position of influence. He handed out the butter in the breakfast food queue. "It wasn't real butter, but shit white stuff that looked a bit like butter," Harry said.

"The breakfasts were diabolical – a shitty square of back bacon was as good as it got, but you were allowed to take a few slices of bread. That was crap too; but having butter, even shit white butter on the bread, made a real difference and helped the food go a lot further.

"We were queuing up and Steve looked after me. He gave me a knob from the top and another deliberately stuck to the bottom of the knife. This big guy in the queue behind me saw what happened and asked for extra butter. Steve quietly told him to move on. Next thing, this geezer put his tray straight into the back of my head. To say I never saw it coming was an understatement. I'd only just fucking woke up."

Claude's cell was immediately next to the prison officer's landing that gave him a full view of the wing. He had seen the incident unfold, and before the screws had moved, he was at Harry's attacker, had dragged him into the nearby toilet recess area and started smashing his head against a bowl. The screws soon came running and asked the bloodied inmate – who looked worse than Harry did when he fell into the ditch at the end of his 100-yard dash – what had happened. "I slipped over, sir," he replied.

"All three of us got nicked," Harry said. "So now I had three prison black marks, radical change of appearance when I shaved my head, and laying a book in the nick, but the stuff with the tray was the problem because it would go down as violent conduct, even though I did fuck all."

***

The merry-go-round of prison moves had one more stop to make for Harry. The three black marks against him meant that, unlike most first offenders, he would not be afforded the more relaxed atmosphere of an open prison on his transfer. He was being sent to Camp Hill on the Isle of Wight.

Harry didn't know one prison from another. On the way back to his cell, he stopped by Claude's door to break the news. "I'm going to Camp Hill," he said. Claude's face dropped. "Fucking hell, Harry. We've got to get you out of that. They don't do choirboys down there."

"Claude had been to Camp Hill with one of his brothers and said he was glad he'd had him there to look after him," Harry said. "I didn't think Claude ever needed looking after. He said it was like Armageddon, where they sent the young tearaways to have a tear up. I began to shit myself.

"The more I heard about it, I genuinely made myself 33/1 to come out of there alive. It was a place where, the moment you walked out of your cell, you had to be prepared to fight. If not, you couldn't possibly survive."

Somehow, Claude and Harry had to figure out a way to get him sent somewhere else. Harry would have to go in front of one of the two governors who ran Brixton. One was known as Jack The Hat, regarded as a straight fellow who wore dark suits with wide pin stripes, and when you entered his office, his big hat was hung on the hook behind the door.

When Harry had been summoned to the governor for bookmaking on the wing, the meeting couldn't have gone any better. There was a screw on either side and just in front of Harry as he stood on the yellow line, giving name and number. "I had the guys almost laughing as I spoke about the recreational advantages of letting the prisoners have a small wager at the weekend," Harry said. "Claude was spot-on about what Jack The Hat was like. It genuinely felt like I was in an audition for *Porridge*, with me as a young Godber as I received a 50p fine, suspended."

Claude and Co had done all they could in the background to try to get Harry off the Camp Hill train, but ultimately it was up to him to convince the governor when he was called back to the office to confirm his transfer. "I've never prayed in my life, but I was really funking my bollocks off that Jack The Hat would be the man sat behind the desk. He was, and just as importantly, his mood hadn't changed."

The pair spoke for about three minutes before Jack The Hat declared: "You're going to Highpoint, they'll enjoy you there. Good luck!"

***

Highpoint was a C category prison in Stradishall, Suffolk, and largely full of older men classified as non-violent offenders but who weren't ready for the greater freedoms of an open prison. Harry was delighted with the landscape, given the disaster he had escaped from.

"Instead of walking into the biggest hellhole on earth, where within a week I'd have been on the suicide block, I was with these guys who all poured their own cups of tea from big pots and helped themselves from a giant plate of Bourbon biscuits. I was chatting away like an old friend on the first day," he said.

"They were talking about how drugs had completely taken over from bank robberies as the No.1 crime of the day. Pete Dixon, from Kent, dapper, early '50s, moustache, convicted robber, said: 'Fucking hell, it was so much easier in my day.' He told us when they used to do banks in the late '50s and early '60s, they'd pull up in Jaguars, side of the kerb, leap out, three bags, balaclavas over their heads and walk into the bank.

"There were usually three birds behind the barrier – a little glass fence six inches high – which the robbers would hop over, then fill their sacks with readies. The girls would scream, but the robbers didn't have guns because they didn't need guns. All they needed was the Daimler and the three black bags. They'd jump in the car and as they were driving off, the police would arrive on bicycles, blowing whistles. He was pissing himself laughing, and so was I.

"I could have been getting raped in the toilets at Camp Hill by lunatics with razor blades in their toothbrushes. Instead, here I was sitting with a lovely guy laughing about robbing banks in the 1960s. And thanks to Pete, the hilarity was set to continue."

Harry had tried smoking a spliff as a 16-year-old watching the newly released Terry Gilliam film *Jabberwocky* after spending the morning at the trendy Portobello Market in Central London. He did it again while on remand in Pentonville, but the effect was the same – a bloody horrible headache. Pete Dixon said: "You silly bastard, that's the tobacco," and promptly stuck a piece of cannabis resin on the end of an empty Biro.

Harry said: "He told me to inhale while he burnt the tiny chunk. The next four hours were fucking hilarious. It was like an LSD trip and I kept thinking he was a small, yellow submarine. The next night, when the lads brought out some food, I just couldn't believe it. Cornish pasties in prison really were a violation of the name, but stoned and starving, and with some of Pete's Heinz tomato ketchup on them, they tasted more like freshly-grilled crayfish in Cape Town."

Highpoint contained a few familiar faces from Harry's days on remand, and he was especially pleased to catch up with the two Senna boys, who were seemingly very relaxed with their five-year sentences and still looked a million dollars.

The lads had quickly sorted themselves out in their new surroundings. They already had a 'red band' (allowing prisoners to leave the grounds to do special jobs) lined up to pick up any prearranged package left by visitors. They gave Harry a Rolex watch and promised him a few quid on top if his mate dropped off a parcel prior to visiting him.

"I never once blamed my pal for not completing on the deal," Harry said. "He'd done the hard bit by receiving it in the first place, and, of course, I never should have asked him. I only did so because he was a genuine good friend and a real top man, but he was a straight goer. I didn't have any pals with a criminal bent. I didn't give a fuck about the watch, I wasn't a big Rolex fan anyway, but I was worried about possible repercussions.

"I was sure that the two boys would know I never fucked them over, but it was Dominic from Basildon who really made sure I didn't have any sleepless nights. He gave them the watch back, told them what had gone on and said that if either of them ever laid a finger on me, he'd hang them up in a tree."

The lads weren't Dominic's cup of tea, anyway. Harry never spoke to the Senna boys again, but he had a new friend – short, stocky with a head like snooker player Willie Thorne, minus the moustache. Not only was Dominic to Highpoint what Claude Thompson was to C Wing at Brixton, he could 'sing like Art Garfunkel and had a heart of gold.'

"The rest of my sentence was a breeze," Harry said. "I had a cushy job on the bins. I finished my morning-only shift over by the incinerator, the old part of the prison where the redundant RAF buildings were. I sunbathed there on the afternoon of the Derby, listening on the old Roberts radio to El Gran Senor get short-headed by Secreto. I thought El Gran Senor's 2,000 Guineas win was the best form of all time, and I knew for sure that if I'd been a free man that day, I'd have definitely been a skint one.

"Highpoint was made up of big houses. We had some great nights in Dominic's room where we'd smoke spliffs, tell stories, and he'd regale us with *Here's to You, Mrs Robinson.* He was great on the guitar. He had a good firm of people around him and I was a bit gutted that I'd nothing I could offer him in return for his friendship, weed and general wellbeing. But he had a plan for me and told me not to worry about it."

***

Harry had spent more than nine months inside, and as it was for a first offence, Dominic knew that, shortly before the end of his sentence, his fellow inmate would be heading out on a 72-hour home leave. It was the allowance made to prisoners in order to help them to readjust more easily to their return to home life. And it was time for Dominic to reveal his 'plan'.

He called Harry over and said that when it was his turn for leave, he'd have to bring some drugs back in with him. Harry once again reminded him that he wasn't going that well and couldn't afford spare cash to buy any drugs. "Dominic smiled, put his arm around me, and said: 'You don't need any money, mate, just arsehole, in more ways than one!'

"My mum hadn't visited me on remand until just before I went to Crown Court for sentencing, but we became good mates again when I was at Highpoint and she was a regular visitor. I spent the couple of days leave with my parents and at the pub, and when it was time to return, Mum drove me to the arranged meet at Micawber's wine bar in East Putney to pick up the gear. Then we drove straight on to Suffolk and stopped at a Little Chef less than ten miles from the prison.

"To be honest, I was quite excited and enjoying it all, knowing there were plenty of wankers in the nick telling Dominic I was a degenerate gambler, that I'd keep the gear to sell it and go on Rule 43[1] when I returned, and they'd never see me again. This job was nothing to do with drugs nor money for me, it was all about trust and honour.

---

[1] *Rule 43 – now Rule 45 – is the segregation of prisoners from their fellow inmates for their own safety*

"Mum said to me: 'Son, have you ever had anything up your bum before?' I could tell by the look on her face that this wasn't going to be fun. And she could tell by the look on mine that the answer was definitely 'No'. At least Dominic's connections knew what they were doing, and the stuff was all in bullet form.

"As you'd expect of a top-class nurse, Mum knew exactly what to do, and 30 minutes later, I tottered out of the roadside restaurant in agony, walking like John Wayne with three-and-a-half ounces of the best hashish you could find in London stuck firmly up my arse."

Arriving to the prison gates, the Highpoint screws second-guessed what had been going on and made the most of the rule allowing them to keep Harry banged up in the reception area for up to 24 hours. He didn't sleep a wink and spent three-quarters of a very long night with his backside perched on the radiator. When they finally let him go back to the houses, he was running and skipping like Billy Hayes when he escaped from prison in *Midnight Express*.

"I ran straight into the toilet area and couldn't wait to drop the load," Harry said. "It never crossed my mind that you couldn't do one without the other, and I pissed myself as the eagle finally landed. Good cannabis was the highest form of currency in any nick, and that Friday night, the place was buzzing. We had puff on our biscuits and weed in our tea.

"Less than 48 hours later, I was watching the most one-sided Wimbledon men's singles final in living history. John McEnroe beat Jimmy Connors 6-1, 6-2, 6-2, but sitting in the Highpoint TV room, halfway through the second set, I was so stoned I couldn't even work out who was winning."

DOING BIRD

The screws timed their ambush to perfection.

"They knew we'd be having a bit of a party on the Monday night and they crashed into the rooms just after midnight," Harry said. "I'd taken a drawer from a small chest of drawers and was using it as a tray for my food – a big bowl of Cornflakes with almost a full pint of fresh milk, a massive chicken leg and a chunk of cheese. I hadn't even started eating – if only they'd waited another 20 minutes!

"They knew for certain that some of our cannabis wealth would be spent in the kitchen, and had us bang to rights. You can't believe how seriously food's taken in prison. Think about Godber and the tin of pineapple chunks episode of *Porridge*! I carried the can and was marched to the reception cells. In the morning, I was back in front of the governor, and an extra week was tagged on to my sentence for stealing or illegally purchasing prison property [food]."

Harry was in a philosophical mood lying on his bed in the cells that afternoon. To be honest, he didn't think the extra week was the end of the world, he had nothing special planned, and more importantly, he wasn't going to miss any major sporting events. But he couldn't stop thinking about young Paddy.

Harry said: "There weren't many other young guys at Highpoint. He was a bit of a loner and very quiet, but a real nice guy. All the lads put on a proper 'do' for him on the night before his release. Everyone dipped into their wages and, in prison terms, it was a veritable feast. They painted his name on a big bed sheet and wished him all the best. We had a great night, at the end of which we all made speeches before asking Paddy to get up and say a few words. He stammered a bit, but was so grateful for what everyone had done. He couldn't hold his emotions and ended up telling us all that we were his only true friends and he didn't want to go home."

Dominic had already told Harry more than once that when he got out, life at times would be a bit of an anticlimax. Paddy's words struck a sensitive chord. So did the reactions of the older lags to his extra seven days inside.

"As I was still thinking of Paddy, I could hear loud banging on the door and couldn't work out what was going on," Harry said. "Then I heard Les' voice. He was a Scouser, mid-40s, sentenced to life for murder, put away for stabbing a man outside a nightclub when everyone in Liverpool knew he never did it. Les' arsehole was like Steve McQueen's character in *Papillon*, a fruit machine that could deliver to order!"

"You bastards, I've got 18 years left to do, stick the extra week on my sentence," he was screaming at the screws.

Les was the ringleader, but there were half a dozen of the top lags in Highpoint demanding that they should do Harry's seven days for him. Their bones of contention were his age, the fact he was supposed to be going home the following week, and they were all eating the same food when the screws swooped.

The prison protests were all to no avail and Harry had to serve out the extra week. But, when the protests were at their height, the governor said to him: "Listen to that, son – burglars, armed robbers and murderers all queuing up to do your extra bit of bird. You're back on the outside in less than a fortnight. Don't ever think you'll find that kind of camaraderie out there."

5

STARTING OVER

Brighton bookmaker John Poulter picked up the old-fashioned green phone in his office on the morning of the 1985 World Snooker Championship final. He rang Joe Coral's head office and said: "Can I have £30,000 at 1/3 on Steve Davis to beat Dennis Taylor?" Corals accepted the wager, and as John put the phone down, he turned to Harry Findlay. "You'd just love that bet, wouldn't you, Harry?" he said.

"I'd have that bet with the Russian Mafia if I could," Harry replied. "I had my last few quid on Davis ante-post anyway, but at 1/3 in the final, I'd have done anything to get a lumpy bet on!"

At eight frames to nil, Davis 'The Nugget' was in complete cruise control. Poulter was telling everyone it was the best bet he'd ever had. "Like finding £10,000 on the floor," he said.

What happened next remained one of the greatest sporting stories of all time as, at 1.30am, nearly 18.5 million TV viewers in the United Kingdom watched in disbelief as Taylor won the final frame on the black to become world snooker champion for the first and only time.

***

"I'll never work out how Carole Hudson put up with me for so long," Harry said. "I met her in a nightclub in Brighton in 1984. I'd never seen anyone with so much fizz on a night out. She was a cracker. Everybody loved Carole, but I spent nearly six years trying my hardest to put her in the nuthouse. One of our saddest moments together was on the front step of Grubbs burger restaurant in Hove, a stone's throw from the Sussex cricket ground just a few days after the Nugget's demise.

"Surrey had a great batting line-up at the time and I talked her into having her whole month's salary as a supervisor at Marks and Spencer on them to beat Sussex at 8/13 in a Benson and Hedges Cup group match.

"Surrey went off at 4/9, although I was a tad nervous when they had to bat first, and truly desolate when they were bowled out with only 170 on the board! After a hellish lunch, I was back on good terms with myself when they took the first two wickets for three runs, but Sussex eventually crawled over the line [174-7 with an over to spare]."

Grubbs did great burgers, but Harry couldn't taste anything that night. It was pissing down with rain and Carole's mascara was running down her cheeks. "Why did we have to have it all on?" she said, through her tears. "Because I thought they were fucking certainties," Harry replied.

He was still potless three weeks later – and absolutely desperate to get some cash in his pocket to back Henry Cecil's three-year-old colt Slip Anchor to win the Epsom Derby – when he read a very interesting article in the *Sporting Life*.

"Mecca bookmakers had decided, for the first time, they would take up to £50 bets by cheque, so long as they were supported by a banker's card," he said. "I knew straight away that I'd found a clue.

"On a normal day's trading, there wouldn't be much we could have done, but Derby day on the first Wednesday in June was a completely different scenario. The betting shops would be jam-packed all day long and it was the perfect time to strike."

All Harry and his best mate Jim O'Rourke needed was a blank, fat chequebook with a card on the day (acquired from a helpful pal), and they were outside the first Mecca they could find in London at 9am. Ten minutes before the big race, they had done 30 shops with exactly the same bet – £40 win Slip Anchor and £10 win Supreme Leader. They didn't take any prices, keeping things as simple as possible.

"Slip Anchor was trading at approximately 2/1 and Supreme Leader was around the 12/1 mark," Harry said. "A win for either horse would return us nearly £4,000. If neither won, we'd be heading back to Brighton without a shilling. It was the best free bet of all time. After I got done for credit card fraud, I wouldn't buy a crooked pair of shoes, but there was no risk involved in this coup, and as the saying goes: 'Never look a gift horse in the mouth.'"

In Lord Howard de Walden's beautiful apricot silks, Slip

Anchor entered the stalls, positioned near the rails. He had made all and won by 10 lengths in his preparation race, the Derby trial at Lingfield Park, crushing the opposition in the early stages. With the pace sensitive, and great American jockey Steve Cauthen on board, Harry was sure the tactics would be the same in the big race itself.

"The way Cauthen eased Slip Anchor into the lead in the first few hundred yards of the Derby was the story of the race, a joy to watch and all over long before halfway," Harry said. "I was delighted when the SP returned at 9/4 straight after they crossed the line. It felt like a Brucie's Bonus. And once again we were back in the game."

***

It was, unsurprisingly, to the scent and swagger of his beloved dog tracks that Harry had returned to gain momentum in 1984, and two of Britain's most famous greyhounds kept his show on the road for the next 12 months. He knew there could never be a greater all-round track dog than Ballyregan Bob. From 480 to 840 metres, he was the master hound. "In those days, the Greyhound Racing Association's asset-stripping attack on the sport hadn't kicked in properly and he was still able to prove it around any type of track," Harry said. "Fortunately for me, I watched not only his first and last races, but also over 90% of those in between.

After winning his maiden puppy competition, coming from behind to take care of the speedy Keeper Tom in both heat and final, Ballyregan Bob ran one of the best races of his life next time out, giving a three-length start and a head beating to

Lulus Hero back at his favoured Hove. "I knew no dog on the planet could do that," Harry said. "I was still shaking half an hour after the race.

"He next went to Hackney to run in the heats of a 523-metre competition. It was his first race away from Sussex but he was heavily supported all morning from 13/8 to 10/11 to win the race and from 9/2 to 3/1 to win the competition outright. The atmosphere on those big midweek afternoons at The Wick was electric. The banter was full-on. Hot Primrose – a super fawn, six-bend bitch from Sheffield – was in the same race. She was also backed off the boards – 14/1 down to 6/1 – and she'd brought a big contingent of Yorkshire supporters with her.

"Knowing that she stayed all day, when she came out of the second bend just over a length behind the leader, their arms went up in unison and they were screaming: 'Aye, aye, Primrose. How far?' so sure were they of victory. The only problem was the wrong dog was in front of her. Ballyregan Bob beat her by six and three-quarter lengths and smashed the track record on the way to winning the event itself in facile fashion – embarking on a world-record unbeaten 32-race winning run."

Scurlogue Champ may not have been as fast as Ballyregan Bob, but he was, according to Harry, 'the most exciting greyhound to race since the beginning of time.'

"The Egyptians would have built a pyramid twice the size of Tutankhamun's in his honour if he'd been around in their time," said Harry. "His style of running was unique. He would invariably tail himself off in the early stages, before powering through the field late on. He was a machine over any stiff six-bend trip and simply unbeatable over the extended two-lap marathon distance.

"I followed him all over the country, betting him at big

odds-on, and in terms of the buzz factor, it was gambling in its purest and greatest form. At Ramsgate in July 1985, he was in an 855-metre marathon and the place was absolutely heaving. I bet £500 to win £100 and £1,100 to win £200 without even contemplating defeat. It was his first run around the Kent track and he looked a little lost on the opening lap.

"For a horrible half a second down the far side, I thought he might get completely detached, but coming out of the fourth bend, and with just over a circuit to go, he just went berserk and broke the track record. Commentators liked to use the expression: 'Like a hot knife through butter,' and his second-lap performance that night was the perfect example of just that.

"He did it on so many occasions. He finished so strongly when catching the super-strong Star Decision over the six-bend 740-metre trip at Hove one night, that as the dogs crossed the line, nobody on the track knew who had won the photo, despite the winning distance being a neck! That won't happen again in a million years, but that was Scurlogue Champ."

***

Harry first came across Barry Flick's name when he was grafting with Terry Harrison at his betting shops in Brighton. They were punting together and Harry was doing some odds compiling. Barry sent a letter on fancy letter-headed notepaper to Terry applying for a betting account.

"Terry had loads of charisma, he was great company," Harry said. "He was the first to cotton on to Boris Becker as a 17-year-old when he won Wimbledon in 1985. Terry backed him before he won the final at Queen's Club two weeks before, whereas I wasn't on him until he beat Anders Jarryd in the Wimbledon semi-finals. We both fancied him to win the next year and backed him from 6/1 down to 7/2, but it was Terry who made him a real good thing."

Harry soon worked out that B.J.F. was going to be very hard to beat. And it wasn't long before the pair teamed up, especially as they had a lot in common – Barry wasn't the first person to take Harry's trousers down at backgammon and Harry preferred him for the many times he helped put him back on the horse. Most people used a pawnbroker's when they were penniless. Harry went to Herr Flicks.

"Barry's second-hand German clothes shop in Coventry was always busy, he said their vintage clothes were of the highest quality," Harry said. "I was glad it was packed on the morning of the 1987 Royal and Sun Alliance at Cheltenham. It was so busy that there were middle-aged women in their bras halfway up the stairs that led up to his office, and I was sure he hadn't heard me coming when, three or four steps from the door, I heard the scream go up: 'No more money.'

"Kildimo was 8/1 to win at Cheltenham that afternoon. I was convinced the race was perfect for him and made him nearer 5/2 than the 17/2 Stanley Racing were offering on the morning of the race. I already owed Barry a few quid and didn't want to take the piss, but I had to get on Kildimo. The previous day at the festival and that night's football had completely wiped me out.

Two hours later, Barry finally caved in. "He said the words I was waiting for: 'What price is he?' There was a Stanley shop less than 300 yards from Herr Flicks still offering 17/2 Kildimo at 1pm. I had £300 on in total – £200 for me and a ton for

Barry. Graham Bradley rode a patient race. I was confident the whole way round.

"Kildimo took up the running at the second last and shit in. After paying Barry back his £200, we went to Hall Green dogs in Birmingham where I won another £300. After an excellent curry on the way home, and with £2k in my kick, it didn't take long to nod off when I crashed at Barry's that night."

***

From the mid-1980s, Harry managed to find his way to almost every snooker tournament on the circuit, not just meeting the players, but discovering their strengths, weaknesses and studying the form. At the British Open at Derby's Assembly Rooms in February 1988, he planned to make a real killing.

Harry involved his old mate Graham Moore whose face 'lit up like Blackpool seafront in late October' when he told him of the plan and showed him the coupon he had specially made up for the purpose.

The World Professional Billiards and Snooker Association (WPBSA) had decided, for the first time, to make the Open a 128-man tournament, meaning the bookies had to price up an extra round – an enormous difference from a punting standpoint as a collection of lower-standard players lined up, many for their first and last time.

"There looked to be eight or nine absolute certainties to put together in a big accumulator," Harry said. "A major concern was whether the big companies were going to price up these matches or not. But I beat them to it, just in case they were thinking of getting cold feet.

STARTING OVER

"I went to a printers with a Rugby League coupon and showed them exactly what I wanted – a coupon grid with space for all the matches, with the banner 'Snooker' I'd cut from *Snooker Scene* magazine instead of the Rugby League headline. It was a work of art when they finished, with all the matches neatly priced up.

"I'd teamed up with the sport's No.1 young journalist, Phil Yates, a couple of years earlier, and before the rounds at each tournament, we went through every match. Phil never understood gambling odds and just gave me a percentage out of 100 he thought the likely outcome would be. His opinion, combined 50-50 with mine, was effectively my snooker tissue for over ten years.

"At Derby, we spent extra time making sure we got the selections right for our golden 'acca' and decided that we would go for a nine-timer. On the homemade coupon, we put eight of the nine players in at considerably better prices than the big firms were likely to offer – where they should have been 1/7, they were 2/7; a 1/9 chance would be put in at 2/9 etc. You wouldn't believe what a difference that would have made to your winnings.

"The bookies all knew Steve Davis, and because he was playing the almost retired Ray Reardon, who was woefully out of form, we put the Nugget in at the right price of 1/12 so they wouldn't smell a rat – knowing full well they wouldn't have a clue about the other matches.

"Independent bookies were all happy to lay our bets when they saw we were just having a hotpots accumulator – apart from Peter Hodson in High Wycombe who just told me to fuck off. Graham and I laid out less than a grand each but stood to win over £24,000 between us. We got a bit on for my brother, Gordon, and a few other pals before heading off to Derby."

Over two-and-a-half days, the 'acca' looked to be truly golden as seven of the nine selections won, either 5-0 or 5-1. Harry and Graham needed Mike Hallett to beat Ian Williamson and Steve Davis to beat Ray Reardon to land the biggest coup of their lives. They thought Hallett was a real good thing, but because Williamson was the slowest and most deliberate player on the tour and might drive Hallett mad, Harry decided on a bit of insurance.

"We were all-in with the accumulator so I borrowed £300 off Mum and had it on Williamson at 11/2 with Corals. Hallett won 5-0 in under an hour. On the left-hand table of the four matches taking place simultaneously in the arena, Reardon walked out to play Davis.

"Reardon was wearing a green plastic visor – everyone thought he was taking the piss. We couldn't believe it when he started playing with the fucking thing still on. But we sat in silence and utter disbelief as the elderly Welsh wizard carved out a 4-0 lead over the unbeatable Nugget.

"Graham couldn't speak at the interval, when Reardon made it 5-0 half an hour later, or at any time on the way home. The bet going down broke his heart. My brother, Gordon, was at a flat with his girlfriend and had a bottle of champagne in the fridge. He opened it in celebration when Teletext declared the two 5-0 results, telling his other half: "Don't worry, that's a mistake. If the score was 5-0, Davis must have been the winner."

"I was often asked how I felt after the All Blacks loss in 2007," said Harry. "I'm never sure of the right answer. But I do know it didn't feel as bad as that soul-destroying night in Derby in 1988."

***

STARTING OVER

Harry had to get himself off the canvas after the Derby debacle. He was grafting away for small stakes and managed to hit a bit of form. He was picking his punches and not playing on the horses. Liverpool were on fire in the First Division, earning him a few quid, and he was doing okay at the snooker. The Nugget was busy showing that his defeat in Derby was a total one-off and all Harry was worrying about was getting a couple of grand together to stick on him to win the big one in Sheffield.

Terry Griffiths was playing the best snooker of his career in the late eighties and managed to hang on to Davis' coattails until just past halfway in the final, when the Nugget pulled away late on to reclaim his title 18-11.

"I was even in Mum's good books because she gave me a lift the next morning down to a lovely small hotel in Tintern, near Chepstow. The Grand Prix of Europe match play golf tournament was on that week. Sometimes you can be in the wrong place at the wrong time. In the clubhouse the next day, Bernhard Langer was telling anyone who wanted to listen that he couldn't possibly win the tournament. The gist of his woes was that, after receiving treatment that involved injections, he hadn't picked up his clubs for over a week.

"As you'd expect, the brilliant German was clear favourite for the tournament and wasn't hard to lay. As well as taking him on in the outright market, I had £300 on Bill Longmuir at 9/2 to beat him the next day. I followed them round, and when the Scotsman teed off at the 16th, he was dormie three up with three to play. He went on to lose on the first extra hole. I don't think Langer shot over par once and he made it to the final, by which time the clue was well and truly over and he beat the short-hitting Mark McNulty 4&3 to win the event."

Usually the view across Tintern Abbey was beautiful to behold, but Harry wasn't in the best of spirits that Monday morning. After paying his bill, and buying the *Sporting Life* and a copy of *Golf Monthly* for the journey, he didn't have enough for the train fare to Coventry, but that never bothered him, and from the station he headed straight to Herr Flicks.

"I was getting a tirade of abuse from Barry as he flicked through the golf magazine and suddenly spotted an ad for City Index, a new bookmaking company. They were all dressed up like those Mother's Pride blokes with bowler hats and suits. Barry said: 'It's a new sports betting firm and you keep telling me you're a betting genius, so give them a call.' He wouldn't take no for an answer, and after dialing the number, it was Jonathan Sparke, the boss, who picked up the phone.

"He sounded like he'd gone to all the right schools but was a witty Jack the Lad and clearly in good form. He told me to ring back the next day and set up a meeting for the following week.

"The next day I rang, not there. The next day, not there. I was driving myself nuts. You know when someone's there but they don't want to talk to you. I tried a couple more times but I was starting to feel like a right prick and then more or less forgot all about it.

"As you'd expect of my mum, she had me doing any odd jobs around the house when I was skint. About ten days later, I was in the kitchen trying to lay cork tiles. I'd heard other men talk about how useless they were at DIY, but I was in a class of my own. I had glue and cork stuck to my hairy legs and everywhere else. I was in a right state. In a genuine temper, I picked up the phone and roared: "Is Jonathan Sparke there, please?' and he said: 'Yes, you're speaking to him, be here at half-past-one today and we'll go for lunch.'

"Mum was the senior nursing officer at Marlow Hospital. I was at home and didn't have 30p to my name, so I called her and said: 'Mum, I've got to be at Tower Bridge by 1.30pm to meet Jonathan Sparke.' Fair play, she said she'd be home in 20 minutes. She drove from Marlow to High Wycombe and into London, and we got to Tower Bridge about 1.25pm. I dived into the office and found Jonathan there with a couple of his younger colleagues, Mark Harbour and Angus Hamilton.

"Jonathan said: 'Let's go to the World Trade Centre in Canary Wharf.' He waltzed me off to this posh restaurant with great big leather menus, put his down and said: 'Leave it to Harry, he can choose the food and wine. When I'd finished with the maître d', Sparkey just started laughing and said: 'You've got the job.' Mark Harbour wasn't even surprised."

Sparke recalled: "He ordered two main courses for all of us. That takes balls. I couldn't believe it. I liked him straight away."

"All of a sudden, I was going to golf tournaments," said Harry. "In fact, any live sport I wanted, and City Index were covering my expenses. All I had to do was come in once a month, fill out a sheet of foolscap paper and they'd give me the money, plus £250 a week on top to cover the sports. I'd ring in the scores, anything I'd heard, and tell them what I fancied. My first tournament was the Woburn Masters. Mum drove me to the course, leaving at 5am, so she could get back to work in time. Getting in without any money wasn't a concern, especially at such an early hour.

"Phoning in at around 4pm, Sparkey was in full flow. 'Harry, you've simply got to come to dinner tonight, meet us at the

Zen Central in Mayfair at 8pm.' I got a lift into London and Jonathan was right, it was the best Chinese in town. Once again, Mark Harbour was in tow, and by the time we arrived back at Jonathan's luxurious flat in the Barbican well after midnight, it was obvious we were going to become good friends."

Mark's was a short but wonderful friendship that would have a dramatic effect on Harry's life. The pair went everywhere together, and in Jonathan Sparke, they had the perfect mentor to teach them about good food and wine. "Sparkey worked out that one of us was very keen on his daughter, Cecilia, and made me much shorter than 1.01," Harry said. "He got the shock of his life when he got up at 4am one morning to go for a piss at his flat and found Mark and Cecilia together."

***

Harry was required in the City Index office once a month but ventured in three or four times a week, just to meet up with Mark. It was on one of these occasions that he fancied a horse in a maiden race at York, but he was acutely strapped for cash.

"I knew Mark had an account at Corals and asked him to get £80 on Gydaros at 11/8," Harry said. "I heard Mark giving his name and account number while I was watching Stefan Edberg play Christo van Rensburg at Queen's on the big TV in the office. Edberg was doing his usual silky serve and volley tennis magic and I only had to see him for a few seconds to know I wanted to be on.

"I asked Mark to check with Corals on Edberg to win Wimbledon. Their 8/1 was the best price, everyone else was 6-and-a-half or 7s. I asked him to make it an £80 double

– Gydaros and Edberg at 8s. He was still no nearer getting the bet confirmed when I checked to see what price Holland were to win the European Championships. I fancied them strongly and Julian Richards, my old pal from the early days, made them a nap. Corals were the standout price, 11/2.

"I shouted across to Mark to make it an £80 treble, 11/8, 8/1 and 11/2. The horse won by three lengths and then became a fucking tortoise and never won another race, but when Edberg and Holland went on to do the business, I had £11,115 to collect, less Mark's original £80 investment."

***

The 1988 Wimbledon final between Edberg and Boris Becker was delayed until Monday because of bad weather, so Harry missed the final stages because he was flying with his mum from Heathrow to Glasgow to cover his next tournament for City Index – the Scottish Open at Gleneagles. Edberg was a set down and the match was on serve in the second set when they boarded the plane.

Harry was the only one of the travellers that day who possessed a mobile phone. Harry said: "As soon as the plane touched down, I rang Mark in the office, just funking for parity in the final, and he told me Edberg was leading by two sets to one and was a break up in the fourth. Mum and I both screeched with delight. The other passengers thought we were mad.

"Jonathan also had a nice few quid on Edberg and I told him he simply had to back Barry Lane at 50/1 to win the Scottish Open. I had £100 on him and another £60 at 33/1. I was a big fan of Barry's game at the time and got on well with his wife, who I chatted with. But this time there was big difference. I had a breeze block phone and Barry was on a birdie blitz. I was on the fairway at the 4th, 5th, 6th and 7th. Barry Lane went birdie, birdie, eagle, birdie.

"I had another £100 at 20/1, £100 at 16/1 and more of the same at 12/1. As he was making the birdies, I was topping up. He went on to win the title by three strokes from Sandy Lyle and Jose Rivero. I watched the final round with my cousin's son, Gary [The Great Garrido], and Barry gave him the winning ball. I was staying at the Queens Hotel in Perth and all my mum's family lived in the town. It was the biggest price winner I'd bet in my life and the world definitely never felt so good."

***

From Glasgow, it was on to Blackpool for Harry to cover The Open Championship at Royal Lytham & St Annes. He spent two days following the practice rounds, but when he turned up at just after 7.30am for the first day's play, it was the blackest July day he'd ever seen. It felt like the middle of the night.

"Plenty of the field had already started their rounds, and looking up at the scoreboard, it was a mass of blue [scores over par]," he said. "Only one man was in red colours – Severiano Ballesteros. As it often was in those days, the bookmakers hadn't changed their odds that early in the morning.

"I had £1,000 with Ladbrokes on Seve at 8/1 to win the Claret Jug when he should have been 5/1 or 9/2. I was out on the course for his spectacular Monday afternoon duel with Nick Price, the South African, when Seve shot 65 and declared it the best round of his life. I flew back to London convinced I'd never need or want a regular day job in my life. I always proclaimed it would be easier to win when you had a proper tank of readies behind you – effectively I had turned £80 into £30,000 in less than a month – and now I had the chance to prove it."

***

Harry wagered £1,100 each-way on John Parrott at 9/1 for the 1989 World Snooker Championship. He also had £100 each-way on Steve James, Parrott's first-round opponent, at odds of 150/1. The draw was such that he was convinced whomever won the match would reach the final. Harry and his driver and right-hand man, Davy Crockett, were staying in Sheffield as long as Parrott survived.

On Saturday, April 15, a day that dawned bright in Sheffield, there were two reasons why the city was in the full glow of the sporting spotlight – the World Snooker Championship and the FA Cup semi-final between Liverpool and Nottingham Forest, being staged at Sheffield Wednesday's Hillsborough ground.

Harry spent that afternoon in the city centre floating in and out of a William Hills bookmakers near the Crucible, following the horses, snooker and football, but, like everyone, his attention was drawn to the unfolding horrors at Hillsborough. The death toll from a shocking crush at the Leppings Lane end of the stadium that housed Liverpool's supporters kept on rising.

The atmosphere in Sheffield was eerily sombre. Harry didn't want to leave his hotel – indeed no one wanted to go anywhere that night. Harry picked at his food before retiring early to catch up with the latest on *Match of the Day*. Serving the tables was a young waitress called Kay Duggan.

Nothing was said that night, but because Parrott won the match 10-9 on a respotted black, Harry was down for breakfast early next morning wondering if he might see Kay. She was a tad shy, and realising Harry was hoping she'd serve him, stayed in the kitchen polishing the silverware. "After I drove her mad for a few days, she told Crockett that staff weren't allowed to go out with guests," Harry said. "But if I was really as keen as I was making out, I could take her out the weekend after the snooker finished."

Harry ended up staying a fortnight in Sheffield because Parrott would, indeed, go all the way to the final. They spoke on the morning of the decider against Steve Davis and Parrott told Harry he could barely hold his cue he was so knackered. He couldn't believe how much getting to the final had taken out of him. The fact he had spent time visiting Hillsborough survivors in hospital simply added to his emotional toll. Parrott lost the final 18-3. Harry got his each-way money.

***

Ramon Duggan, Kay's father, met Harry at the front door. "You're not going to lose her in a game of cards, are you?" he said. Canasta wasn't on the agenda. Harry was taking his new date to an evening at Wembley dogs to see Chicita Banana.

Harry had bought the bitch for £11,000 after she finished second to Odell King in the first round of the 1988 Irish Derby. He had backed Odell King at 8/13 to win the heat, and coming out of the second bend, thought he'd win by ten lengths, but Chicita Banana took off to get to within a length-and-a-quarter on the line. "I knew she had to be a superstar over six bends," Harry said. "Before I'd even paid for her, I backed her with all the

STARTING OVER

Shelbourne Park bookmakers at prices from 20/1 down to 12/1 to reach the final and told them she was a certainty to do so."

The whole track knew about the wager, and the East Dublin aficionados went crazy when she delivered another flourish to finish second in the semi-final. Harry had won back the £11,000 he'd paid for her before she even left Ireland. The deal was that she would fly to John McGee's kennels in Ockendon, Essex, after the final – in which she came fifth.

To say she made an inauspicious start to her career in England is an understatement.

"At one stage it looked so bad that, in desperation, we upped her in distance to an 850-metre, ten-bend race at Catford," Harry said. "Nelson's Palm, a big, black slow-boat, beat her by seven lengths, and afterwards she sat down on the track. I'd never seen another dog do that, and as John picked her up to place her into the antiquated kennels, I asked him what the fuck we were going to do now. John replied: 'Don't worry, I'll find the key to unlock her.' I thought it was him who needed locking up.'"

Chicita Banana went on to the Steward's Cup at Walthamstow as a 33/1 chance to win her heat and 100/1 for the outright honours. "Personally, I'd have added two noughts to the price," Harry said. "But she came from behind to beat the odds-on Fort Leader by a head in her heat. The next morning I was on the phone to Mr McGee. 'I found it,' John said. 'She will make all in the final on Saturday and win by six lengths.'

"He was nearly right," Harry said. "After flashing out of the boxes, she led all the way to win by six-and-a-quarter lengths. Down at the winning line at the presentation, I didn't think it was possible to feel so happy."

Two nights later, he was knocking on the Duggan's front door.

***

With her best friend Dawn Biggins at her side, Kay stood by the winning line at Wembley while Harry climbed the steps to the Royal Box to get a better view. Wembley stadium was a noisy, raucous venue, and Kay was mesmerised as Chicita Banana ran the race of her life, breaking the track record of the illustrious Ballyregan Bob by 0.05 of a second.

"The cheering died down and suddenly there was this riotous din," Kay said. "I looked up and there was this figure running down the steps screaming 'Where's the £50 for your gun now, you bastards?' It was Harry."

Kay had no idea that on a previous run at Wembley (two weeks prior to her lamentable Catford effort), Chicita Banana was three lengths clear before being caught by the moderate Frontyard Kay, owned by Dudley Roberts. After the race, Harry was only looking for a hole to crawl into before being accosted by two of greyhound racing's real characters – Georgie Brown from Daventry, and Ladbrokes' Alan Isherwood. Alan brandished five ten-pound notes. Harry asked: "What the fuck's that for?" "That's to buy a gun to shoot that bit of Irish shit you paid £11,000 for," he replied.

Kay saw her date in a real rage. "Dawn and I looked at each other and I thought: 'What have I done?' It took Harry hours to calm down from his riotous high. He promised me a night out at a club in London but we ended up going to a Chinese where no one ate anything, then walking around until the early hours before Crockett drove us all back to Sheffield because I had to be at work. It was a bit of a whirlwind."

The next time Kay was in London was watching Chicita

Banana win The International at Wimbledon, beating Sard by seven lengths. Harry was with his best pal, Mark Harbour. Harry had been backing Arsenal to win the First Division all season, and stood to win over £16,500, but Arsenal needed to win by two goals at Anfield that night and were 10/1 to do it. Mark and his late father were season ticket holders at Highbury. Ten minutes after receiving the trophy for Chicita Banana's win, Harry and Mark were rolling around the floor of the Diamond Room bar at the track as Michael Thomas scored one of the most famous goals of all time at Anfield to secure Arsenal's title success and Harry's money.

They were all at a nightclub until 2.30am and spent the early hours sitting on a bridge across the Thames between Windsor and Eton until the sun came up and they went for breakfast.

Harry said: "Mark's father died in his early 40s from a heart attack, and Mark was sure he would go the same way. When Barcelona were tearing Arsenal apart at the Nou Camp in April 2010, in a Champions' League tie, he had to go for a lie down at the family home at half-time. Ten minutes later, his mother heard a heavy thud and Mark was gone, exactly the same age as his dad. Cecilia Sparke and I both spoke at his funeral."

***

Kay learned pretty quickly what life was going to be like if she stayed with Harry. "We were in Scotland in the summer of 1989, Crockett was driving us. He and Harry were grafting at the greyhounds in Edinburgh and Glasgow and had turned £2,000 into £13,500. But then along came Signore Odone."

Harry picked up the story: "If you were ever going to back a novice chaser, you did it at Perth because they were the easiest fences to jump in Britain. At the opening price of 2/7, I thought Signore Odone was the bet of the year. I made him ten on. I wasn't the only one. Everybody in the ring wanted to be on, and it was a mad scramble to get accommodated. His starting price was 2/13. I'd bet him all around the ring and wasn't sure of my exact stake. I watched the race on the rail with the water jump in front of me.

"After one fence, the race was over as Signore Odone romped into a 15-length lead. He was even further ahead as he took the water. He didn't make a mistake, but after landing safely, the jockey just jumped off his back. He had felt him go lame. All the cash we'd accumulated was in a linen bank bag, and when we returned to the car, the only thing left was one red £100 Scottish note."

Kay had seen Harry and Crockett counting out the money before they left for the races. "I was earning £72 a week at the time and I'd only seen cash like that in the movies," she said. "Then they went and put it all on one horse. Harry told me what happened. All I could think of was that lovely deep bundle of money and now it was all gone. How the hell was he going to cope with that?

"The Signore Odone loss must have put Harry off the horses for quite a while because I can't remember the next time we went racing, but we did go to every snooker tournament for years."

***

Harry and Kay's first daughter, Jade, was born the night Manchester United won the European Cup Winners' Cup against Barcelona in Rotterdam in May 1991. That was why Harry, initially at least, wasn't at the hospital for the birth.

A new mouth to feed affected Harry's punting. He started to get a bit negative and had a dodgy run, but he concentrated more on his snooker betting and it became his reliable source of income. Ken Doherty, from Ireland, was a rising star on the circuit at the time.

"Harry knew more about me and Peter Ebdon [a fellow young professional] than our managers did by the time we started our professional careers on the tour," said Doherty. "He got plenty of money out of both of us. There was always a group of punters at the snooker in those days, but you didn't see many of them at the qualifying events. Harry turned up everywhere."

Ebdon added: "Harry had the ability not only to talk to people, but extract opinions from them without them knowing it. Many punters only seemed to worry about their own opinions; Harry wanted to know what everybody who knew what they were talking about thought. He always told me I was the best final-frame winner of all time. And he was right."

***

Like everything else in the punting world, snooker had its sell-by date, and things started to get a lot harder for Harry and his snooker-betting pals when William Hill employed Steve Tucker as their No.1 odds compiler.

"The tour was in Belgium for a Masters tournament in Ostend," Harry said. "After an average dinner in town, five of us returned to our hotel bar. Everyone was staying in the same three-star Campanile hotel, bang in the middle of an industrial estate. It was pissing with rain. Glen Gill, a new punting pal, and I had done our bollocks on Martin Clark; Tony Knowles had been knocked out in the first round; and Dene O'Kane, the Kiwi, was homesick at the best of times, so you could guess what kind of mood he was in. Jimmy White must have thought he'd been parachuted into the cast of *Mad Men*!

"In the hotel reception, Rex Williams, chairman of the WPBSA, was sitting with Anne Yates, the press officer, when Martin Turner of Sky Sports walked in with a big briefcase and a Sky TV baseball cap on and joined them.

"Half an hour later, I asked Jimmy to come with me to talk to them and asked Glen what price I could have on being offered a job on Sky before 9pm, which gave me 45 minutes to make an impact. Within 20, Martin asked me if I'd ever thought of being on TV before. Ten days later, I was in front of the cameras in Bournemouth for the 1995 International Open."

The main presenter there was a young Jeff Stelling, and although they went on to work together at the darts, to say they didn't hit it off straight away didn't do the situation justice. It took a few tournaments before they became pals. Stelling said: "I interviewed Harry when one of his dogs won at Peterborough and afterwards told him: 'I've got a lot of people wrong in my life, but nobody quite as wrong as I got you.' The players of both sports enjoyed Harry's company and he got on especially well, both on and off screen, with Sid Waddell, the great darts commentator."

***

Harry's job on Sky was to inform the viewers before play of the best bets of the day. By now, Tucker had proved so hard to beat, the pair were sharing opinions, so Harry was concentrating on trying to beat the other betting companies. "Tucker didn't trust me entirely at first, but after a few tournaments, I'd won his confidence and he knew I wasn't putting him away. And then I struck.

"When we went through the draw for Bournemouth, I told him exactly how I'd priced up each game, and why. Then we came to James Wattana against Euan Henderson. I was 1/5 Wattana and 100/30 Henderson. As I expected, he made it much closer. 'No, I said, all the Glasgow boys say he's gone, he's letting them down for practice, can't pot a ball when he does turn up, and is completely disillusioned with the sport. James is flying, he's really settled in the UK, practising ten hours a day, couldn't be happier and can't miss a ball. I've got three very strong bets in the first round, and he's one of them. I'm having a big treble.'

"Tucker never said a word and we moved on to the next match. He swallowed the bait with a mighty gulp and went 1/5 Wattana, 100/30 Henderson. I almost pissed myself when I saw those prices in the paper on the morning of the match.

"On the afternoon of the game, I told anyone watching live on Sky Sports that Henderson was the bet of the year, explaining why, at the very least, he had a 50% chance of victory and yet they could bet £30 to win £100. I said on TV: 'This is too good to miss, you've simply got to get on.'

"Henderson went off as a 7/4 chance and trailed 4-2 after the first six frames. I'd averaged out just over £3,500 at just under 3/1, but I knew it was the only chance I was going to have of getting one over on Tucker and told everybody to lump on. I feared the worst.

"Henderson's final-frame victory was one of the best buzzes I ever had at the snooker. Euan was a smashing lad but kept himself to himself. After the game, he was heading to Burger King but ended up in a Chinese restaurant with us until well past midnight. We were more than 12-handed around the table and I don't ever remember drinking a toast to anyone at dinner, but that night we did. To Euan Henderson.

"It didn't do him any harm because it ended up being his best tournament, reaching the quarter-finals before losing 5-2 to John Higgins.

"I was certainly right about how hard it was becoming to win at the snooker. My friend Andy Carter drove us to Sunderland for the 1995 Skoda Grand Prix where the both of us and Phil Yates all fancied the same five players. We thought they were real good things.

"I said to him on the way: 'It's not about winning or losing in Sunderland, Andy; it's purely a matter of how much we're going to get.' But not only did all five players get beat, not one of the matches went to the final frame."

At the services on the way home, Andy Carter described it as the worst night of his life, predicting he would never recover. Over the same pot of lukewarm tea watching the traffic go by on the M1, Harry Findlay knew it would be his last snooker tournament.

***

In the early 1990s, Harry and most clued-up racing punters found a new game to play – backing ultra-fit, interval-trained winning machines of Martin Pipe's, normally with Peter

Scudamore on top, after he had nicked a 20-length lead at the start.

In late January 1993, Capability Brown didn't need any favours as the tape went up. In a three-mile, two-furlong novice chase on officially soft ground that had turned heavy, all he had to do was jump round safely. He was an 8/15 chance that should have been 1/6. "I had every penny I possessed [£1,800] on him," Harry said.

By off time, conditions had got so bad it was barely raceable. Heavy ground wasn't a problem but it was so dark you could hardly see what was happening. The Pipe odds-on shot had the race well sewn up with a circuit to go. Turning into the home straight, the other horses were nowhere to be seen when, at the third last, disaster struck and Capability Brown fell.

"I felt as if my life had ended, and barely would have had the train fare home, " Harry said. "Then, suddenly, Scudamore was grabbing hold of the horse's reins and re-mounting. The second horse still hadn't entered the straight and Peter was turning his mount around to re-take the third from last. At the time, I'd no idea you were allowed to do it [re-mounting was banned in 2009 for the safety of horses and jockeys]. By the time the horse had cleared the next two fences, I'd not only worked out what was going on, but realised I was about to be paid out on a winner. It was as good as I'd ever felt on a racecourse, and when Scudamore and Capability Brown returned alone to a dark and sodden winning enclosure, I was there to greet them. I couldn't thank the jockey enough and felt like the kid in the Ready Brek advert, my whole body covered in a warm, red glow. Scu was pissing himself laughing."

6

LAS VEGAS OR BUST!

The Race and Sports Book at The Mirage on the Las Vegas strip was a veritable punter's paradise, even if this particular heaven was an oasis of concrete, bawdiness, glamour and slot machines in the middle of a desert. "The first time I saw the place, I was pawing at the scenery to make sure it was real," Harry Findlay said.

It was the autumn of 1996, and here was Harry like Captain Kirk on the bridge of the Starship Enterprise. "There was a massive screen on the front wall offering the big live horse racing meet in the US, and smaller screens showing every other one," he said. "On one side in neon was a sports betting show-board, with the odds for the weekend's NFL, college football and ice hockey action. Every big fight for the next year was priced up. It was 20 years ahead of its time. Beam me up Scottie!!

"Sunday was the 'it' day – live NFL from 10am. The atmosphere at full bore five minutes later with really knowledgeable people going crazy after every play. Downtime didn't exist. Seven-and-a-half hours later, in leather armchairs, we watched the late game. Everybody had a bet. How couldn't you? The place was mobbed.

"It was pure theatre. Kahlua and Bailey's with plenty of ice served by film stars in referee's striped shirts. And can you believe it – the drinks were free! I couldn't wait for the Monday night game. If anything, the craic was even better 24 hours later – what a buzz it was to have a bet, all these shrewdies lining up at the counter at the end of every quarter trying to be the first man on if the house made a rick on the handicap or the unders and overs. I was hooked.

"After the buzz of Monday NFL, returning the next day was a genuine downer. No college football until next Saturday, and a day later for the NFL. The event all the faces were talking about was in a sport I knew absolutely nothing about."

Yet it was on one of these downer days, when the conversation turned to high sticks and hip checks, that Harry had the encounter that would shape his gambling philosophy forever.

He recalled the significance of the moment in an 'Off Piste' article in the *Racing Post* he wrote a dozen years later. "The only big live action was the ice hockey between the Blazers and the Penguins," he said. "With a 10/11 line and a five-and-a-half point handicap[1], I didn't have a clue.

---

[1] *Both teams 10/11 to win, but with the outsiders given a five-and-half-goal start.*

"The cashiers looked great in their smart black-and-white striped referee uniforms. But there was one guy behind the counter who clearly stood out – in his late 30s wearing an Armani suit, Corcoran tie and pocket handkerchief, the best in the world. He looked and acted like the boss.

"Getting his attention, I leaned over the counter and asked: 'With a gun to your head, who would you take?' He even smelt good as he leant back and drawled: 'Sorry pal, I don't know nothing about the Blazers nor the Penguins, but if you're seriously looking for some proper advice and really want to make the game pay, then never ask a fucker with a day job what he thinks.'"

The memory of that chance discourse over a betting counter remained as fresh to Harry as the cashier's aftershave. "He was standing there practically mugging himself off, saying: 'I've got a day job, so how can I be any good at gambling?' The smartest, greatest-looking bloke in the whole joint, with probably the best job, and it was so right what he was saying."

Of those eye-popping trips to the Sports Book, there was one that he would regard as the most exhilarating and traumatic day's punting of his life. "I won a lot more on other occasions but never had nearly as much fun doing it," he said. That day, there was a new addition to the group who travelled with Harry on these gambling expeditions. His name? Tony Bloom.

***

Harry Findlay was formally introduced to Tony Bloom at the NatWest Trophy quarter-final between Sussex and Yorkshire at Hove cricket ground on July 30, 1996. Tony's father, Ron, was a Sussex season-ticket holder, but the match was a sell-out and he was on the outside peering in.

Harry had booked a marquee for a few pals, and with access to the big tent came 12 ground passes to help ticketless fans gain entry. "I managed to get about 40 people in before they worked out what I was doing, and one of them was Tony's old man," he said.

How much did the result of the coin toss that morning influence the evolution of Harry's life and betting career? Heads and he'd never have met Tony. "I'd lumped on Yorkshire and if they had been batting first, I'd have been watching the match live, praying there were no wickets, rather than grafting other guys into the ground," he said. But Sussex had won the toss and chosen to bat. Harry was busy grafting.

Ron Bloom was delighted to be inside the ropes, but without his usual seat and nowhere to watch the game, Harry suggested he come to the marquee for a cup of tea and a slice of cake to settle down. "He stayed there until lunch, was a different man when he left and said he'd be back at tea," Harry said. "He said he wanted us to meet his son."

When Harry and Tony met, the conversation soon turned to sport and betting. Harry remembered two things – "First, he knew his punting and clearly had something about him. He was a real spark," said Harry. "Second, was how much he loved chocolate éclairs. He was relentless. I thought the fresh cream was going to start coming out of his nose.

"The last thing he said was that he's really good on American football. I said I didn't bet on it, but I went to a couple of games a year for the thrill of it as much as anything else. He offered his number and said I should call him if I ever needed any advice."

By a quirk, Harry and a bunch of his gambling buddies were heading across to San Diego a few weeks later to see the Chargers against the Oakland Raiders live, before heading to Vegas to take in the Breeders Cup, the legendary race meeting. It was as he was packing for the trip that Harry suddenly remembered Tony's love of the NFL and called to see if he had an opinion on the Monday night game.

Bloom's response was that the Chargers (San Diego) was his best bet of the week, he had backed them at minus 2.5 (to win by at least three points). Before Harry had taken the message on board, Tony asked if he could join the group. "He said he'd had 'a proper bet' and wanted to watch the match live," Harry said. "I told him to be at Heathrow at 11am the following morning.

"I actually forgot about him until we were at the check-in desk and just as I thought: 'What about Tony Bloom?' a head appeared from behind a couple of giant suitcases and he shouted out: 'Hi guys, hope you're on the minus 2.5.' Off we all went."

All that mattered was getting into the Jack Murphy Stadium in San Diego for the game. Harry was grafting for tickets around the ground and was bartering with a local tout when the police arrived and tossed the scalper into the back of their truck. Harry did his best to argue the tout's corner but was then threatened with arrest himself. He backed off. The group had their tickets. San Diego shit in. They were in the money.

"The next day, we were driving through the old part of the city," Harry said. "It was stinking hot and we stumbled across a pitch and putt golf course. Tony challenged me straight away. It was nine holes for $1,000. I know I'm fucking useless at golf, but because of that, I often used the putter from up to 100 yards out whereas I guessed that Tony might fancy himself with the nine iron or pitching wedge.

"The course hadn't seen rain for months and was rock hard. Tony ended up in a few cactus bushes and eventually the nuthouse. As we walked off three hours later, he was $16,000 behind. I found out for the first time that day what everybody he did business with would discover, that he was the best and fastest payer in the world."

Tony Bloom would also become 'The Lizard', known and feared for his cool, bloodlessly calculating demeanour, especially at the poker tables of the world. Harry would name one of his dogs 'Lagato Dorado' (the Golden Lizard), after the small trinket Tony placed on top of his poker chips as they regularly mounted in front of him. On this day, though, Bloom was down a few bob and Harry was feeling good about himself.

With the takings from his pitch and putt success in his pocket, Harry phoned his partner, Kay, and said she had to bring their daughter Jade to Vegas for the weekend. The girls were buoyant. But before they had boarded the flight, the positive vibes from Harry's golfing success had begun to dissipate. What came easily, disappeared in much the same manner.

"We all did our brains on the horses," Harry said. "We had a murderous two days. We always used to bet British horses in the US and US horses in Britain – something we did every year. This time, it didn't work out. We also had a few match bets on the Breeders Cup races and never backed a winner.

"Ross Jackson was our man for sporting tips and had been for years, especially on college football. He was a lairy, good-looking Portsmouth bookmaker who drove a white Jag and had three betting shops all by his early 20s. He'd mellowed a bit since then and was now based in Vegas after marrying an American girl, Wanda Miller."

The marriage was on the rocks in 1996 when the legendary Country and Western singer Kenny Rogers walked into the restaurant where Wanda was a waitress, and by the time he had walked out, he knew he had met his fifth wife. In 2017, Kenny and Wanda Rogers celebrated their 20th wedding anniversary. "With that severe blow to his morale, Ross' alcohol intake went through the roof, and with it, his winnings dried up," Harry said.

On this particular trip, though, Ross had a pal who knew his college football inside out. The one chance Harry and the clan had to recover from the whipping they'd taken on the horses was to bet Stanford – the California college – at minus 7 (to win by more than seven points) in the big college game on Saturday night.

Ross Jackson's man made them the best bet of the season so far and the instruction was for Harry and the boys to lump all their cash at minus 6.5. Try as they might, across half a dozen different casinos on the Strip, that price had dried up. To make matters worse, after the racing on Saturday, all the minus 7s had also disappeared. It was with much trepidation that Harry took Stanford at minus 7.5 for all he had.

"With seven points awarded for a converted touchdown, it was a horrible number to take because at least at minus 7, you get a push [your money back] if they won by that number," he said. "It was the most painful game I've ever watched, three-and-a-half hours of purgatory. Stanford could and should have won by 27 points but everything that could go wrong, went wrong. A late touchdown for the underdogs meant Stanford won by the dreaded seven points. I was wiped out."

Harry retired to bed wondering what on earth he could do. Kay and Jade were on their way, there was no turning them back.

"Breakfast at Kokomo's used to be as good as it gets, but mine had lost a lot of its flavour the next morning because the girls had left England and I was potless," Harry said. "In those days, every meal, every round of drinks, everywhere we went, we played 'Spoof' and the loser paid. When I lost to Glen Gill [one of his foremost betting buddies], I explained I couldn't pay for breakfast, asked what he had left in readies and how much he could let me have to play on the morning's NFL games.

"Glen took $2,000 from his bedroom safe and gave me half. Ten minutes later, I was in the queue at the cashiers when Simon Roberts, the baby of the group, walked past. I told him what I was doing and he gave me his four $100 bills. I laid out the entire $1,400, having three doubles and a small treble, and needed at least two of the three teams to win to keep myself alive. The three games were close, but all my selections obliged. I had $3,800 for the afternoon games.

"Tony gave me two selections, while Simon and Ross' man fancied one each. I was really grafting. I laid out $3,600 once again needing at least two winners from four to stay in the game. We were all starving by this time and decamped to the California pizza kitchen in the back of the Sports Book surrounded by televisions showing all the live stuff.

"All four picks absolutely shit in, done and dusted before half-time. We were having pizza at 3.30pm and I was banging my knife and fork on the table in sheer delight. The Cab Sav had never tasted so good. I'd turned a grand into just over twelve in two NFL sessions.

"Next thing I knew, Ross appeared with a bounce in his step, telling us his ice hockey man had a real nap – the San Jose Sharks at plus 1.5. His man thought both teams had an equal chance in the game and should be the same price, and couldn't believe he could get a goal-and-a-half start. The only down side was that it wasn't the live TV game, so we couldn't watch it anywhere and would need score updates.

"I had $3,000 to win $2,700 on the Sharks +1.5, and $1,000 to win $1,700 that they would win the game outright. It's tough having a big bet and not being able to see the action. All the Casino Sports Books in Vegas had a ticker tape that moved around showing you all the latest scores. I made sure they were at least halfway through the second quarter before checking the score for the first time. The opposition was at home so I knew their score would flash up first.

"Funking for the elusive bagel [a zero], I got exactly what I wanted. I was saying: 'Now please just show a '1' next to the Sharks because then I knew I'd really be in the pound seats. When the number '4' popped up, I had the broadest smile Vegas had ever seen. I knew my tank was up to almost $16,000.

"The girls were arriving from Chicago in two hours time, but as far as I was concerned, the best was still the bet to come. There were three marathons [eight bends], all heat races that night at Flagler greyhound park. Ross was convinced that the three favourites were good things, especially the last one. Caesar's Palace was the only casino where you could bet on the dogs, but it was hard to get a proper big bet on. If you wanted a chunky investment, the only way was to split the money up and just hope you could keep getting on.

"I had just over $2,000 on the first dog, which got a decent early pitch before powering clear on the second circuit. I won $1,800. Chatting up the cashiers, I reinvested my winnings on the second hotpot – approximately $2,500 to win $2,200. She was a tiny bitch drawn next to the fence, but after pinging out of the boxes, she led all the way to a facile victory.

"With $19,600 in the hod, I couldn't wait for the last heat. Although a much shorter price at 2/5, I was more than happy because Ross thought the dog had already won. Defeat was out of the question. I gave Glen and Simon $1,500 each to try and help me get up to $6,500, but we were all knocked back every time we tried to place the wager. The hare started to run and I hadn't managed to get a single penny on. I was begging the final cashier to take at least something, but all to no avail.

"I looked up at the big screen expecting to see Ross' best bet of the day absolutely bolt up. Instead, he resembled a fucking canine tortoise, lost ground on every bend and was beaten by about 15 lengths. He barely picked up his feet at all."

Harry's $19,600 was still miraculously intact. And his day on the punt was finally over. He glided out of Caesar's Palace and hailed the first limousine in the lot to take him to Las Vegas airport. During the week, the gang had spent one morning at Circus Circus playing $100 a man at the fairground sideshows, coconut shies, basketballs and donkey derbies.

Whoever got the highest score in each game won the pot. It was just like the old days at Butlins in Great Yarmouth as Harry walked away with $800. He collected as many cuddly toys as two bin bags could carry and transported them back to the Mirage.

"It had been an horrendous journey for the girls, they were shattered when they arrived, but I remember Jade's face when she came into the room and the bed was completely covered in toys," he said. "After a bit of room service, they were soon asleep, but I was wide awake for hours, sat watching the late-night news on CNN but mainly staring at the three beautiful pink $5,000 chips in my left hand and nearly five grand in cash in the right."

7

A FELLOW TRAVELLER

Julian Snow was Britain's real tennis amateur singles champion a record 19 times and won the equivalent of the lawn tennis 'Grand Slam', seizing four British Opens, the US Open twice and both the French and Australian Open titles once apiece. The fact he played real tennis and not its more exulted racket rival had to be why he was neither a household name nor lauded for a sword-tap.

Not only was Snow's haul of titles remarkable, but also that he had the energy reserves required to win so much, given that every hour was spent living on his wits, either gambling with his own money or dealing with hundreds of thousands of other people's in an atmosphere far removed from the aristocratic flavour of the real tennis courts of London's Queen's Club.

HARRY FINDLAY

He was another man taking gambling to a punishing extreme.

During a garlanded athletic peak, Snow all but exhausted himself as a trader at the London Financial Futures Exchange – "a crazy way to earn a living, full of foul-mouthed, excitable, aggressive, competitive people," he said – and devoted a fair part of each day to betting on the horses. He was a professional gambler, which could be said to be a crazy way to earn a living, full of foul-mouthed, excitable, aggressive, competitive people. Julian Snow was a less extreme version of Harry Findlay. They became and remained firm friends.

Snow was a touring amateur player, a journey that brought the financial hardships he hoped he could offset by delivering a steady flow of winning bets. He would go to as many race meetings as possible, given his frenzied trading existence and the requirement to stay physically sharp to continue his real tennis dominance. He sought to grow into his surroundings as an eager young bettor about town and be accepted at the track, where he found an initial soulmate in Glen Gill, Harry's go-to racecourse man.

"Professional punters were mostly middle-aged men, whereas Glen and I were two youngsters, and we saw each other more or less every day," Snow recalled. "In those days, you'd bet on a photo finish if you were in the right place on the course. A close one might take four or five minutes to develop, and there was a good and exciting betting market with brilliant repartee, and we'd be standing in the line, talking the usual talk. Through Glen, I was introduced to Harry.

"It was in the Kempton Park ring. He was shouting the odds as loud and boisterous as usual, and I couldn't believe who this person was, let alone he was a friend of someone I knew. Harry always said the first time we met properly was at Lingfield Park when he watched me eat a whole pavlova, which sounded entirely plausible.

"Harry rang one Saturday evening in November '92 and said: 'I'm coming to London tomorrow, let's have lunch.' I had to tell him I was playing real tennis. Eventually he realised I wasn't pulling his leg and I invited him to watch. I got front row tickets for him and Kay. He got a bit boisterous in his support. In those days, I could win (and did) easily, 3-0 as I recall, which was all very satisfactory at the time but regrettably I was nearing the peak of my powers. Harry asked where I was going next and I said to Melbourne for a World Championship eliminator. He said: 'I'll come.'"

Julian, Harry and Kay spent Boxing Day 1992 at Kempton Park, clambered into a taxi to Heathrow and took the overnight flight via Singapore to Melbourne, where they checked into the Hilton on the Park, with its extravagant views of the MCG (Melbourne Cricket Ground), and just across from it, the Rod Laver Arena, the centrepiece of the Australian Open tennis championship.

Harry was far too hyper to sleep that first night and flicked on the television to try to find some live sport, anything that would fill the hours before Kay stirred. He couldn't believe his fortune when he heard the shout: 'Set to go, Bendigo!' The dogs were on.

Snow said: "The concept of watching greyhound racing in a hotel room in those days was terribly exciting for Harry. He was straight into his element. The third evening we were there, I had to attend a dinner with the real tennis committee. He was waving the evening paper and said: 'But there's dogs tonight,' then uttered some unpronounceable name."

The place, Snow later discovered, was Warragul.

"I said: 'Where the hell is that?' and he said: '250 miles away, but I've got to go — how can I be there by 6.15pm for the first race?' There was no way he could do it by road — he didn't drive anyway. No taxi driver in their right mind would want him in their cab for four hours. The next thing I knew, he'd got hold of some poor sod in the [Kerry] Packer organisation and told them he wanted to hire their helicopter. He did it, too. I've no idea what it cost but it couldn't have been cheap, not at such short notice.

"Off he flew. He said that kids just came up to the helicopter and gawped at him when he landed, it was as if a spaceship had arrived. He loved it — he'd never been shy of being centre of attention. I bet they still speak about it now, the time a spaceship landed in Warragul and this fat bloke got out."

Harry recalled the place, even if he could not spell the name: "Everyone at the track was wearing their jumpers back to front, and in what passed for a café, they had hexagonal tables and plates piled high with chips, with big pies on top. It was my kind of place. I had a good night's punting."

That New Year's Eve, Julian and Harry decided to go to the dogs in Melbourne. "I was first down to the lobby where the taxi was waiting," Julian said. "The driver asked: 'Where you going, mate?' I said: 'Sandown dogs.' He said: 'You like the dogs, mate?' and I said: 'Yes, but my friend likes them a lot more than me. What about you?' He said: 'I love the dogs more than I love my missus.'

"He said his brother was Adelaide's leading trainer. I thought: 'This is handy,' because Harry and I used to have side bets on every race. I said to the driver: 'Before that fat bugger comes down, mark my card.' When we got to the track, I had an opinion on all the Adelaide form. Harry hadn't a clue how I was so knowledgeable."

Snow and Findlay were unlikely bedfellows and yet maintained a trusting alliance and professional appreciation of each other's talents. The communication dwindled when Snow decided he had more chance of living the fine life in Australia, especially as the money from gambling ran out, and the life of a city trader was becoming less and less one of natural instinct and ever more at the mercy of technological advancement.

"For a gambler, the arrival of Betfair was a godsend. I used to pay a girl £40 every morning to traipse around local betting shops – there were half a dozen within a 10-15 minute walk. Even that took the edge off the profit. We paid [a commission agent] 3% that felt like nothing until you added up how much you bet each day and that 3% killed you. It drove you mad because in those days, it was all on the phone and the aggravation of speaking to Ladbrokes' minimum wage telephonists 20 times a day did your head in. Particularly when they were basically trained to say 'no'!

"In '92, I was employed by Citibank as a financial futures trader. I sweet talked them into giving me a good deal where I could take ten weeks off and play real tennis tournaments. I'd go to the US twice, Australia twice, France once and play two tournaments in this country. There was the 10 weeks. I was betting heavily, and that's why I left my job, because it was ridiculous when you were betting a month's salary on an afternoon's racing. That didn't make sense for too long, win or lose.

"The great thing about futures trading was that the pit opened at 7.30am and closed at 4.10pm. You could trade out at the closing prices for two minutes until 4.12pm or you got fined. [There were] twenty minutes to clear up and then I was out of there and on the real tennis court at Queen's at 5.30pm, almost every weekday. I know a lot of my colleagues would spend that time in the bar, drinking too much and imbibing illegal substances, but I used to go and shout at the pro and hit balls at Queen's."

Harry would often share Snow's London living quarters, a flat festooned with copies of the *Racing Post*, inked circles around the horses and dogs they fancied, television on in the corner, shouts and screams interspersed with howls of anguish if they lost and Harry constantly reaching for the phone.

"Harry has never known what normal people stand for and, therefore, he's never been able to cope with normal life," Julian said. "If he came to stay with me, he'd leave a trail of destruction – towels, cigarette butts, pieces of paper – he was incapable of making a cup of tea, let alone putting anything into a dishwasher. I don't know how Kay dealt with it. He never booked his own airline ticket. Who knew how it all worked? What was it Dostoyevsky said?: 'A small number of people have their single passion and aspects of their life they are dedicated to.' Harry was always an extreme version of it."

Snow witnessed first-hand Harry's relationship with Tony Bloom, one that rose and fell in equal, seismic measure. "We travelled quite a bit together, especially in Australia. Lizard wasn't my cup of tea. I always dissed him. He was a mean guy, and very successful, which was probably why I didn't much like him. We must have been bored because we went to play bowls one evening and he turned up with a tape measure. He said he wasn't having any rows. That's him.

A FELLOW TRAVELLER

"Harry was a distinct one-off. Most of the successful gamblers these days are like Lizard or those from Hong Kong, with massive computer programmes. Harry did his own thing, with his own thoughts for his own reasons. He was an original who didn't need a staff of hundreds in an office in Camden like Lizard has. They're all so smug and MI5, it makes me angry. I'm just jealous because he's a billion or two ahead of me!

"Nowadays, there are an increasing number of people who are basically computer scientists who have a swish algorithm. Lizard wouldn't blow his nose unless the algorithm told him to. People like myself think: 'Crikey, that's a value price.' It's what judges call 'instinctive synthesis', you just put all the factors together and say, that's a bet or that's a lay.

"If you went racing and someone said: 'What do you fancy?' it depended on the prices. You could back anything at some price, so it was a question of assessing in your own mind the true odds and being able to recognise when the odds offered were bigger than those true odds.

"Harry is *the* expert at that, and part of his MO, particularly in the old days, was betting short priced, which the regular punter and the media wouldn't conceive could be value, but just because the horse was 8/13, it didn't mean it wasn't value. All the stuff about 'I never bet odds-on' – good luck with that! That's what he was most well known for as a punter, fearlessly lumping on short-priced favorites.

Asked to describe his former punting partner, Snow said: "Unique, but that's a bit fatuous. Exuberant, enthusiastic, principled, single-minded, keen, he just loved it. Sometimes when we would be together and start in the morning on the football and the horses, by the evening I've had enough and I'd like a glass of wine, but no, there was this and that still on. No offence, but when the last dog race was run, I wanted to take it easy. His phone was going 'jibber, jabber' the whole time to people in Sydney giving rugby league tips, or if there was a nap at Randwick tomorrow.

"He was brilliant at befriending sports people. In the old days we used to go to Melbourne Park the day before the Australian Open and he'd be chatting with Roger Federer and Paul Annacone, his coach. I couldn't do that, I'm too English and expensively educated. Harry had good chat. We were in the swimming pool at the Crown Towers and he started chatting to Rafael Nadal and his uncle Toni, who are granite and wouldn't give the time of day to anyone for ten dollars. But he got through to them all.

"He couldn't live a day without risk. I'm reasonably relaxed nowadays, but in those days I was straight living and fit and he was smoking spliffs and would be ready to go all night if necessary. I'd like to ask his mum: 'How the hell did this happen?' I had a similar experience at Ascot when I was nine and fell in love with the horses and gambling, but I didn't turn into Harry."

8

BIG FELLA THANKS

George Armstrong Custer coursed his dogs on the eve of The Battle of the Little Bighorn. Knowing he would likely go to his death the next day, General Custer wanted one last look at the animals he revered. Having pitted a group of them, one against another, he petted and then dispatched 20 on a train with cavalryman James H 'Dog' Kelley, who would become the mayor of Dodge City.

In time, it was said to have been almost impossible to walk the streets of Dodge without tripping over a descendant of one of Custer's greyhounds. One of the offspring named Fly was, according to *Tales and Tails*, among the highest ranked coursing dogs of the 1870s.

"Custer also had a superb greyhound called Byron that was

devoted to the General, and after many a successful chase, was rewarded with a demonstration of affection," they wrote. "He was the most lordly dog, powerful, with a deep chest and carrying his head in a royal way. When he started for a run, with his nostrils distended and his delicate ears laid back on his noble head, each bound sent him flying through the air. He hardly touched the elastic cushions of his feet to earth, before again he was spread out like a dark, straight thread.

"This gathering and leaping must be seen to realise how marvelous is the rapidity and how the motion seems flying, almost, as the ground is scorned, except at a sort of spring bound. As soon as the General tossed himself on to his bed, Byron would walk to him and was invited to share the luxury."

Harry Findlay purred when he heard such stories, for they reminded him of one greyhound he would own, treasure and often share his bed with. Big Fella Thanks was the name of the dog whose story would assume a status in Ireland's long and colourful coursing folklore, second to no other of its kind.

The tale of the Big Fella, an often cantankerous dog, his larger-than-life owner and a quiet, undemonstrative trainer, stirred ready echoes of Seabiscuit, the horse of American legend that gave succour to the nation through the Great Depression of the 1930s.

Seabiscuit was more of a little fella, a small horse that became the equine hero of the small-town masses in need of something to lift their spirits in times of hardship. In the final year of the 20th Century, in the deep south of the Republic of Ireland, the legend of Big Fella Thanks took defining shape. Like Seabiscuit, he was a symbol of hope over the odds.

The story was fired by the twin flames of innocent ambition

and heartbreaking tragedy. At first, all Harry wanted was to own a decent coursing dog. He ended up needing a dog that could mend the broken heart of an entire town.

The pieces slotted into place, Big Fella Thanks became a *cause célèbre* and a giant of his time. It was ironic that Harry should nickname him 'The Horse', because he wanted a champion greyhound, not an equine superstar. But this dog would become more than even Harry could ever have expected.

***

Harry Findlay walked – in not a particularly straight line – into the TV room in the bar at the Hotel Minella in Clonmel, Co. Tipperary, in January 1997, with his old friend, the Cork bookmaker, Edward Donnelly. "We'd both had about five pints down in the town, so we were very happy," Eddie said. "I introduced Harry to Denis O'Driscoll from Skibbereen."

It was not so much an introduction, more an acclamation as Denis was feted by Eddie as "the greatest fucking trainer of coursing greyhounds that ever lived." In reality, Denis O'Driscoll had only worked with track dogs and had never trained a coursing dog in his life.

Through the haze, Harry recalled a shy, red-faced lad who looked about 16. "I immediately wondered what the fuck Eddie was talking about," he said. "About 15 years earlier, I'd been given a tour of the great Mickey Murphy's house in Tralee. Over the years, dogs that were placed into Murphy's hands in the days leading up to the National Meeting had become three times shorter in the betting. Not to mention he'd already won a record seven Derbies. What could this kid do?"

A few further pints later, Harry had purchased a big 90lb black pup named Albert The Great. Denis O'Driscoll was his trainer. Albert The Great cost Harry £500 for a half share – the other half belonged to Denis' elder brother, Michael 'Curley' O'Driscoll, noted as having one of the keenest minds in the greyhound business.

Albert was not great enough to secure Harry, Curley and Denis the 'golden ticket' of a berth in the Clonmel finals, as he was beaten in the latter stages of three trial stakes that took place up and down the land in the weeks prior to the National Meeting. But their appetites had been more than whetted.

Denis O'Driscoll was a full-time chef at his father Noel's restaurant in Skibbereen, working dogs in the morning, going in for a 10-hour shift in the kitchens and then returning to his dogs in the evening. Harry told him: "You'll have to give up making fucking sherry trifles." They had a mission to complete.

***

Harry was 19 when he first set eyes on Powerstown Park, the home of the National Meeting, soon after he had spent the day at Mickey Murphy's knee. The Murphy homestead was not a luxurious spread befitting a legend in his sport, but an ordinary tenement in an unremarkable street. The front door opened into an old-fashioned sitting room – armchair in the middle of a linoleum floor, crucifix on the wall, bare and uninspiring – but when Harry walked through a second door, it was as if a Pandora's box had been opened.

It was the entrance to the dog's world that dominated the secluded section of the house. Harry had never seen such spotless kennels, shining steel and a kitchen area any chef from a five-star hotel would have been happy to serve from. In the kennels were two coursing dogs, leaping excitedly. "Beautiful bloody animals," he said.

"Coursing dogs were generally 20% bigger than track dogs and one of those first two I saw had the shine of a fresh conker. He took my breath away," Harry said. "After watching the first course on that initiation in Clonmel, I nearly pissed myself with excitement realising I was going to see 60 more of these two-dog courses in a single day. I knew I wouldn't want to leave."

It was to the Tipperary town each winter that coursing habitués descended en masse. Historically, the meeting had been staged on the first Monday, Tuesday and Wednesday of February before it was switched to Saturday, Sunday and Monday in 2013. Three days off work became one, to the outrage of many.

The decision to become a long weekend event had minimal impact on the economy of Clonmel and surrounding areas (worth around £15 million in 2017) that looked to a sudden intense concentration on the town as a means of inuring it against eleven more fallow months that followed.

Hotels trebled their rates and finding a room if you arrived the night before was virtually impossible. Latecomers begged and bunked down in whatever space they could find, but such inconveniences were of little import to the pub owners whose premises were clogged to overflowing and only closed for the shortest of adjournments. Pints of the black stuff stacked up. Most evenings ended with the singing of rebel songs that spoke of the Irish nationalism redolent of the south. The craic was incessant.

The Irish mingled with Australians, Americans, Englishmen

and Scandinavians, all hearty regulars immersed in the coursing customs where sport and alcohol meshed and wads of cash changed hands in a blur of bets, banter and burgeoning bookmaker's briefcases as the dogs flashed by every few minutes.

For those not from the region, much of the banter was a blur. Harry seemed to understand everyone perfectly, but then again he spoke the language of the punter and this was unfettered punting territory.

All roads led to Clonmel's racecourse, Powerstown Park, which could have passed for just another field were it not for a couple of stands which cried out for a lick of paint. The moment you walked into the grounds, the sounds and smells resonated, especially if your head was uncomfortably heavy. There were yapping dogs in their temporary kennels, short-odds punters shouting their prices, burgers aflame, Guinness being supped, while the previous night's excesses and the current day's courses were feverishly debated. Bleary eyes abounded until the betting stalls opened for business.

The format of coursing was straightforward – one dog against another, red collar against white collar, dashing across a field in pursuit of a hare. The dogs were released simultaneously by a 'slipper', who held both on an extended leash until the hare was a required distance up the field in the middle of the racecourse and moving strongly enough to ensure it had a direct route into the escape. Once the hare darted beneath a padded wall at the end of the course, the dogs could not reach it.

In 1993, a change in Irish Coursing Club (ICC) rules rendered compulsory the wearing of muzzles on the dogs to minimise the harm they might cause to their quarry, should they unnerve, corner or potentially upend it.

DJ Histon, chief executive of the ICC, told RTÉ, the national broadcaster, in 2017: "Coursing is not about killing the hare, which is presented with nothing it can't handle. The hare is one of the most successful prey species, and it's because of its ability to evade capture that it's so prolific in Ireland. Genetically, they have 360 degree vision, stereophonic hearing, they can make a turn in a single stride and they have tremendous speed, stamina and agility as well."

The winner of each course would be the first dog to 'turn' the hare. The pursued animal, sensing one or both dogs closing in, would deviate from the straight course it had been trained to follow. The judge, on horseback at the side of the course, raised a red or white flag to denote which dog had made the hare jolt sideways first.

There was the occasional disruptive protest against the existence of something the anti-blood sport groups insisted was not a sport at all, but legalised cruelty. The decision to muzzle all dogs was a step in the right direction but it did not deter repeated calls for coursing to be banned altogether. The protestors railed against the forced removal of hares from their natural habitat, that they were held for two months while trained to run and then placed at the mercy of two dogs who – though they could not kill it – might maim or petrify it.

To Harry, coursing was the purest of sports – "Dogs doing what their instinct and breeding trained them to do." Julian Snow, though not a dog man, appreciated his friend's love of the sport. "For Harry to be an advocate and an enthusiast of coursing went down well with the locals, especially when the rest of the country was full of socialist bureaucrats trying to stop it," he said.

Sir Mark Prescott was no socialist bureaucrat. The nobleman, a 3rd Baronet, had a distinctive past about as far removed from Harry's as it was possible to be. He was the Harrow-educated son of an art and theatre critic for *Punch* who broke his back at the age of 17 in a riding accident and then became an apprentice trainer at the famed Heath House yard in Newmarket. He was appointed head trainer in 1970, earning a reputation as a caring, patient man who also developed a love of all things blood sport, cockfighting and bullfighting his unbridled favourites.

Sir Mark was a ferocious advocate of coursing, and when the Waterloo Cup – England's premier event, first staged in 1836 in Great Altcar, Lancashire, and described as the 'blue riband of the leash' – was outlawed in 2005, he believed it to be a hugely retrograde step. "That was very sad," Sir Mark said. "The hare was the principal sufferer, because it wasn't conserved on the estates any more, so it was a lunatic piece of legislation, both vindictive and illogical."

Harry was present at the last rites of the Waterloo Cup. "There were so many people there from different walks of life and countries. The winner, Shashi, and five of the last eight runners had Pakistani handlers. I'd never known a sadness like it," he said. "For the last half an hour, Sir Mark looked as if he was going to be physically sick."

But Clonmel continued to afford Sir Mark an opportunity to spend three days with like-minded coursing aficionados, and it was there he first heard Harry Findlay. You could find Sir Mark at the same spot every year, three-quarters of the way up the field on an upturned tea chest that carried his special mark. That was the way of it at Powerstown – you got to the racecourse early, claimed your box, chalked your identity on it and that was your podium for three days. Woe betide anyone who might try to muscle in on your territory.

The Findlay tones made Sir Mark spin around on his wooden vantage point. "Harry hadn't been to the coursing before and he was at the back of the stand making lots of noise," he said. "He was good fun, he livened it up and he was betting quite big, bigger than most people. We all looked upon him as someone who was going to enhance the richness of the place."

Harry had known of Sir Mark through a horse he once trained, Spindrifter – 'a machine', as the trainer described him. "I was helping out in a betting shop at 18 as a board man [putting the prices up on sheets on the wall], and Spindrifter was a two-year-old that won more races than any since the beginning of time," Harry said. "In the old days, Spindrifter would start at 4/7 – now it would be 2/7. Spindrifter regularly kept me in the game when I was a teenager."

Harry's youthful idolatry of one of Sir Mark's horses had become full-blown admiration for the knight's love of coursing. "The great man wrote an article once about why it shouldn't be banned, and made me look like a selling plater in terms of his eloquence," Harry said. "I preferred the Doctor Dolittle approach, and if I'd asked a roomful of hares if they wanted coursing banned or not, they would all have screamed: "No, please, please can we keep it."

***

Most nights, when he repaired to the Hotel Minella in Clonmel after a few pints in town, Harry would be in bed not long after midnight. The chances of him winning a few quid from the coursing relied on him being fresh on the boxes the following morning. He was not a big drinker. But he was a heavy sleeper.

In February 1996 – the year before his introduction to Denis O'Driscoll and the purchase of a half share in Albert The Great – Harry was sharing a room at the hotel with Kelvin Richardson, one of the 'originals' in his support group who had worked on the London futures exchanges, became a professional punter and possessed an astute head for numbers. Richardson was another Clonmel regular.

One night, after Harry had gone to bed and as Richardson watched on, the card tables in the Minella were overturned amid chaotic scenes when five masked men burst into the room and a gun was pointed at the head of one of the guests who'd been mistaken for the hotel owner.

The gunmen demanded to know where the safe was and eventually made off with £12,500. Not a single shot was fired but half a dozen guests – those not scrambling for what was left of their card money – threw themselves out of the first floor windows to escape any potential gunfire. At least three broke a leg in the process.[1]

Kelvin Richardson made his way back to the bedroom where Harry was snoring and clambered under the sheets of his twin bed without speaking a word. Next morning, oblivious to the night's events, Harry was in the breakfast room, demanding his kippers. "I should have thought something was up when I

---

[1] *Three months later, the Irish Times reported the murder of John Kelly in Dublin, allegedly at the hands of an associate with whom he had fallen out after a series of armed robberies, including the one at the Hotel Minella. Kelly was watching TV at home when a gunman burst in and shot him first in the chest and then in the back of the neck.*

noticed the waitress' head was bandaged and all the windows were broken," he said. "I didn't have a clue the chef was in therapy."

***

There was no repetition of gun-toting or any less fearsome interruption to the smooth running of the National Meeting two years later, although Harry was on a distinct edge. He finally had a runner at Clonmel and knew the bitch was potential champion material.

Just before Christmas 1997, Harry told Julian Snow, who was staying with the family at their home in Sheffield, he had asked to meet the headmaster of his daughter Jade's school. Julian didn't ask why, he shrugged his shoulders and drove Harry to the gates.

He presumed there was something amiss academically, or Jade's attendance record was poor. Instead, Harry wanted to persuade the headmaster that Jade simply must go with him and Kay to the National Coursing Meeting in the Republic of Ireland.

"Harry had an armful of cuttings about a dog running in some distant place the headmaster had clearly never heard of," Julian said. "The story was so absurd it couldn't be untrue. Having Jade watch her dog run was more important to Harry than if she'd been asked to be a bridesmaid at a royal wedding."

The year 1997 had not been kind to the Findlay finances – "I was basically skint and bang under pressure," he said. One bright spark, he hoped, was the purchase of one of the litter sired by Needham House, the stud dog of the moment. The expensive pups had all gone and only the runt of the litter was left. Curley O'Driscoll acquired her for £2,000 and Harry said he would pay half, though he couldn't find the money straight up. They decided to name the bitch Jades Dilemma, after his daughter.

Harry had cobbled enough money together for an earlier than usual trip to Australia, where he grafted away with his good mate and former AFL footballer Simon Beasley at his bookmakers' offices at Canberra racecourse to try to generate some funds. Then a call came from Curley that Jades Dilemma was making her trial stakes debut in Charleville, Co. Cork. Door to door from Canberra to Charleville would take about 40 hours.

Harry arrived at the baronial Longueville House near Mallow barely able to keep his eyes open. "I hadn't seen Kay or Jade for the best part of a month and they were buzzing," he said. "Their excitement, and hotel chef Will O'Callaghan's superb digestion menu that evening, were just enough to keep me awake. I can't remember enjoying a meal more and it ended up being the best weekend of my life by a country mile."

Before Jades Dilemma's first-round course, five of the previous run-ups had resulted in one or both dogs being unsighted (not seeing the hare) and Harry wondered if his bitch had ran a trial in preparation for her big moment. "I suddenly thought 13,000 miles was a long way to come without a single rehearsal and when Denis said: 'No,' we both pissed ourselves laughing," Harry said.

Jades Dilemma flew out of the slips, pulled six lengths clear and won her first-ever course comfortably. Three hours later, she did precisely the same in the second round. Not only was she through to the next day's quarter-finals, but was a 2/1 joint favourite to win the Oaks trial stakes outright.

"I didn't get much sleep that night, and it wasn't so much because of the dog – I was all-in and more on Jacques Villeneuve to win the F1 world title," Harry said. "It was D-Day for him as well as Jades Dilemma on Sunday.

"The bitch couldn't have been more impressive, storming to victory in all three courses. As the judge raised his flag in the final, Villeneuve still had 20 laps to complete in the Spanish Grand Prix to become world champion. It was a straight shoot-out between him and Michael Schumacher, who had come off worse after a shunt early in the race. All Villeneuve had to do was to keep going.

"Eddie Donnelly's car was parked next to his betting pitch in the middle of a field in the middle of nowhere. We opened all the doors so everyone could hear but, as usual, BBC Five Live was shit reception on medium wave. We just about managed to hear the last few laps. Villeneuve was the champion. The journey to the local pub was like a dream. We not only had a runner at Clonmel, but a genuine contender. I was still in the game."

Eight-year-old Jade was sent forward at the award ceremony in the pub at Charleville to collect the trophy. She didn't know whether to laugh or cry, everyone was screaming her name. Her delirious father said: "I can't ever remember being so happy. The Guinness tasted really good that evening."

The success of that venture and the fact that the O'Driscoll family had an entrant in the Oaks, the bitch's classic, was the magnet that would draw hundreds of locals on the road from their home town of Skibbereen to Tipperary in the first week of February 1998. Among the travellers were two dashing men about town, Mick McCarthy and Jack Pat Collins.

***

Though he had a bitch in the National Meeting, Harry Findlay still hadn't paid Curley O'Driscoll his £1,000 share for Jades Dilemma before she was to run her first course at Clonmel. But he didn't have long to wait.

Frank Harvey, from Derry, a longtime friend of Harry's, who was one of hundreds who drove the length of Ireland each year to attend the meeting, knew the challenge they were facing in the first round. Her name was Alcaty, who had been beaten by three lengths in the final at Frank's local East Donegal meeting.

Alcaty was only in the Clonmel field because the bitch that beat her was injured, and Frank considered it a moderate trial stake anyway. Needless to say, the boys helped themselves. On a trawl of the local pubs and hotels the night before the championships, Harry and Frank were getting as much on as they could at odds of 1/2 down to 2/5 on Jades Dilemma.

Once Harry was on his tea chest at Powerstown the next morning and dominating the flow of cash in the short-odds betting, he had to be quick as Jades Dilemma was running in the first course of the day. He smashed her down from 2/5 to 1/5 and the dog never gave them a moment's worry. "She duly shit in," Harry said. "You didn't have to be a good judge to know she was a genuine contender. She was as strong as an ox and seemed to thrive on the tough uphill finish of the field."

All the Skibbereen gang was on ante-post at 25/1 and 20/1 for the bitch to win the Oaks. "The excitement was unreal,"

Harry said. "She made it to finals day without any difficulty and genuinely looked stronger every time she went up the field."

Indeed, on Wednesday morning, Jades Dilemma won her quarter and semi-finals with a healthy advantage on the clock and was considered an almost unbeatable 1/7 favourite to beat Dunsilly Pride in the final. Harry and the boys thought she might be led in the early stages (courses barely took 15 seconds to complete), but there was total conviction she would win.

As they left the slips, though, Jades Dilemma and her opponent bumped and it was Harry's bitch that came off worse from the collision. Her opponent bounded into a three-length lead and try as she might, it was simply too much ground to make up, especially as the slipper had let the dogs go a fraction early and it was not the longest of hares.

Dunsilly Pride was bearing down on its quarry. Jades Dilemma closed to within a fraction but crucially faltered as she hit the rising ground near the end of the course and the decision went to the rank outsider.

***

The walls of the O'Driscoll home on North Street, Skibbereen, were covered with photographs of greyhounds and family coursing victories. The sideboard was adorned with cups and trophies (Denis won the Irish Cup in 2017 to add to the collection). One of the defining images was that of the supporters who travelled from the town to witness Jades Dilemma's attempt to land the 1998 Oaks.

The picture was taken after the presentation of the runner-up trophy. The bitch herself was flirting with the camera and looked as stunning as ever. Harry, at the foot of the steps of Powerstown Park, failed to force a smile. An air of 'so near yet so far' prevailed.

So sure had everyone been that Jades Dilemma would win for Harry and the O'Driscolls that a party was scheduled for those rollicking on the roads back to Skibbereen. The glasses were lined up and extra Guinness ordered. "It was going to be the best night of all time, but now we had nothing to celebrate and nowhere to go," Harry said.

Harry, in a slough of despond, decided that he, Kay and Jade would stay an extra night in Clonmel while Curley O'Driscoll said he was going to travel home in a car with two of his best mates, 'Small' Mick McCarthy and Jack Pat Collins, twin embodiments of the life and soul of Skibbereen, as well as a teenage pal of theirs, Daniel O'Brien.

McCarthy had played Gaelic football for the local club, O'Donovan Rossa, captaining them to an All-Ireland Club victory, and he was talented enough to represent the Cork inter-county team, winning two senior All-Ireland medals in 1989 and 1990. Curley said: "Though nicknamed 'Small' on account of his height, Mick was an awful big thing around the town, and Jack Pat was a real ladies man. We went everywhere together."

Mick and Jack Pat said they were going to stop for dinner on the way home, and Curley – though not a big eater – would have joined them nine times out of ten. Instead, at the last minute, he said he'd stay and help Harry drown his sorrows. "Harry was at rock bottom, so down about the loss," Curley recalled. "I said to him: 'You have to take your beating in this game,' but he wasn't for cheering up."

BIG FELLA THANKS

Mick McCarthy and Jack Pat Collins set off for nearby Rathcormac, stopping at a local inn on the off-chance Harry and Curley had changed their minds about eating. When there was no sign of them, the lads clambered back into the car. At the next roundabout, less than two miles on, it slammed head-on into a Jeep and both were killed instantly. They hadn't stood a chance. Young Dan O'Brien, in the back of the car, walked away with a few scratches.

The town of Skibbereen, which had been preparing to celebrate a magnificent Oaks victory, was instead tossed into a maelstrom of desolation. A community in which everyone knew everyone else was in mourning and enough tears were shed that terrible night to have swelled the levels of the River Ilen ten-fold. Curley O'Driscoll was desolate. He had lost his two best friends in the world.

"I was in an awful state and felt so guilty because they had come to Clonmel to support us," he said. "Mick and Jack Pat were the two brightest, nicest guys in Skibbereen. The whole place was devastated."

The *Irish Independent* wrote a touching commemoration of Mick McCarthy, who left a young wife and two-year-old son: "We will always have visions of this curly-haired corner-forward turning defences inside out with his finely honed skills, brilliant ball control and sheer tenacity. He was not alone a superb footballer, but a very special person."

***

It was about six months after the shocking deaths of Mick McCarthy and Jack Pat Collins that Harry thought he might try to find a dog that could bring back some sparkle to the still-crushed town of Skibbereen, one good enough to win at the National Finals in Clonmel.

But with the 'Skib' boys still brokenhearted and not following the sport as closely as they used to, and Harry based in England, it was a thankless task. There was really no point in doing it unless they found a really top dog.

The new coursing season was well underway and Harry hadn't heard or done a thing when he received a call from an excited Martin McDaid from Derry, late one Sunday evening. A fine judge and a man who never missed a coursing weekend in his life, McDaid told Harry he had just seen a dog win a trial stakes at Killimer-Kilrush, and that it was impossible he would see a better athlete that year.

There were two problems. The dog wasn't for sale, and if he had been, Harry would have a major fight on his hands. The legendary handler and big-money buyer from Newry – Brendan Matthews – had been at Killimer that day. He was on to Big Fella Thanks' owner Anthony O'Connell before Martin had rung Harry. Matthews was telling everybody that night that the Big Fella wasn't for sale and if he did become available, he would get him.

Harry soon worked out that O'Connell was a real gent and a fine family man who wouldn't particularly be turned on by pound signs. That gave him a chance. Everybody in coursing knew what had happened to the 'Skib' boys the previous year and Harry told Martin exactly what to say when he phoned the owner. Half an hour later, the deal was done.

The agreed price was £19,000, a lot of money for a coursing dog back in 1999. But Harry always preferred to pay extra for a proven dog rather than half as much for an inexperienced pup or sapling. O'Connell caved in to Harry's request late on a Monday afternoon. The slight problem was he was flying to Cape Town at 10pm the following night.

There were no bank transfers when buying dogs in Kerry in 1999. It was cash in hand. Harry left Sheffield at 8.30am on Tuesday and was at his bank in Chesterfield to pick up the readies bang on 9am. The cashiers had it waiting for him. He flew to Ireland, met Denis at a coursing meeting at Bandon, Co. Cork, where they trialled one of their dogs, and headed north to Abbeydorney to pay for their purchase.

O'Connell's sons remembered the day Harry arrived to buy Big Fella Thanks, much for the fact that he couldn't stay still, walking back and forth from kitchen to sitting room to keep up with Teletext, checking on a European tie that had kicked off early in Russia.

When the time came to shake hands and Big Fella Thanks was tucked up in the back of their van, Harry and Denis placed a bag of readies on the kitchen table. At the end of the count, they were staggered that it contained £17,000. They were two grand short. Harry and Denis returned to the van, turned it upside down and found the dog lying on top of the missing £2,000. Big Fella Thanks was Harry's.

Anthony O'Connell had been reluctant to sell to Harry – despite all the emotional buttons being pressed – because he worried Denis O'Driscoll's lack of experience as a trainer in the coursing world would restrict the dog's chances of a successful career. Anthony might have been selling the dog, but he still wanted him to win. Despite Jades Dilemma's performance at the 1998 Oaks, Denis was still regarded as something of a novice in the game. Harry convinced O'Connell that Denis was up to the task.

Curley O'Driscoll gauged the temperature and the talk around the local towns. "Everyone thought Harry was mad spending so much money on the dog and that giving Denis the dog was mad, mad, mad, but he bought it for Denis because of what happened [to Mick McCarthy and Jack Pat Collins]."

There were a couple of months before the Derby to get the Big Fella in perfect shape. Denis O'Driscoll would not be making any sherry trifles for a while.

***

On the way from Kerry to Skibbereen, the boys stopped at the No.1 greyhound vet in Cork – Chris Donovan. Alongside Harry and his £19,000 purchase, waiting for his turn was a local farmer who also had a white and brindle greyhound. His dog had cost £50 and had a piece of string for a lead. Other than that, the dog was magnificent, as bright as a button, in great condition with a beautiful coat. On the contrary, the Big Fella looked like an old man, his feet as big as his legs were long, which gave him a hunched back, and his droopy bassett hound eyes did little to suggest a *joie de vivre*.

Harry reckoned if he had randomly selected 100 people in the street who had no idea about greyhounds, shown them the pair and asked which they thought was worth £19,000 and which was the £50 dog, 99 of them would have made the wrong choice. "You wouldn't have had Big Fella Thanks as a champion in a million years," he said.

BIG FELLA THANKS

When asked for a word to describe Big Fella Thanks, those closest to him said 'grumpy' or 'miserable'. His mother was Emmerdale Rose, and Tom Horgan, a local breeder, booked pups from the litter, given her impressive pedigree. "One or two of them sold and this fella was left, possibly no one wanted him," Tom said. "I wouldn't have kept him myself. About four or five months old, he was like a giraffe, all legs, no body. He was an ugly duckling."

Harry's initial inclination was to change the dog's name, and not because it evoked an infamous event in Irish business history. The dog had been initially named after an incident between former Taoiseach Charles Haughey and Ben Dunne, from the family that owned Dunnes Stores, one the country's largest department chains.

Dunne was alleged to have paid Haughey substantial amounts of money for undisclosed favours. At a tribunal hearing into the affair, a conversation between the two was revealed. [Dunne:] "Here's something for yourself." [Haughey:] "Thanks big fella." O'Connell was not allowed to register 'Thanks Big Fella', so he called the dog 'Big Fella Thanks'.

Harry was concerned people would think he'd bought Big Fella Thanks because the name mirrored his personality and that it was a gesture of self-importance rather than because the dog had serious Derby-winning potential. Master Kieran – the name of one of Anthony O'Connell's sons – was his chosen alternative.

One among the number of Harry's band of coursing brothers simply would not have it.

Finbar Giltinen was nearly 70 years old the day the Big Fella was bought. He had been bookmaker Eddie Donnelly's clock man since the beginning of time. His duty at the coursing was simple but vital. A flagman at an appointed position at the start of the course would signal when the dogs went past him. The clock man immediately pressed the button on his stopwatch and when the winning dog reached his designated eye-line, the watch was stopped. The time would be relayed to Eddie and had a direct effect on his odds for the forthcoming courses. For a bookmaker, a good clock man was the difference between winning and losing.

"I'd been on long journeys with Finbar. We'd supped pints in each other's company, but in over ten years he'd never said a fucking word to me," Harry said. "Not for the first time, it was pissing down with rain at Bandon. Eddie jumped into the driver's seat, with me alongside him, and as Finbar clambered into the back, I told Eddie of my plan to change the dog's name. Finbar growled: 'Change the dog's name and you change his luck.'

"For once in my life, I was speechless for nearly a minute. Eddie asked why I was changing the name, and I said: 'How the fuck can I change it when that old bastard hasn't spoken to me in nearly 12 years and the first thing he says is not to!'" Big Fella Thanks remained Big Fella Thanks.

Now came the important part, knocking Big Fella Thanks into shape for the Derby. It was no straightforward undertaking. Denis O'Driscoll said: "He was a very lazy dog, he wasn't the best to gallop, so we walked and walked him, miles and miles up and down the hills outside Skibbereen. We did that every day. He was a poor grubber, poor at eating his food. We were worried about him all the time."

It was a sentiment echoed by brother Curley. "He was big,

lanky and all over the place," he said. "We had to employ young lads from the town to help us walk him. And when you did, he'd drag you in the bushes for a piss every 20 yards. But Harry knew he could run. The lads who tempted Harry to buy him had seen him run, so they knew he could run. But he had a miserable attitude and was very fussy about what he'd eat. A terrible dog he was.

"Denis would spoon-feed him, but he wouldn't eat. Denis was with him the whole time, trying to build him up. The Derby was real tough and you had to have the dog at the peak of everything. You need them in that way to go up to Clonmel to have any chance of winning."

Harry had flown from South Africa, where he had stayed for three weeks, on to Australia for his annual winter break, and not a day went by when he wasn't on the phone at least three times to Denis for updates on the dog's progress. "Nothing else seemed to matter," Harry acknowledged. "I was with Kay's father, Ramon, in Sydney, and it wasn't like any other trip. We were trying to relax but all we could think about was the Derby. Big Fella was the 4/1 ante-post favourite and the pressure was immense."

A group of Harry's closest friends, including Frank Harvey, drove from the borders of Northern Ireland to Skibbereen to watch the dog's final workouts on the gallops to guarantee that he was 100% and help iron out any last-minute problems. There were none.

And so, once more, a year on from a trek east that ended in such tragedy, the people of Skibbereen were on the march to Clonmel – a group consumed by sadness, excitement and trepidation in equal measures.

***

The winner of the Derby at the National Meeting would have to be victorious in six courses across three days, one on Monday, two on Tuesday and in three on Wednesday, the finals day. Big Fella Thanks could not have been any better prepared, nothing had been left out, he was ready to go.

The dog was an overwhelming 1/8 to win his first-round course, taking on a challenger with vastly inferior trial stake form, but as the two dogs left the slips, Big Fella Thanks inexplicably lurched to the left and off a true line. He hadn't sighted the hare. The groan from the crowd was stomach-turning.

"We thought: 'Fuck it, we're going home, we're beat,'" said Curley. Big Fella Thanks was three lengths adrift halfway up the field when he got sight of his quarry and showed amazing pace to get up and take the flag by a couple of lengths. Stood on the boxes afterwards, plenty of faces were crabbing his performance.

Before Harry left that afternoon, he went to the kennels area to see his dog. Jerry Desmond, the Irish Coursing club chairman, had been standing by the slips gate to watch the course. He told Harry that though Big Fella Thanks was in grave danger early on, the balance he showed for such a big dog when he got on line was incredible. It was a mantra repeated by many farmers and gnarled dog folk throughout the three days.

Big Fella Thanks was still an uneasy 5/1 favourite to win the Derby that night. The boys repaired to the heaving Jeremiah Moynihan bar on Upper Gladstone Street, where the hordes from Skibbereen were already in full flow. "We were disappointed with his performance and grateful for the result,"

Curley said. "And we never lacked confidence because we had Harry on the team."

The following morning, Big Fella Thanks copped a break when his second-round opponent withdrew through injury. He had to go up the field on his own in a bye course, so as not to have an unfair advantage over the other dogs in the competition. He clocked a decent time but the second day was always going to be about his third-round afternoon clash with Barney Mooney's flying machine I Say.

The short-odds betting on the boxes was furious and fair. You could get 4/7 on the Big Fella and 7/4 about I Say. Coming out of the slips half a length in front, Big Fella Thanks opened a length-and-a-half lead he maintained to the crucial turn of the hare. The official part of the course was over, the favourite was through, but the hare turned again and ran back the way it came, away from the padded protective wall. A huge sigh rose from the crowd. The dogs' instinct was to keep chasing the hare it had no chance to catch. Any extra exertion for the winner – who may have to run three times the following day – could seriously damage his chances.

It took over a minute – a lifetime in coursing – for the hare to dodge, weave, spot its escape and dart beneath the barrier where the dogs could not reach it. The bookies had seen enough and the chorus was that Big Fella couldn't conceivably win the Derby.

No stone had been left unturned to make sure Big Fella Thanks was comfortable and safe. 'Fierce' Pierce Connolly was in charge of looking after him, and the team had turned a horse box trailer into a mobile kennel with Pierce as *de facto* security, staying in it with the Big Fella at home in Skibbereen, on the trip to Clonmel and during the championships themselves.

Everything had gone without a hitch until that Tuesday night. The dog's extra exertions in the field had really taken their toll. He was crashed out in his trailer but wasn't doing much else. Worst of all, he wouldn't touch his food. He'd have been a million-to-one to win three courses the next day without grubbing up.

"He loved the fatty, cheap bits of chicken – the parson's nose and greasy undercarriage were his favourites," Harry said. "Finally, feeding him that alone, he got his dinner down at about 11pm. We still had a chance."

When Denis came to walk the dog at first light the following morning, 'Fierce' was sleeping so soundly in the trailer that the trainer was able to take the dog out, walk him for half an hour, bring him back, settle him again and security did not stir.

Though the target was obviously to win the event outright, qualifying for the third and final day was a huge relief and – though no excuse was required – reason enough to down a few more pints of the black stuff on Tuesday night in Moynihans.

At the same moment, entering the pub by different doors, in walked Noel O'Driscoll, the patriarch of the family, and Harry Findlay. Anyone asleep in the nearby houses – and that was highly unlikely – would have been woken by the Irish roar that greeted their arrivals. It might even have woken Fierce Pierce.

***

Morning had broken fair over the hills surrounding Clonmel on finals day of the 1999 National Meeting. The eyes were red but the spirit was strong as the crowd descended, agog with anticipation. The Derby was the pinnacle of the meeting, so the courses in that event were staged last, after the plate competitions, the Champion Stakes and the Oaks.

Handsome Billa was the most impressive dog Harry had seen in the first two rounds. "I knew we were in for a real tight buckle in the quarter-final," he said. "I was surprised and delighted when the Big Fella burst two lengths clear in the first few strides and was never in danger." Despite this convincing victory in a good time, there was new name at the head of the Derby betting – Toy Razor. He was simply taking off in the other half of the draw, the freshest dog in the competition, he was well ahead on the clock and was in more than capable hands.

The semi-finals were set: Toy Razor v Forever Minstrel and Snipefield Glory v Big Fella Thanks. Both favourites had the look of good things but neither was considered absolute certainties. Their opponents had been in the top eight of the betting before the competition started. The cream had risen to the top.

Ultimately, the hotpots obliged, but in significantly varying styles. Toy Razor pounded into a five-length lead against a good-class dog and clocked the fastest time of the 1999 meeting, indeed one of the fastest in Clonmel's history. "You had to be there to see how fast and strong he looked," Harry said.

In the second semi-final, the Kerry-trained Snipefield Glory was neck and neck with Big Fella Thanks as they approached the incline when he missed a stride and switched sides. "Usually if dogs do that they have no chance, but he came right back at the Big Fella and we were lucky to beat him by half a length," said Curley O'Driscoll.

Harry saw it slightly differently. "Big Fella was just doing enough in front and when Snipefield almost came alongside, he kicked again and pulled out a bit more." Harry was fully aware that his dog wasn't overly impressive in his semi-final, but that wasn't the problem. Toy Razor was. "I couldn't believe anything could do that to Forever Minstrel," he said.

The knowledgeables in the crowd were of like mind. Curley O'Driscoll said: "They all said our dog looked fucked, he looked very down and out after that course. But that was just his make-up. Brendan Matthews, who wanted to buy him two months earlier, said: 'Even if our Lord Himself came down from the cross, he couldn't help Big Fella win the final.' But by God, he didn't know we had two lads in heaven looking down on us."

There would be a 45-minute interval between the end of the semi-finals and the start of the succession of finals, of which the Derby would be the finale. The others races went by in a blur for anyone connected with Big Fella Thanks. Harry didn't bet on any of them.

Curley O'Driscoll, thinking of Mick McCarthy and Jack Pat Collins, had never experienced such diverse emotions: "We were 4/1 before the start of the whole competition and now 3/1 in the final, the rank outsider. We had Toy Razor to beat and no one gave us a chance. But we knew our fecking dog was fighting fit and was better than people thought. I went up into the stands five minutes before the off and bumped into Jimmy Barry-Murphy, the great Cork hurling man, and he said: 'Well Mick, what do you think?' I said: 'Jimmy, we're not dead yet,' and he said: 'The best of luck.'"

On the upturned wooden boxes at the front of the stands, the air was thick with anticipation. Harry clambered back onto his tea chest next to Frank Harvey. "I told him we still had a squeak," Harry said. "I'd spoken to Joe O'Driscoll [another brother of Denis and Curley] during the interval, and he agreed with me that Big Fella was only toying with Snipefield Glory in the semi-final and all was not lost. Frank had tears in his eyes, his nose was running and all he could say was: 'Will you not fuck off, he has no chance.'"

The 'slipper' for the Derby final was the evergreen Johnny Doyle. He'd been around coursing all his life. "It was like officiating at an All-Ireland final," he said. "The Derby was always special, but in those days there was a lot more money around and people were carefree. Big Fella Thanks, now he was an outstanding dog. You didn't see too many like him."

The slipper had to make sure that the hare was strong enough for the course as it bounded past the leashed dogs. That day, Doyle realised the first hare was neither fast nor straight enough for proper course, so there was a momentary pause as a blue awning was drawn across the front of the dogs. A deathly hush descended over 15,000 people as they waited for the next hare.

Harry looked down at his programme and then up at the sky. "I realised that this was the last course of the century at such an historic venue," he said. "I'm not remotely religious, but I looked at the cosmos or whatever was out there, and said to myself if I could have £10 million in cash and ten Derby winners further down the line, I wouldn't take it. I'd rather just have the winner of this course. I knew I'd never want or ask for anything again."

Not only was it the last course of the 20th Century, it would prove to be up there with the best in living memory, a stirring battle between two stunning animals. This time the hare was strong and straight, the dogs were released and Big Fella Thanks jumped out into a neck advantage, only for Toy Razor to pour up on the inside and take a half-length lead halfway up the hill.

From somewhere, Big Fella Thanks found a second burst of energy and, as a sound like thunder rolled across the racecourse from the stands, overtook Toy Razor, bounded two lengths clear at the top of the field and broke his challenger's heart. Race commentator Mitchell Fortune shouted that the crowd was going 'stark-raving mad.' Big Fella Thanks had won the Derby. Clonmel had not seen the like of it for years.

***

Everyone was pouring onto the field – well at least they were trying to. Tom Horgan, the breeder, leapt the wire on the side of the course and fell flat on his face trying to untangle himself from the netting. Anthony O'Connell's sons thought they could bound up the course but found the hill too knackering and ran out of breath.

Johnny Doyle heard the roar of the crowd from the slippers' hut, knew how the course had finished and dabbed a tear from his cheek. A huge percentage of a devoutly Catholic crowd believed the result had been written in the heavens. The Big Fella had done it for Mick and Jack Pat.

Harry's instinct was to turn to where Curley O'Driscoll had gone the colour of his bright red rain jacket. "His head looked like a snooker ball," Harry recalled. "What I remember most was the sheer emotion. Noreen McManus [wife of legendary Irish racehorse owner JP McManus] and all her Greenbottle syndicate pals were right behind Curley crying their eyes out. So was everybody else."

Denis O'Driscoll, who watched the final from the slipper's hut, did have the energy to run the length of the uphill course and jumped on his tea chest to give Harry a bear hug. Everyone wanted to shake the owner's hand, so much so that when he came to try to raise the trophy, Harry couldn't even grip it properly. "Those massive farmers and dog people with their huge hands, they'd crushed my tiny mitts," he said.

All roads led to Skibbereen that evening. The celebration was held at the pub run by the sister of Jack Pat Collins. As the entourage from Clonmel approached the town, the highway was marked on both sides by a stream of bonfires – every bin and basket seemed to be aflame. It was to be the first night of a party that lasted for weeks.

When Harry was allowed to adjourn to his room at the West Cork Hotel at 6.30am, after 'what will always be the greatest day and night of my life,' he realised his waistcoat and jacket pockets were stuffed with cash. Eddie Donnelly had collected half the Big Fella's winnings and didn't have anywhere else to put the money. "I had £20,000 at 9/2 on Big Fella Thanks and it was my only bet," Harry said.

Curley O'Driscoll relished the celebrations but couldn't help remembering two friends who would loved to have been a part of the day. "Very few people from Skibbereen knew much about coursing before the accident," he said. "And now everyone followed it. Denis won the Oaks twice more, once for Harry with Mountain Guest in 2006.

"Harry always involved Anthony O'Connell and his sons – the previous owners of Big Fella Thanks – in everything. He made sure the family was looked after if they came to see the dog run. He set up a free bar in every pub in Skibbereen for a week after Big Fella's win. That was Harry – too generous. When Harry was going well, everyone was going well."

To underline the quality of Big Fella Thanks' success in Clonmel, three of the dogs he had beaten on the way to his Derby success – I Say, Handsome Billa and Snipefield Glory – all retired successfully to stud. As for Big Fella Thanks, he was never quite the ladies' man – although, to be fair, he didn't get to see many bitches. Most stud dogs would go to stay with a stud master, but Harry insisted the dog remained with Denis in Skibbereen.

But Big Fella Thanks had secured cult status in Ireland. There was a huge crowd for the following season's meeting in New Ross where he once again took on Toy Razor. They reached the final with ease, and this time, Big Fella Thanks raced away with the All Age Cup, opening up a two-length lead from the off and extending that advantage before he turned the hare.

From there, the Big Fella went on to win the Mallow All Age Cup and a similar event at Killimer-Kilrush. When he won his quarter-final at the Champion Stakes in Clonmel in 2000, Big Fella Thanks had racked up a record 31 consecutive victories. The great run ended in the semi-final when his old adversary Snipefield Glory finally got the better of him.

Harry and Denis decided to take the Big Fella back to Killimer-Kilrush once more later that year, where he was to face the 2001 Derby favourite, Matt Hyland, in the second round of his defence of the All Age Cup. "Plenty of faces you didn't normally see on the first day turned up to take on Harry and the Big Fella in the short-odds betting," Curley said. "Matt Hyland went off the marginal favourite but he was beaten three lengths by our dog." Matt Hyland would be the losing finalist at Clonmel in the Derby three months later.

Killimer was a remote spot in Co. Clare, but the pubs were buzzing that night. The next day when Big Fella Thanks went to slips against the weakest of opposition, the biggest concern for his connections was if he could maintain his interest in the thrill of the course. Although well in front, he lost sight of the hare and wasn't on a true line. The judge drew the white flag.

It was pouring as only it can in Ireland and Harry went wandering out of the field for a few minutes on his own. Suddenly, from behind a huge bush, the judge, resplendent in red jacket, appeared on horseback and stopped him in his tracks. The judge took off his cap. "How sad to see the Big Fella finally beaten," he said. "I so nearly pulled the other flag and gave him the decision."

It was one of Harry's favourite Big Fella moments. The night before, in the best pub in the main square of Kilrush, there were pockets of people from Portsmouth, Derry, Sheffield, Perth and Skibbereen, all having a great time because of one dog. "I wondered then when the dream was finally going to end," Harry said. "Now I knew."

On their next visit to Skibbereen, Kay thought Big Fella Thanks was looking especially sorry for himself – he always did for the most part – and started to get emotional. She asked Harry: "Can we have him at home now?"

At their resplendent pad near Bath, the Big Fella was afforded an almost regal status. Julian Snow remembered: "This big ugly dog, snorting and farting in a corner of Harry's office, but he was treated like royalty until the day he died. You had to give him respect."

As the months went by, even famous greyhounds were worn down by the cares of life. The Big Fella developed cancerous tumours around his backside and in his testicles, and when he contracted a serious virus in 2009, no one thought he would survive more than a few days. Harry kept vigil over Big Fella in his office, and one evening, when he had been called down for dinner, left him wrapped in a sleeping bag with his head near the door and returned 15 minutes later to find the dog had disappeared.

Kay and Harry shouted for their friend Bradley Montague, on holiday from Australia, to help them look for the old champion. From 9pm until 1am, aided by torchlight, they searched high and low. "There was a little limestone cave against the back of the house, and though we must have gone past it a few times, we flashed the light again and there he was, stuck in a crevice. He'd obviously crawled in there to die," Harry said.

"Bradley always was a skinny bastard and we pushed him into the crevice, scratching himself to bits in the process, and he slowly hauled the Big Fella out, back end first. I said we should let him die with a bit of dignity in the boot room. Kay got his bed down from the office, we laid him on his mattress, and effectively said our goodbyes.

"We woke up before 7am and the whole house smelt of death. I'd never known anything like it. In the boot room, the walls were covered in thin black shit, but he was wide awake, exactly where we'd left him. He lived another ten months. He was a bloody amazing dog."

The local veterinary surgeon, Andrew Chivers, was injecting the dog with anabolic steroids to keep him going, and two days after what Harry described as 'a dose of Jungle Juice' was administered, the dog chased a deer almost twice its size across a nearby field for 500 yards. It was like the old days. Chivers recalled: "Harry was thrilled. In my 40 years in this business up to that time, I am pretty sure that was the first time I'd ever been described as a fucking legend."

BIG FELLA THANKS

In return for keeping the Big Fella going, the vet received two gallons of cognac awarded to the owners of Denman as their prize for his victories in the 2007 and 2009 Hennessy Gold Cups. Neither Paul Barber nor Harry drank the stuff.

But the day Harry hoped would never come could not be put off forever. He asked Chivers to come to the house one afternoon to put Big Fella Thanks down before Kay headed north to visit her family in Sheffield. Everyone was there to say their last goodbyes, but the vet still saw signs of hope. "Let's try this," he said, brandishing another potion. "I think I can keep him going."

Another terrible night followed for the Big Fella and the next morning Chivers was summoned once more. The poor dog couldn't even get to his feet. Harry cradled his head and Georgie Welsh – a sculptor commissioned to work on a life-size model of Big Fella Thanks and who had fallen under the dog's spell – took him at the other end. The vet put him to sleep. "He went very peacefully," Andrew Chivers said. "There were a few tears."

"All three of us were balling our eyes out," Harry said. "In the end, I was so pleased Kay wasn't there, it would have been too sad. If she loves me half as much as she loved the Big Fella, I am a very lucky man."

9

THE 13TH MAN

There is no special mention of him in the nation's record books, he cannot to be located between Matthew Elliott and Adam Gilchrist in their alphabetical list of players, and yet, for one day, one glorious summer day in 2006, Harry Findlay donned the apparel of the Australian cricket team and became the unlikeliest 13th man in their history.

It could, of course, only have happened to Harry. He had not flown to Melbourne with the intention of being involved in cricket for any reason other than the usual adrenalin rush of making hay from the success of the baggy greens at the same time as enjoying R&R in perfect temperatures, a few games of tennis, some archetypal Aussie horse racing at Caulfield – "The place always reminded me of *The Sullivans*," he said – and spending days and nights with one of the best mixes of mates anyone could have.

He thought his days as a sportsman were over when he was unable to maintain the goalscoring record that had been the talk of the playing fields of High Wycombe when he was 12. He scored a lot of goals that season, knew what he was doing and had plenty of confidence, but in his own words: "Had no pace or class, and in my first year at John Hampden, I just about managed to get on the sub's bench for the reserve team.

"If someone told me I'd end up being on the sub's bench for the Australian cricket team one day, I'd have thought they'd had one spliff too many," he said. "But it fucking happened."

As ever, the Crown Towers on Melbourne's Southbank was Harry's comfort choice, the perfect relaxing antidote as the gambling dollars flew back and forth. The Crown's casino was a haven for the amateur punter, but Harry never got the fascination for the one-armed bandits and blackjack tables where money vanished in a blur of card deals, arm thrusts and generous gulps of VB.

Even as an eight-year-old at a Butlins holiday home in Great Yarmouth, he worked out that playing the bandits was a real mug's game. "A cherry on the first reel only paid evens," he said. "What was the point of wasting all those 2ps?" As for dabbling at blackjack, he'd had enough of trying to win his mates' pocket money at three-card brag before he was 14, and hadn't played cards since.

The only time you would have found Harry anywhere near the gaming area of the Crown was in the Sports Bar late on a Saturday night, watching a short-priced hotpot bolt up in a trotting race at Perth.

It was better to use that time of year to replenish the soul in surroundings that mixed sociability with sport, unbeatable seafood with classic wines, which Harry indulged in the hotel's superior restaurants – Rockpool and Silks. That said, he appreciated that the next wager was never further away than a rustle of the racing sections of the *Herald Sun* or *Melbourne Age*.

They were spread across the desk in his room at the Crown in January 2006. The television in the corner was tuned to the cricket on Channel 9, where the velvety tones of Richie Benaud were attempting to trace an objective path through the barely disguised partiality of his co-commentator, Bill Lawry.

Australia were involved in a series of five One Day Internationals against South Africa, and during one of the lunch intervals, Glenn McGrath, the fast bowler, was being interviewed. Harry turned the volume up a touch. "I wasn't listening that closely but I heard Glenn mention something about an auction for the Flying Doctors [Australia's famous air service which transported lifesaving medical supplies to the Outback]."

McGrath was announcing that the winner of an auction, where all proceeds went to the Flying Doctors charity, would have paid for the right to be Australia's 13th man for the upcoming day-night match in Melbourne. Harry, in the room with his best mate in Australia, Bradley Montague, couldn't quite believe his ears.

"It had to be a joke – something for the kids," he said. "But the lady interviewer said you had to ring 0800 something or other and you've got a chance to be the 13th man. This was the real thing, you were on the bus, part of the team, in the nets, in the dugout, every bit of it.

"McGrath said they were looking forward to having the highest bidder on board, and straight away I said to Bradley: 'This will happen once in a lifetime, it's a one-off, I've got to be top of that list.' The next day, the auction closed and the highest bid received was \$35,000."

The winner and next 13th man for Australia was none other than Harry 'The Dog' Findlay.

The only minor element of disappointment for Harry was that he would not be making his first and last appearance for Australia at the Melbourne Cricket Ground (MCG), the iconic venue famed for its high-rise white floodlight towers, massive pitch acreage and the fact that it could house over 100,000 patrons. The One Day International was, instead, to be played at the somewhat less salubrious Docklands (now Etihad) Stadium.

Never mind. It was with a jolly swagman bounce in his step and the odd butterfly in the pit of his stomach that he made his way along Southbank from the Crown to the Quayside apartments – directly across the Yarra River from the yellow-bricked Flinders Station – where he was to be introduced to his team-mates for the day. "I thought the Aussie team would be staying somewhere a bit smarter," he said.

Harry was met by the same lady who had interviewed McGrath on Channel 9, who was clearly flustered that Harry Findlay, with his big glasses, ample girth and Cockney accent, was to be sharing the Aussie locker room that afternoon with McGrath, Ricky Ponting and Brett Lee. "She kept going on about how lovely it was all going to be, but I bet she was thinking: 'Fucking hell, how do I explain this one?'" Harry said.

"We were at the foot of the stairs at the apartments and Andrew Symonds, a charismatic Queenslander, appeared on the landing. I couldn't have been a bigger fan, even in his early days playing for Gloucestershire, but he was a bit of a frightening sight first thing in the morning. The lady says: 'Oh, Andrew, here's Harry Findlay, your 13th man today.' He grabbed me by the hand, crushed it, looked me straight in the eye and growled: 'Behave yourself!'"

Perhaps Symonds had remembered encountering Harry nine months earlier, when they were staying in adjacent hotels in Colombo, Sri Lanka. The Australians were touring in the sub-continent and the team made regular trips across the bridge separating the hotels because the one where Harry was staying not only had a superior swimming pool, but served the better food, especially their pizzas.

"The Aussies never seemed to be able to get to our place quick enough," he said. "I broke the ice with a few of the lads telling them how much fun a group of us had at the MCG when they beat India in a One Day International the year before. I said: 'I've supported you lot for years, home and away, but never more than that day.' India were cruising to victory [134-1 chasing Australia's 288 from their 50 overs] when Sachin Tendulkar was brilliantly caught by Ponting.

"It was one of those out-of-this-world catches, the ball was flying over his head and it looked as if he had grown a second arm to catch it. When [Sourav] Ganguly was run out for 82 and smashed his bat into the ground as he walked off, he must have heard the cheers from up in our box. The game had been turned on its head, we were having a right party as we'd all made a big day of it and had more money on than we probably should have done.

"As I was relating the story of one of our best nights ever to the Aussie lads, I remember Damien Martyn pissing himself laughing. He was supposed to be the shy one of the group. Little did he know that I was soon going to be in the dressing room with him!"

At the Quayside apartments on matchday, Harry and his shadow from Channel 9 were on the pavement waiting for the team transport to arrive. Harry assumed it would be a luxurious trip across the city in a posh single-decker coach decorated in the Aussie colours, which would be roared on by the cheering hordes as it snaked towards the stadium.

Not quite. A Budget Hire van suddenly braked hard in front of the apartment building with a grinning Andrew Symonds behind the wheel. Harry was beckoned to clamber in, where he found Ponting and Martyn squashed together in a couple of seats in the back.

"It was like going to play for Hithercroft Colts under-12s, but without the smell of wintergreen," Harry said. "I squeezed in next to Ricky, introduced myself and remembered a pal of mine from Tasmania once assured me that his brother, Mike Donaldson, not only played with Ricky as a youngster, but was a better batsman! I hoped he hadn't been bullshitting when I mentioned him, but Ricky remembered him very fondly.

"We began chatting and I already knew he was as much of a mad greyhound fan as I was. His nickname was 'Punter'. One of my favourite tracks in the world was the old White City at Launceston, where he was born, and, like me, he was heartbroken when it had closed a couple of years before."

The pair were getting on so well that Harry felt emboldened enough to ask the captain a direct question – "I'm not being funny here, Ricky, but for all the times I've seen you, what were you thinking when Adam Gilchrist decided to walk when given not out in the 2003 World Cup semi-final against Sri Lanka?' I knew I was fuming at the time, and when Ricky passed Gilchrist on his way to the crease, I was sure that he was, too. His answer confirmed it."

Ponting – possibly distracted by the hubbub over Gilchrist's decision to walk that day – made only two runs before he was the second Australian out, but a typically surging Symonds innings of 91 not out put his team in command. They won by 48 runs. "Roy [Symonds' nickname] was laughing along in the driving seat when I put Ricky under that bit of pressure," Harry said.

Symonds steered the Budget van into the Etihad, parked under the stands, discharged its cargo and Harry was ushered into the Aussie dressing room – "One of the biggest fucking rooms I'd ever seen," he said. And there, in the centre of it, sat David Boon, the team manager, walrus moustache and all.

"The TV girl had done it again, walked up to Boon with me a step behind saying: 'Hello, David. Meet our 13th man.' I said: 'Hello, David. Harry Findlay.' Well, his face was the colour of fucking tomato ketchup. He'd have paid 40,000 Aussie dollars to strangle me there and then. He just couldn't believe it. Their ideal 13th man would have been a 10-year-old from New South Wales with an autograph book who'd sit in the corner quiet as a mouse, and here was a big, fat 40-year-old Pommie punter with opinions on everything. Well, it was their idea to auction the spot for the Flying Doctors, not mine!

"The Aussies had a session in the nets before the game. Glenn McGrath asked me to collect the balls and throw them back after they'd finished bowling. I never was a powerful thrower but one ball I chucked caught Glenn flush on the back of his arm. Shaun Pollock, a real class act I'd met as a young man in Cape Town a few years before, was in the South African nets pissing himself laughing."

Much to Harry's relief, McGrath was passed fit to play. But in the dressing room preparing for the match, Harry was approached by one of Australia's team of security men who asked point-blank if he was a gambler. He bluffed his way through it, but his mobile phone was confiscated all the same. "Fucking hell, now I didn't have a phone all day. How the hell was I going to survive?" he wondered.

As crowd numbers grew, Harry marched out into the middle of the Etihad for the coin toss. South Africa's skipper Graeme Smith briefly acknowledged him. "He didn't say much when he saw me, he probably wondered who the fuck I was. But we all posed for a picture together – him, me and Ricky," Harry said.

Trying to appear incongruous, slap bang in the middle of the Australian team bench – "I made a few comments, but no mistakes," Harry said – the 13th man watched his adopted side amass 245 from their 50 overs. On the face of it, it was a very beatable total, but Harry's intuition and reading of the circumstances and conditions told him that Australia were a nap.

"I knew it was a massive amount of runs in reality, because they were played on a ruddy football pitch. I had never seen anything like it," he said. "I'll tell you how bad it was, the players were wearing cleats, proper football studs. Not one of them was wearing cricket boots. It was almost impossible to score fours on that pitch.

"I was already on Australia pre-match and all I wanted to do was press up and have more on at the end of their innings.

But my phone was gone. The Aussies were only just favourites with the bookies at half-time, but I knew they should have been much shorter odds."

Keeping his opinions to himself – as hard as it was – Harry picked out a table set away from the team for lunch, where he was amazed to be joined by Glenn McGrath. "I had 20 minutes on my own with him – you'd want to marry him, a 24-carat gent," Harry said. "I'd known him previously as the ultimate tormentor, steaming in time after time and getting the crucial wicket you were funking for.

"He told me all about his late wife's charity, a foundation that had turned the original six specialist breast cancer care nurses across Australia into 300. The lunchtime food on offer may have been sub-standard – they'd incinerated the pasta – but the company was first class. Glenn asked me about the score and what I thought of it, and I told him, but I don't think he knew I was a true punter.

"I was certain they were going to start to discuss the tactics before the South Africans went in. I thought I'm going to jump up here and say: 'Listen, lads. It ain't none of my fucking business but that 245 is worth 285. You've got to allow so much for the fact they won't score any fours.' And how right I was.

"But the Aussies never discussed the merit of how many runs they'd scored. Just before taking to the field, Ricky got the team in a huddle next to the dugout and said: 'Listen, we lost our last One Day game and nobody, nobody beats Australia fucking twice on the bounce.' That was it. Unbelievable.

"They never began to think or talk like gamblers or laptop punters would, looking at the stats and seeing how much those runs were worth. Look how it's changed. Run the clock forward ten years, there would be two or three statisticians on the firm and a geezer whose only job was working out the run rate. Gamblers, punters, we're miles ahead, absolute miles ahead. We think of everything when it comes to odds and maths.

"I was right about the outcome. South Africa were bowled out for 186 – the Aussies shit in. When they were two down for a dozen, I wanted to set fire to the dugout to get some smoke signals started to get some more money on."

True to his lifelong obsession with learning as much about sport as he could, Harry discovered something that made him slightly mistrustful about the supposed camaraderie of a cricket dressing room. "It's not a team game in the real sense," he said. "I played football from six to about 20. I'd have played until I was 40 if I'd been good enough. I always considered football a massive team game, even if you had Cristiano Ronaldo in your team!

"Having been born in Scotland, I never knew anything about the ethos of cricket, but I assumed it was a team game. Okay, there are 11 lads on the same side, but the bowlers and the batsmen hardly talked, they were playing for their own figures. In football, a centre-forward tries to score, but it's all about the team. The big important matches aside, I'm bloody sure the No.3 or No.4 batsman wants the No.1 and No.2 out fast so they can get in.

"I began to understand why it is that cricketers suffer in the way they do. I've read the autobiographies – the stress, the despair, the depression, the suicides. It might look like a team game, but it really isn't.

"If you were a young cricketer playing in your first match and you took 5-63, scored 54 not out and your team lost, would you be happy or sad? It didn't quite add up to me.

"Andrew Symonds was bullying Brad Hogg – he never left

him alone. And the Aussies had a first-timer, Brett Dorey, a real big guy from Western Australia, and when he came on to bowl, all Symonds did was laugh at him. 'Oh my God, it takes him longer to turn at the end of his run than the Queen Mary,' that sort of banter. He knew he wasn't up to it after three balls. They were ruthless. Symonds just pissed himself all day. Michael Clarke was a relatively new kid in the side. He was Symonds' best mate. Symonds kept saying: 'Where's Pup, I've got to look after Pup.'

"They all called him Pup, but even at that age I could tell he had a bit of the tiger about him. I'd had my bollocks on the Aussies to beat England in a One Day match in Adelaide in 2003, and they were in all sorts of trouble at 104-6 [chasing England's 152] when this blond boy came to the crease on his debut and single-handedly won the game. The Aussie commentators were eulogising about the new wonderkid, and they were right. Pup scored 39 not out off 47 balls in less than an hour to steer them to victory. I personally thanked him for that the minute I saw him in the dressing room."

The Budget van dropped Harry back at the Crown at a quarter-to-one in the morning. Boon and Ponting were the only two left in the back seats when it pulled up on the forecourt. "I didn't patronise anyone, I just did a professional day's work. It felt as if I'd done a proper shift," he said. "I knew I was full value for my $35,000. I shook Boon's hand and firmly believe he'd come to respect me."

Clearly he had: "I couldn't believe it when I saw him," Boon said. "But for a big fat Pom, he wasn't too bad. But thank God they took the phone off him!"

Harry's rewards were a signed shirt from the squad and the

esteem of Australian cricket. There weren't many Poms who could say that.

***

The former Australian captain turned legendary commentator Richie Benaud climbed into a hotel lift at the Crown Towers that Melbourne morning to be confronted by the sight of Harry Findlay in what passed for his cricket whites.

Harry had seen Benaud many times at cricket venues across the world and would nod in a gesture of recognition and admiration without saying anything, which was a rarity. This time, he couldn't help himself: "Morning, Richie. Guess who's going to be Australia's 13th man today? Richie didn't say a word, but looked at me as if I was seriously fucking mad," Harry said.

Benaud had become as much an unmistakable part of the English summer as he was Australia's – his commentaries the lilting backdrop to those of a certain vintage. With his rather more stoic English co-commentator, Jim Laker, Benaud was a stalwart of the BBC's coverage of the Sunday League cricket for decades.

For a gambler in those days, Sundays were anathema. "There was next to no live football and no Sunday horse racing, except the Prix de l'Arc de Triomphe on the first weekend in October," Harry said, "The exception was the Sunday League cricket, which started at 2pm on the dot. The bookies priced up the day's games, but they closed bang on 2pm. No more bets.

"When rain was about, you had to be on the team batting second. Chasing the runs gave you a massive advantage with the scoring system. If it was overcast, any team with half a brain was going to bat second if they won the toss."

One Sunday afternoon in May 1995, Harry and his pals decamped to the United Services Ground in Portsmouth the worse for wear, having been to the dogs the previous night and later, after a lavish Chinese meal, to a nightclub.

"When we woke up at midday, we worked out we had just over £2,000 between us, and with Hampshire playing Sussex, we were happy to have it all on Sussex at 4/7 [to win £1,200], but only if they won the toss. It was overcast, and in the pre-Duckworth-Lewis days [the complex system by which victories were determined when rain interrupted play], it was even more important to bat second.

"I was looking at my watch because they usually had the toss at 1.55pm, announced it over the ground and you had five minutes to get your money on. It was 1.57pm – no one was saying anything – and I was thinking there was no way I could have a bet. Then Mark Nicholas, the Hampshire captain, appeared at 1.58pm with the umpires and they walked to the middle.

"I worked out I had to get myself out to the middle for the toss because if Sussex won it, I'd have less than two minutes to get on. I timed it to absolute perfection. I was wearing a huge white Sergio Tacchini tennis shirt, orange and black shorts and sandals, but I didn't give a fuck what I looked like, this was the only clue of the day. It was our only chance to get any readies.

"Just as Nicholas was about to toss the coin, I was at his shoulder. He tossed, it landed and started to roll – at least 20 feet. By the time the umpires, Nicholas and the Sussex skipper got to the coin, I was walking off the pitch. I was going back to bed.

"I was at least five yards off the square and Nicholas suddenly noticed me and screamed: 'Oi, who the fucking hell are you?' I turned round and said: 'Mark, don't fucking worry about it. You won the toss.'"

Sussex won by eight runs, so Harry and the boys would have won the money, but he never put the bet on. He was fast asleep!

10

YOU WIN SOME...

Flight QF002 from London to Sydney via Bangkok landed safely after the first leg of its journey on January 8, 2008. Harry Findlay was in the first class section even though, only three months earlier, he had lost £1.9 million on the All Blacks' shocking defeat to France in the Rugby World Cup quarter-final in Cardiff.

Such inconveniences would not be allowed to interfere with Harry's travel plans. Nor did he believe it was the moment to back off, betting-wise. There were sufficient funds to play with, which was all a gambler required for life support.

Harry had long been an expert at wiping his mouth and moving on. The Millennium Stadium experience just required more tissues than usual.

YOU WIN SOME...

A few weeks Down Under were always good to replenish heart and soul, and more often than not, the coffers as well. There was the 2008 Australian Open tennis to mock up for. Roger Federer remained the major player and cash cow. Rafael Nadal was a worthy challenger and Novak Djokovic was emerging as a breezy Serbian contender worthy of consideration.

The first week of January meant one thing, hopping on a plane. Harry had never turned right, unless he could help it, and chose the highest grade of travel to fly to Sydney with pal Alex Williamson, who had taken the Cardiff devastation as badly as anyone else in Harry's box.

Harry, a frequent flyer, had been fascinated by the development of the Airbus A380 – which had come into full service in 2007 – and a pilot acquaintance had told him it was the only way to fly long haul. "He told me to stay away from the 747s, because most were over 30 years old and had done a helluva lot of flying time," Harry said. "In a nutshell, a lot of them were knackered.

"First class is a lot of money, but when you're on an A380, it's value. On a 747, it ain't. I arrived at Heathrow in good spirits and saw my bag disappear down the chute only for the girl at check-in then to say we were on a 747. I was screaming: 'I don't want to fly, get my bag back.' Alex tried to calm me down. 'Let's just go Harry, let's just go,' he said."

Alex recalled that Harry was in a real funk all the way through the boarding procedure. "He was arguing with everyone and was on the phone shouting at the guy who'd booked the flights – 'I don't want to be on this crap plane.'"

As he tried to settle into his seat, Harry counted four fellow first class travellers – Alex among them – so privacy was never going to be an issue, but the fact he wasn't on an A380 still rankled. "I was sulking like a pig," he said. "The food is never that good on a plane, even in first class, but they do provide top-quality caviar and Dom Pérignon, so I did my usual, had a bit of both before taking two sleeping tablets and I was fast asleep."

There was nothing unusual about the flight, or the landing in Bangkok, so Harry and Alex were taken aback to be summoned over the loudspeaker, asking that they should make themselves available at a certain check-in desk as soon as they were in the airport lounge.

They were told that there was a connecting BA flight to Sydney leaving in less than half an hour, and if they wanted to get to Australia by the morning, they should make a dash for it. Because Harry had kicked up such a stink about being on the flight, and he and Alex were first class passengers, the pair were offered privileged treatment. Harry and Alex did what any other passenger would do in the circumstances. They ran. Nobody else who had been on the flight to Bangkok would be able to leave the city for the next 36 hours.

"We arrived in Sydney first thing next morning. We were staying at the Hilton Hotel on the Harbour, down by the rocks, having a five-star breakfast just in time to watch the football," Harry said. "Before we'd left England, Clare Balding had interviewed me for TV and asked for a tip for the year so punters could win a few quid. I said: 'There's no doubt, Clare, it's Spurs at 11/2 to win the League Cup. They should be 5/2, the odds are completely wrong.'

"There were only four teams left in the competition and I said everyone should lump on Tottenham. Their semi-final against Arsenal was over two legs, the first was 1-1 at the Emirates and the second was an absolute nap. [Spurs would win 6-2 on aggregate]. I had £150k on them. The other semi-final was between Chelsea and Everton. At half-time, the news came on.

"We weren't paying that much attention and then, at the bottom of the picture, it said something about a miracle flight, and they were interviewing Qantas staff in Bangkok about this plane that had landed on battery power because everything else had gone. We turned up the volume. I said: 'Fuck me, that was the plane we were on.'"

Unbeknown to any of the 346 passengers and many of the 19 members of cabin crew on the flight, a water leak in the first class galley had knocked out electricity to a series of the plane's systems that began to conk out one by one when it was around 25 kilometres from its destination.

The formal air accident investigation reported two years later that, had the flooding occurred more than 30 minutes from the airport, or had there been a delay in the landing procedure (it was, fortunately, a clear day with unrestricted visibility), the plane would have been at 'considerable risk', with more systems likely to shut down.

The leak – caused when an anti-ice heater failed and the ice that formed blocked a drainpipe – had already knocked out power to the radar, cabin pressurisation, autopilot, auto-throttle and a number of fuel pumps as the plane descended 10,000 feet.

"If I'd have done what everyone else usually does in first class, which is going on the piss, drinking the best part of two bottles of wine and having to use the toilet five times, the leak would have happened much earlier and the plane would surely have gone down," Harry said. "I reckon I saved the flight.

"If we'd been further out to sea, they'd have had to wake us all up to tell us what was going to happen. Imagine hearing this over the tannoy: 'I'm afraid we've run out of power, we've got to ditch in the sea, so you can text all your relatives because we're all going to die.' That was it. If the power had gone half an hour earlier, our price for survival would have been 100-million-to-one."

Indeed, when the plane landed, it had been flying 16 minutes on emergency battery power that was designed to last, at most, for half an hour. In another 14 minutes, the Qantas 747 would have become a giant glider carrying over 360 people to their doom.

"Who was the one person who would have suffered the most? Me," Harry said. "I had to be dragged on, kicking and screaming. Alex was blown away by the news about the flight. He couldn't speak for a day."

Alex was indeed rendered speechless, though more because the Chelsea-Everton first leg – on which he and Harry were betting in-running – was decided by a late own goal by Everton's Joleon Lescott. "I couldn't believe that Lescott was outjumped by Shaun Wright-Phillips, who was about 5'5", and we saw our money – a lot of it – go up in smoke," he said. "But it was true that the news of the flight completely sideswiped us. We couldn't get our heads around it."

The loss of six figures on Everton was bad. Replaying in your head what could have happened over the Bay of Bengal the previous day was enough to make anyone wretch.

At least once a week, between the ages of 15 and 35, Harry would endure a recurring dream where he was in a plane that was going to crash and he'd always survive. "I'd wake up just before it happened," he said. "Jade had those dreams all the time as well. Every time you wake up you think: 'Cor! Fucking hell, I got away with that.' That's the surrealist in me surfacing again.

"Despite those dreams, I've never been scared of flying. But the thought of being told that you're going to ditch in the sea in 30 minutes' time when you owned the Gold Cup favourite and didn't want to get on the plane in the first place would have been too much for anyone to take."

On another of the Findlay visits to Las Vegas – where Harry said: "I'd had it right off" – the team regulars had flown on to watch the Dallas Cowboys for the Monday night game. They were flying high, both literally and in the financial sense. Their first port of call was a Dallas mall where they splashed out on coats, crocodile shoes, all sorts of luxury goods. Harry would have surprise upon surprise for Kay when he got home.

No sooner had the flight crossed the Atlantic coast en route to Heathrow, than the pilot announced they were heading back to New York. One of the engines had failed. "It was a full-on emergency, everyone on the plane was shit-scared, apart from Glen Gill, who was so fast asleep that only the cheering from the passengers when we landed at JFK woke him up," Harry said.

"Even when the pilot made his announcement, I remember thinking: 'Even if this goes down, I'm not going with it.' I was so confident, it was like an out-of-world experience. I had loads of readies in the suitcase, all these lovely coats, this wasn't going to happen to me. You think how are you going to handle things and how you'd react, and although you might think you're going to completely fall apart, you don't. I felt a massive surge of confidence, almost like I had a force field around me.

"When we landed, I'd never seen so many fire engines in my fucking life. We clambered off and all the guys on the ground were applauding. Then we came into the terminal and there were loads of passengers, all waiting to get on flights, screaming about how late they were going to be. I went straight over to the desk shouting at these stupid Yanks: 'Are you lot completely off your fucking heads? Are you deranged? We've just had the greatest result of all time and all you're worried about is being fucking late.'"

JFK might have been one of the world's busiest international transport hubs, where the din was constant and invariably full-on, but that night, in the one corner of it where Harry Findlay was raging, it had otherwise fallen strangely silent.

***

Most people have experienced a failed alarm call at a hotel and written it off as an infuriating inconvenience – a flight long departed, the breakfast kippers all gone or the motorway full of the cars they had booked the call in order to avoid. It was perfectly okay to protest, but the damage had been done. But what if such an inconvenience cost £100,000? It happened to Harry in October 1989.

"I think I've been so blessed in many ways, and then there were the times when I wondered: 'Fuck me, how did I ever pull myself around after that?'" he said.

A flight to Newcastle to lump on a dog at Brough Park trained by John McGee, one of Ireland's finest, brought Harry his expected reward and the felicitations of everyone at the track who had been told to back it with all they had. He couldn't remember the dog's name but he was a light brindle and won

Coltish footballer: Harry Findlay (third left, back row) in High Wycombe's Hithercroft Colts U12 team in 1973. Coach Geoff White had a big influence on the boy and kept Harry in the squad later when "on ability alone, I had no chance"

Into his stride: "Even at U12 level, I was used to being readily outpaced by boys half my size – if I had my time again, I'd have been a full-back, not a centre-forward, Harry said. "It was Peter Osgood's fault"

A night to remember: Harry in a state of shock with mum, Margaret, after his beloved Chicita Banana had broken Ballyregan Bob's track record at Wembley in 1989

First date: Harry chose Wembley as the venue for his first date with Kay Duggan (left) who brought her friend Dawn Biggins as a chaperone. Chicita Banana's victory made it a very special occasion

Saddest picture: Harry's bitch Jades Dilemma had been beaten in the final of the Oaks at Clonmel in 1998. No one could raise a smile. Jack Pat Collins (yellow jacket centre) and Mick McCarthy (far right with medallion) would be killed as they drove home

In the pink: With the prodigious Chicita Banana and many of the trophies the bitch won in a thrilling career. "Not bad for a dog once described as piece of shit," said Harry

As good as it gets: Harry with Big Fella Thanks after his Derby victory at Clonmel in 1999 and below, sharing the spoils in Skibbereen with Curley O'Driscoll (far left), Denis O'Driscoll (holding trophy) and friends Patrick and David Hourihane

Bloody Marvel: Harry proudly walks around the track at Romford with the bitch Metric Marvel who was his first-ever runner as a trainer and had just won on her debut

Viva Las Vegas: The trip to the Nevada desert in 1996. Left to right – Glen Gill, Clifford Dennis, Jade, Nigel Troth, Kay, Simon Roberts and Harry keeping a tight hold on first-time fellow traveller, Tony Bloom

Next-door neighbours: Denman (left) and Kauto Star captured in the build-up to the 2008 Cheltenham Gold Cup

We did it!: Harry embraces jockey Sam Thomas at the end of the race. Frank Harvey, back right, relishes the moment

Doing a Dettori: Thomas spectacularly dismounts from Denman in the winner's enclosure at Cheltenham as Paul Barber leads the horse in

Royal patronage: Equestrian Olympian and huge sports fan, The Princess Royal, shares a lovely moment with Margaret Findlay, Harry's mum, as she hands over the Gold Cup

Glorious Goodwood: Harry, back right, and company enjoy a day at the races. Seated – Gordon Findlay with Ron Bloom (Tony's father) and greyhound trainer Don Cuddy opposite their wives. Inset: Kay meets her sporting hero, boxer Chris Eubank

Lunch at William Haggas' home: Frank Harvey with his No.1 sporting idol Lester Piggott, Harry and Michael Holding, the horseracing-mad former West Indian fast bowler who is good friends with famed trainer Sir Michael Stoute

Day at the cricket: Harry (seated second left, front row) on a trip to Lord's is joined by, among others, Mark Harbour (back left), Julian Snow (to Harry's left) and Tony Bloom (seated second right). Inset: With another boyhood hero, former Chelsea and England goalkeeper, Peter Bonetti

Word from the wise: Peter Thomas in the *Racing Post* described the relationship between Denman co-owners Paul Barber and Harry as 'like a sage septuagenarian trying to control his hyperactive grandson in a sweet shop'

Harry The Dog: Harry in his element walking his dogs in the woods near his home in Bath. Force of Habit, a retired track sprinter, left, seeks his master's affection with the most famous of them all, Big Fella Thanks

by three-and-a-half lengths. He'd backed it from 2/1 to 4/7, and when it romped home, he couldn't have been happier. "A professional in-and-out job," he called it.

"We had a great night, a full monty Chinese, a bit of time at a nightclub and all the hotel had to do was wake me up at 6am because I was booked to fly from Newcastle to Gatwick early morning. We were backing three good dogs at Pompey the next night. But the alarm never went off."

The sight of a dishevelled, unshaven Harry Findlay would be alarming if he was in a contented mood, but this was not one of those mornings. The two hotel receptionists on duty at 9am (two hours after Harry should have been on his way to the airport) were at first stunned and then grovelingly apologetic, but clearly unable to turn back the clock and assuage their raging guest. All they could say was: "Nothing we can do, sir." Returning to his room, Harry reached for the *Sporting Life* and described picking it up that particular morning as: "The worst thing I did in my life."

"I wasn't doing the horses full-time in those days, it was mostly snooker and the dogs for me. I looked at the paper and there were a couple of race meetings that day, one at Hexham. I didn't even know where Hexham was, but there was a little chart in the *Life* showing the outline of the course and it said 17 miles from Newcastle. I couldn't get a flight until 5pm, so I thought I'd have a day out at Hexham racecourse to kill the time. It almost killed me.

"In the first race, the favourite was a horse called Ben Ledi. It was 1/4 and there were four runners. I bet something like £1,600 to win £400. As it jumped the water, its legs splayed, it stumbled and fell. One down."

As Harry chased his tail, trying to make up for the first-race loss, the favourites succumbed and the day got progressively worse. He said his behaviour was shockingly unprofessional. He backed five horses odds-on and they all lost.

"To make me more nervous, there was a guy there putting the money on for Ladbrokes, running around betting the same horses as me, they were all getting shorter and shorter and I ended up doing my brains. I never chased as a gambler; I'd always been so professional. I knew what I was going to bet beforehand and the worst thing was to start to chase when you were hotting up.

"When you've missed the early morning call, you're at a racecourse you shouldn't even be at and you've got a Ladbrokes rep on your shoulder, well my head was gone. I got into a taxi outside the course and realised I'd done over £100,000 on those five races.

"I lost to a few bookies that day and paid them off, but there was one I really did my bollocks with. It took me over four years to pay him back. I settled up through his clerk, an old guy called George, who I became mates with. I'd send him a few quid whenever I backed a winner."

To add insult to the pain of a six-figure loss in one afternoon at a meeting he'd had no intention of attending, the evening flight was redirected to Heathrow rather than Gatwick, so the trip to Portsmouth dogs was never going to happen. Harry decided to take a taxi to Windsor and check into the Sir Christopher Wren Hotel.

"I got pissed out my brains with the pain of it, and because I had loads of cheese and port after the vodkas, I had a bloody stormer the next morning," he said. "I had the *Life* delivered, and though my head was pounding, all I was saying to myself was: 'Please don't let all those dogs have won.' Of course, they all had, and I never had a dollar on them. In those days, it was all about being there and cash on the day. There was no odds-checkers or internet. Worst day of my life."

This wasn't the only time a grizzled Harry appeared at a hotel reception in full, unexpurgated flow. "I was staying at the George V in Paris for the French Open," he said. "They charged two grand a night and all I wanted was a decent shaving kit. You assumed they'd have a half-decent Gillette Blue disposable, nice and smooth. In my opinion, a Bic is as bad a disposable as you can get, but in their white box, they'd obviously found something even cheaper. I was in the bath, fully soaked up and cut myself to fucking pieces, there were nicks and blood everywhere."

Brandishing their 1p razor, Harry marched down to reception with only a pair of boxer shorts to cover his essentials. "I said: 'You're charging me 2,000 Euros for the room and you give me this? Get the hotel manager, get the head of housekeeping, and explain to me why they're charging someone this much for a room, giving them a 1p razor and doing this to me.' I was going mad. I wasn't having it. The manager came out, he couldn't have been more apologetic and I managed get one night's stay in the hotel for free, but I never went back again."

***

Once every four years, the football World Cup was the planet's biggest betting event by a furlong, no other gambling market retained such a high percentage of mug money, and for the knowledgeable football bettor, it was a one-off opportunity to make some really big money. Harry had done his homework but wasn't in the best of form as the 1998 tournament loomed. He was desperate to up his stakes in the big competition and knew exactly what to do.

"Our house in Aughton, Sheffield, was worth about £90,000, and though you can't sell a house overnight, I knew the Lizard was a master operator and he just told me to sign it over to him and he'd give me the ninety. 'When we win during the World Cup, you can buy it back for the same price,' he said.

"That was what Tony Bloom was like, no fucking about, money transferred straight away and he didn't believe in interest. We had the same solicitor, I signed the house over and bang, the money was there. I even sold Kay's lovely sporty red BMW. I got £10k for it and that got me to £100k for my World Cup betting fund while Kay was driving around town in a Rover hire car that cost £115 a week."

With the fund sorted and the World Cup a few days away, Harry wanted some downtime to get away from it all. He decided on a few days in India with his pal Jim O'Rourke for company.

"I loved India so I thought we'd go to Delhi, chill out in Goa first and then head somewhere like Bombay," he said. "On the first day in Goa, I fell asleep for about four hours by the swimming pool and woke up looking like a Maine lobster, fresh from the pot. I was in agony and screaming like a pig because no one had bothered to wake me up. Plans for dinner at a recommended restaurant 30 minutes away were cancelled and I was pugged up in our room sulking and trying to feel comfortable. That was when Jim turned the TV on and there was a Test match between the West Indies and England at the Kensington Oval."

"Surely we've got to bet the West Indies," Jim said after the first English wicket fell. Harry initially resisted but had the first £10,000 on as the second batsmen trooped off. His avowed intent not to bet on the trip was beginning to melt like a hot fudge sundae under a tropical sun, but the boys were on good terms with themselves when England reached 55-4 with Graham Thorpe, the Surrey batsman, off the field hurt. They'd had nearly £40,000 on. There was no betting in-running back then, but the Test matches were different because they lasted five days and that meant you could have a bit more on, knowing that, at the end of each day, you could change your position.

Arriving back at the hotel the next afternoon, Harry and Jim saw the latest score and nearly started to cry. England were three hundred and something for six and eventually made 403 all out.

"I was having a nervous breakdown. I'd sold my house, Kay's car, and England had done that. I said to Jim: 'We've got to get out, we've got to back the draw. I can't lose on this Test match. Forget the profit.' So I ended up with roughly £38k on the West Indies at around evens and more or less the same bet on the draw. With hindsight, the draw was a bit of a panic bet. I shouldn't have done that, but instead laid the West Indies and just taken a loss on the match there and then. Instead, I'd left myself open. If it was a draw or the West Indies won, I had enough to buy a bowl of rice. If England won, almost the entire £80,000 was gone."

Harry and Jim flew on to Bombay, but they were restless on the flight. Things were not looking good. "The West Indies started their reply okay, then collapsed," Harry said. "They were all out for 265, then Thorpe had another blinder on one good ankle and England declared their second innings at 233-3. The fourth night the West Indies were batting, and if England bowled them out, I was going to shoot myself.

"The opening partners – Clayton Lambert and Philo Wallace – went in with nine or ten overs to bat to see the day out. More than life itself, I didn't want a wicket to fall that night."

In their suffocating twin room after a tortuously hot day, Harry and Jim were watching the match unfold with the bed covers pulled up over their noses. They knew one wicket could change the entire destiny of the Test and their futures. If one, or maybe two wickets fell, England would go into the last day with their tails up – a nightmare scenario for the pair of them.

"Then one of the weirdest things ever happened," said Harry. "I think it was the first match and almost certainly the first series where they were using a red and green light system to determine run-outs and stumpings. There were only two overs to go in the day and these two stupid bastards went for a run. I nearly died because there was no need for it, it was worth a tenth of a run, the wickets were shattered and you couldn't tell whether it was in or out.

"In the old days, they'd probably have given it not out because it was really close, but they went to the third umpire. They showed a replay two or three times, the bat was down and he was half an inch short of the crease. The third umpire was watching it. I knew he was out and I knew I was fucked.

"With the new technology the third umpire had at his disposal, I'd have bet my eyesight to win a penny he was going to give him out. It was impossible to get the decision wrong, but he did.

"Even with him not out, which truly was an act of God, the fifth day was going to be knife-edge. It was the draw or England.

The West Indies needed 375 to win, so had no chance. At the end of the fourth day, they were about 20 for no wicket, and now I had to sleep on it knowing I could do £80k with nothing to gain. I needed the West Indies to bat all day for a draw. I couldn't think of a worse situation in all my life. With the betting as it was in that situation, there was nothing I could do. I couldn't move. It was glory or the bullet."

With the match being played in Barbados, the time difference meant that Harry and Jim would have to spend the daylight hours in a state of torment. "We had the whole day to shit ourselves," Harry said. "I couldn't speak." Harry decided to go to the hotel pool, but before he had finished one length, he felt as if he had been trying to swim in dark treacle. "I was under so much stress, I felt as if I couldn't move.

"I was at a hotel on the beach, it was Sunday lunch, they put on a barbecue, beautiful tender tandoori chicken, rosé wine, and I couldn't taste it. I was so fucking scared. I thought: 'Why can't I just be a normal person so I could really enjoy that lunch? Why do I have to put myself under so much pressure?' Jim hadn't helped, but it was my own decision to get involved and I knew if I hadn't have fallen asleep by the pool that first day in Goa, I wouldn't even have known the bloody match was on.

"I just about managed to get through the day without topping myself and then, at about 6pm, we'd never seen a storm like it. It was Noah's Ark stuff. There was massive forked lightning, the electricity was lost, the place was plunged into darkness and there were no phone lines from the hotel, no TV. It was a horrible place to be and the match was due to start in half an hour.

"Then the old-fashioned phone rang in the room, Jim answered it and it was Ranjeet, the Indian bookie. I said: 'What the fuck does he want?' Jim hadn't realised the significance of what he'd asked. Ranjeet wanted to know what the price the draw was. I thought: 'That's fucking handy. It's 20 minutes before they start play and Ranjeet wants to be on the draw.'"

The TV in the room still wasn't working after the electric storm so Harry and Jim set off for the bowels of the hotel, down from the reception area, to the rows of shops below ground level, where bookstores, gift shops and small cafés proliferated.

"We went into this old Bombay bookshop. It was all blacked out, but this guy had a little generator and he was watching the match on a tiny screen. We sat there waiting for the play to come on, the picture was grainy and suddenly all you could see were these guys in sou'westers, lovely big, bright yellow plastic coats, pulling the covers on. It was pissing down – a second act of God. The start of play was delayed until well after the lunch break, and when they did manage to get on, it was only for a couple of hours before it rained again and it was always going to be a draw. As a young boy, the *Great Escape* was almost certainly my favourite film and now I had a leading role in the sequel."

***

The Scoop6 launched in July 1999. The Betfair website in 2017 said that this special bet offered: The possibility of winning vast sums of money, which makes it an appealing proposition to infrequent bettors and professionals alike. It comprises both a 'Win Fund' and a 'Place Fund'. In order to land the more lucrative Win Fund, you must correctly identify the six winners of the designated races; if your six horses are placed, you have the consolation of the Place Fund.

YOU WIN SOME...

"Rather like the National Lottery, the amount you win is dependent on the size of the pool divided by the number of winning tickets. Those who have the successfully chosen the six winners and scooped the Win Fund are then eligible to have a crack at the 'Bonus Fund'. Winning the Bonus requires the punter to correctly choose the winner of a designated race the following weekend.

"Although the minimum unit stake for the Scoop6 is higher than both the Jackpot and the Placepot, it stands at a relatively modest £2. You'd be forgiven for assuming that the small-staking punter has little chance against the might of the large syndicates and professional gamblers who often stake tens of thousands in extravagant permutations; you'd be wrong, though.

"The Scoop6 has transformed the lives of many an infrequent, small-staking bettor. No case is more relevant than that of Agnes Haddock, who scooped £688,620 when correctly choosing six winners in 2007. Tony Wonnacott, a 45-year-old father who also played a straight £2 line, won £310,000 in 2009, further bolstering his winnings by landing the Bonus Fund in conjunction with renowned professional gambler Harry Findlay, a week later."

Scoop6 was in its infancy when the Findlay family flew to Naples, Italy, for a break in 2000. But Harry had the hump. He didn't like travelling early on Scoop6 Saturday because all he had to hand was the *Evening Standard* with Friday night's information for the next day, and one tissue man, Barry Beesley from City Index, to call to price up the races.

Harry had booked a lovely hotel – the Santa Caterina, a location favoured by many high-profile people, including the former US President Bill Clinton and his family. When Harry arrived, he was feeling a ton of pressure. He and Kay had been trying to shield their daughter Jade from news of the Concorde plane crash in Paris a few days earlier for fear that she would be frightened about stepping onto a plane. It was all a bit fraught.

What stressed Harry out further was a lack of information on the form of those horses in the Scoop6 he was about to back. "All I had were the tissue prices from the *Standard,* and I was trying to work out the permutations," he said. "I had the hard races sorted. The fifth and sixth races were small fields with seven or eight runners. The first four or five in the betting were close and then there were three outsiders in the last two legs.

"I had five horses in leg five and five horses in leg six. The first four legs were done. The last two races were five by five. If I put five horses in leg five and five horses in leg six, the bet came to £184,000. I had that perm all laid out, which meant I was in for 60%, Tony Bloom 30% and Glen Gill 10%.

"As I was getting ready to put the bet on, I realised that in leg five and leg six, really what I should do – because there were two horses in both races going ahead of the others – was to have two in leg five and five in leg six and then do another ticket with five in leg five and two in leg six.

"That meant I'd only be laying out £122,000 instead of £184,000 [the more selections you have, the more perms you have], but more importantly, it was the right thing to do because if one of the front two in the betting won both races five and six, I wouldn't show much of a profit. Kay was putting Jade down for an afternoon nap as I was putting the bet on. 'What are you doing, Dad?' she said. 'I'm putting the Scoop6 bets on,' I answered. She said: 'Dad, you never win the Scoop6,' before dropping off to sleep.

"I'd got to make a decision and knew what I should do, but under so much stress, I just couldn't face missing out on a big win if two of the bigger-priced horses won the last two legs, so I staked the full £184,000. I took the split-second decision to be unprofessional. I'd never done it before. Around 99% of times in this game, if you were unprofessional, you paid for it. But this time it went in my favour and was a real life-changer, because the fifth horse in the betting won the fifth race and the fifth horse in the betting won the sixth race. We won £2.2 million – 60% for me, 30% to Tony Bloom and 10% to Glen.

"If I'd done the right thing and gone two by five and five by two, I wouldn't have had a penny. Because I did the wrong thing, I won £1.4 million with £800,000 on the Bonus. I won it because I was in the wrong place at the wrong time, stressed out of my head.

"The most amazing thing was when Jade woke up about three hours later. I said: 'What did you say about the Scoop6?'

"That night we ordered room service, the moon was high, it was the most gorgeous weather. Kay's favourite dish in the world is spaghetti vongole, and though she was the smallest eater in the world, she had three main course portions and we sat there about three hours looking out on the most beautiful moonlight. We'd won a lion's share of £2 million and were knocking back a couple of lovely bottles of Montepulciano.

"I never won the Scoop6 for another two years, and in that spell I must have given £1.5 million back. I had an absolutely abhorrent run on it. I reckon I've probably been 10-12% in front on it over the years, but the bet is a massive risk – it has wiped out a number of syndicates and a lot of very shrewd gamblers.

"Imagine how much I'd have lost over those months if I hadn't won the £2.2 million in Naples? If I hadn't been unprofessional, the Scoop6 would have wiped me out long before I owned a horse."

11

HORSES FOR COURSES

Harry Findlay had fulfilled his desire to have a greyhound great enough to win Ireland's coursing Derby. That was really enough for him. He'd happily see out his days with Kay and Jade, betting for all he was worth and training his dogs. Maybe he would find another one to enhance his standing, and there would be more nights full of smiling Irish eyes.

Had anyone suggested to Harry that he might one day stand in the winners' enclosure at Cheltenham on Gold Cup day, watch a horse he owned earn royal acclamation at Ascot, or that a beast he bought for his mum would contest against

Sheikh Mohammed's finest in Dubai, he would have said they'd read too many fairy stories. He was Harry The Dog.

"When I was a youngster in Blackpool, I had a £170 treble on three horses trained by Philip Hobbs. I saw his picture in the *Sporting Life* and thought: 'I bet he's a lovely fella,'" Harry said. "I couldn't imagine 25 years later I'd be at his place having breakfast and Mum and I would have horses with him, the first of which was Monticelli. Jimmy Barry-Murphy, the Cork hurling legend, told me to buy him, and the plan was to absolutely lump on first time out.

"A hundred yards from the winning line, we were held in second place when the leader, without any reason, veered across the course and threw the race in our lap. It was the luckiest winner we ever had and he ended up being a free horse rather than a very expensive one!

"We had a genuine potential superstar with Mr Hobbs in Canaradzo [named after the winner of the 1861 Waterloo Cup coursing event], but after bolting up in a decent bumper race, he was injured in a freak accident at home and never raced again."

***

The word 'superstar' would be properly ascribed to Shergar, the stunning equine beast who would go down in racing folklore for a classic Derby victory the like of which had not been seen in a generation, before he was kidnapped from a stud farm in County Kildare, Ireland, in 1983, never to be seen again.

Two years before his abduction, in one of the major unsolved mysteries of the era, the horse was in his absolute pomp. Harry

– 19 at the time – followed the advice of *The Observer* racing correspondent Richard Baerlein that 'now is the time to bet like men' on Shergar to win the 1981 Derby. Harry had only £200 to his name but managed to talk his dad into giving him another £200 in order to double his stake.

"With Shergar around even money, it was £800 or I was skint, and the old man would have given me almighty grief," Harry said. Shergar won by ten lengths in one of the most awe-inspiring Derby performances in a generation.

The bay colt's next outing in England was to be in the King George VI and Queen Elizabeth Stakes at Ascot at the end of July. A fortnight earlier, Harry's pals were in their local, the Bricklayers Arms in Downley, discussing their upcoming holiday. They were leaving on the day of the race.

Now potless – £800 could disappear rather rapidly – and with no chance of going on the trip, Harry was distraught, until his mate Pooch offered him a lifeline. Pooch strongly fancied two cricket teams the next day, pulled £50 from his wallet and told Harry to find a couple more winners and have an accumulator. In effect, it was a betting slip that might end up getting Harry a place in the cranky Ford Escort van that was going to take the lads on their European adventure.

The cricket teams bolted up, Harry dug out a rugby league winner, and decided to stick in 'any American' to win golf's Open Championship at Royal St George's at odds of 4/9, to which the unheralded Texan Bill Rogers duly obliged by four shots. The last leg of the 'acca' was Shergar at 1/2 to win the King George.

"If Shergar won, I had £750 to collect from Corals, but the lads were leaving on Saturday morning, so I had to watch the race in Dover," he said. "If the horse lost, I'd have been trekking back to High Wycombe on my tod, without a shilling to my name. I never had a passport either, but that was the last of my worries. Shergar wasn't as impressive as he was at Epsom, but duly obliged by four lengths."

Harry was right about the passport, and the boys quickly devised a plan for their newest passenger to travel incognito by covering him with their sleeping bags and using him as a cushion in the back of the van while driving through customs on either side of the English Channel. No one was ever the wiser.

Having negotiated their way through France, the troupe stopped in Monte Carlo, the very Mecca of gambling haute couture. After loaning a hosepipe from one of the local gardens for a communal shower – "When we got back to the van we realised how badly the fucking thing stank," Harry said – the lads were persuaded to march into one of the principality's casinos. They could not believe their eyes.

Julian Richards, the leader of the gang, said: "Here we were, this smelly bunch, striding in to watch Harry play the tables. God knows how we got past the doorman. He won around £300 in four or five rolls of the dice. That was what made being with Harry so exciting because those sort of things didn't happen if you hung around normal people."

***

Were it not for Kevin Ball, the elder brother of the singer and actor Michael Ball, Harry Findlay would never have owned a horse. Harry was working for Sky TV as a darts pundit and Ball arrived for the World Matchplay final at Blackpool in a top-of-the-range helicopter, breezing into the arena like a film star. "He was so smart and one of the best-looking men I'd ever seen," Harry said.

Kevin Ball liked a bet and the two soon became pals. Harry and Kay were invited to a garden party he was hosting in Surrey. "We didn't get asked to many dos like this one, and certainly we'd never been to anything as classy as this. The home, gardens, wine and entertainment were all ten-star," Harry said.

At this stage of his life, in late 2001, Harry was fulfilled working his favoured greyhounds with trainer Don Cuddy at Lindrick Dale and busy cracking the Asian Handicap code with Tony Bloom, so the unscheduled arrival of Ball at his kennels was a bolt from the blue. As was his request. Did Harry want a leg in a horse that Kevin Ball had just bought at the Doncaster sales?

"I wasn't interested in owning horses," Harry said. "But Kevin was persistent and said that the horse – Garruth – would be trained by Paul Nicholls, who he assured me was the next great National Hunt trainer. He got that bit right. I only knew Nicholls at the time as the jockey of Playschool, who I'd won a few quid on.

"I bought a leg in the horse but the other investors failed to pull up their shares, so I ended up owning nearly all of him. Kevin Ball ruined me, not because Garruth was a major disappointment, but because I'd have never owned horses at all if he hadn't turned up unannounced that day."

Garruth was sent to Nicholls at his yard in the Somerset village of Ditcheat, premises owned by a wily dairy farmer and horse owner, Paul Barber. Harry went down to sort out his affairs with regards a new world of horse ownership and met the guv'nor. "I explained to Mr Barber that I didn't want any horse running in my name or have to set up my own colours, and he offered to run the horse in his," he said. "I think he must have liked the way I handled the whole business.

"Like anybody else from outside the game, I was nervous getting involved in bloodstock," he said. "But I knew I could trust Paul Barber the first time I shook his hand. He was a total gentleman from the off and I knew his word was his bond. How many top people who deal in horses can you say that about? Probably one in a thousand, but I had that man – Paul Barber."

That said, how could either man have expected from that encounter between farmer and gambler on the Somerset Mendips would be forged one of the most unconventional and successful partnerships in National Hunt history?

***

Garruth won his first race for Harry Findlay and Paul Nicholls at Plumpton in November 2001 with AP McCoy in the saddle at odds of 2/9. "It was one of the worst novice chases of all time and I wasn't impressed with the horse at all," the new owner said. "We bet the big odds-on and I was grateful to get away with it. I didn't fancy him next time when upped in class at Newbury, and he was a well-beaten favourite."

After two more disappointing runs at Uttoxeter, the team returned to Plumpton in February 2002. Two things etched themselves in Harry's mind that day – first how deplorably Garruth ran and then talking to Tony Bloom's father, Ron, in the unsaddling enclosure after the race. Harry said: "Don't worry about Garruth, Ronnie. Your son will become chairman of Brighton and Hove Albion and they'll be a Premier League team within ten years." "Do you really think so, Harry?" Ron Bloom replied. "Gauging from the look in his eyes as I said it, I thought he made it about a 9/4 chance to come true, but he certainly wasn't shocked at the prediction," said Harry.

If Harry thought Tony Bloom was on the up and up, the career of Paul Nicholls was on a similar trajectory. He had his first Grade 1 success in 1993, and six years later – a month after Harry's canine pride and joy Big Fella Thanks won the Irish coursing Derby – Nicholls trained three winners at the garlanded Cheltenham Festival: Call Equiname in the Queen Mother Champion Chase; Flagship Uberalles in the Arkle Challenge Trophy; and finally, with the Barber-owned See More Business in the most coveted of all, the Gold Cup.

Nicholls flourished, but it was not until having been runner-up as Champion Trainer for seven years that he would reach the pinnacle from where he became exceedingly difficult to dislodge. In 2008 came an experience like no other, as he trained the first three horses home in the Gold Cup.

The victor – and in many eyes the most celebrated winner of the blue riband of National Hunt racing since the regal Arkle in the 1960s – was a mighty animal named Denman.

Garruth would win only once more with Harry as his owner, a success rate he considered was an indication that he was not best suited to having horses of his own. He would rather go back to his dogs and helping Tony Bloom cement his increasingly dominant position in the world of football odds. Then fate dealt another defining hand.

Margaret Findlay was still in the nursing profession into her 60s, until one day she stumbled and was trapped beneath a wheelchair. It took an eternity for anyone to come to her aid. Gordon Findlay, Harry's younger brother, got to the scene as quickly as he could and Margaret's sons decided their mum should not work any more – it was time for her to retire.

But Margaret wasn't one to tolerate inertia; she wanted to remain as active as possible. Horse racing gave her an enormous thrill and Harry decided the sport would be the outlet for her to engage more fully with the unwelcome prospect of retirement.

The plan was that Harry would purchase a couple of horses and his mum could drive to Wincanton, Taunton, or Exeter – the West Country courses she fell in love with – for a day at the races, spending time amid decent folk who would watch out for her. The telling factor was that Margaret was to be in partnership with Paul Barber, so Harry didn't have anything to worry about and knew she would relish his company. If they had a couple of wins, so much the better.

"Mum really loved the fun of owning a horse and the people she met in the game," Harry said. "I hardly ever went racing, and when I did, I was astounded how charming and nice the two top jockeys at the time – Mick Fitzgerald and Richard Johnson – were to her. Mick was trainer Nicky Henderson's No.1 jockey. He never rode for Mum but always looked after her and treated her with so much respect. I loved that.

"But, to be honest, I still preferred the dogs. The first horse that won for us at Royal Ascot was High Standing, and I wouldn't know High Standing if he walked in here now. I used to sleep with my greyhounds. Owning greyhounds was a different kettle of fish, you had them at home as pets, you fell in love with them and they'd do anything for you, great animals.

"Beshabar, who won the Scottish Grand National for Mum,

bit all his stablehands, his trainers, everybody. He was a bloody nightmare. I started working at racing kennels the day after I left school. I'd been around dogs ever since and never been bitten by one in my life. Owning horses was a bollocks game, meant for kings and queens."

***

Harry's arrival in the upper echelons of the sport – though his mum was officially listed as the joint owner with Paul Barber – met with grudging approval. Harry's longtime racing pal Jim O'Rourke soon discovered how hostile people were to his presence.

"Harry's mum hadn't even had a horse jump a fence with Paul Nicholls as her trainer before he'd been told by another owner in the yard with links to a betting company that Harry was a drug dealer," Jim said. "Nicholls' mind was poisoned from the start. It killed certain people when Harry came into the yard. They tried to get to Paul Barber as well, but he was the boss and he and Harry were becoming genuine friends."

Nicholls preferred to run his horses as well as speak for them when it came to dealing with the racing media. Harry's presence meant that the press would often gravitate towards him for a quote. He was, after all, eminently quotable.

"I had a few differences of opinion with Nicholls, mostly about race tactics and because he didn't like the fact that I had an opinion," Harry said. "He often said that I was a loudmouth looking for a megaphone to speak into, but that wasn't fair.

"Not being flash, but people used to come to me looking for interviews, not the other way around. But I had a horse called

HereComesTheTruth that I named after Nicholls, because when the press interviewed him, he'd always tell the truth, and so did I. I was a gambler and the only time I wanted to speak to people was to mark their card."

Clare Balding, the omnipresent BBC and later Channel 4 racing host, would make a beeline for Harry whenever she saw him on the course. "He was great TV. Oh God, so approachable," she said. "He came across so well. Anyone who could jump through the screen and make everybody care about their horse was fantastic for any broadcaster. I was always thrilled when he was there."

There was to be an increasing barrage of media requests for Harry and Paul Nicholls after March 2005, when a telephone call from Paul Barber to Harry was to shape all three destinies in a manner they could not possibly have imagined.

***

Paul and Marianne Barber were in Ireland attending a point-to-point meeting to see if they could spot a horse with a difference. On a lousy day of lashing rain and strong winds, the one about which they had been tipped the wink fell at the first fence. With time on their hands, they drove on to trainer Adrian Maguire's yard where Paul Nicholls joined them.

They weren't the first set of potential owners to get a look at the horse they were about to see. Indeed, Maguire was becoming sick and tired of telling people that this horse was something special. He had already notched up a 12-length victory in a point-to-point in Ireland, and Maguire couldn't work out how he hadn't already been sold. His sire was Presenting, Paul

Barber's favourite. His name was Denman, and seconds after walking him into the main yard from his box in front of the Barbers and Nicholls, Maguire didn't have to worry about pressing the horse's case any more.

Paul Barber said: "I saw the horse. Nicholls turned to me and said: 'I'm having him,' and I said: 'No you're not, I am.' I bought him there and then. It was his stature, he was such a big horse who stood out there. He looked at you and you knew immediately he would be a good horse – if you were lucky. He had so much character. Of course, he was to be one of the greats."

The initial asking price for Denman was £180,000 but Paul Barber argued it down to £120,000. He was immediately on the phone to his partner. "What do you mean you bought a fucking hairbrush," Harry said when told Barber had purchased Denman. His £60,000 half-share of the price was in his partner's account the following morning.

The earlier prospective bidders were made aware that Denman had undergone a wind operation, which many horses required if they had trouble breathing. Paul Nicholls believed the operations were a necessary evil and did not detract from the horse's potential, but it made other possible buyers nervous.

Henrietta Knight, a shrewd old-fashioned trainer who had already won three Cheltenham Gold Cups with the beloved Best Mate, had been to the Maguire yard and fallen in love with Denman, but declined to bid because of the operation. For the same reason, the late David Johnson, who was trainer Martin Pipe's wisest owner and punter, turned him down. It wasn't even a problem for Barber, and Denman was on his way to Ditcheat.

***

Denman won his first novice hurdle race in Britain for his new connections at Wincanton. The horse was more workmanlike and resolute in victory than anything else, but it was a flat, right-handed speedster's track and far from ideal for a big, staying horse like him.

It was with some trepidation that the connections returned to the trainer's local track for his next outing. This time they had a serious opponent – Karanja – trained by Victor Dartnall, who went off as even-money favourite. Denman was 2/1, but he powered away up the home straight to win by a staggering 16 lengths.

Harry and Paul Barber were both on a high amid the throng waiting for the horse in the unsaddling enclosure. Harry said: "It was a tough ask for Denman to go right-handed on a sharp track like Wincanton, and Christian Williams, the jockey, did a great job from stopping him running out. I was amazed what he did to Karanja.

"Paul [Barber] was in bits afterwards, shaking like a leaf, and I think from that day onwards he believed he'd got the ultimate horse he'd dreamt of since he was a boy. And don't forget, he'd already won a Gold Cup.

"Denman must have been behind me in the winners' enclosure when Karanja's jockey, Andrew Thornton, dismounted and started talking to his shrewd old trainer. Suddenly, his eyes widened. He looked almost scared. I knew exactly who he was looking at and I heard what he said to Mr Dartnall: 'That is a fucking monster.'"

Harry relished the company not only of Paul Barber, but the group of mates who were always with him on race day. They all more than knew the time of day, and the conversation – even at this early stage of his development – was about Denman having Gold Cup potential. It was 'The Colonel' John Wood who said something that made everyone sit up: "Bugger him running in the Gold Cup, Denman will *win* the bloody Gold Cup." The Colonel was the first man ever to say it.

When Denman won his next race – the Challow Hurdle at Cheltenham on New Year's Day, 2006 (by 21 lengths) – Harry was successfully wagering a few more thousand quid on Roger Federer to win another Australian Open in Melbourne, but was back in time for a scheduled novice hurdle at Bangor-on-Dee, North Wales, on February 10.

The race was set up as a duel between Denman and Black Jack Ketchum – two horses of immense potential and both trading at around or just above even money. An overnight frost prompted concerns for the two sets of connections. Black Jack Ketchum was withdrawn, but at the last minute, Denman's entry was confirmed.

"Bangor-on-Dee was an impossible place to get to on a sunny day and we had no chance with conventional transport at such late notice," Harry said. "I couldn't even find a helicopter from my usual contacts to take us. But you couldn't meet a bigger enthusiast than Paul Nicholls, and he rang to say he'd found an old military chopper to take us from Bristol. First of all, he said I had to ring Paul Barber and talk him into it, because we all simply had to go to Bangor-on-Dee. Paul Barber didn't take much convincing."

Harry leapt into Kay's Range Rover – "I promise you, Jackie Stewart couldn't have got us to Bristol any quicker," he said. A few minutes later, the chopper took off. Harry would normally be the front-seat passenger, but not in a three-ball with the two Pauls. "There was definitely some form of heating in the front, but fuck all in the back. I'd never been so cold in all my life – I was sure I was going to die of hypothermia," he said.

Paul Barber recollected the flight in much the same way. "It was a big red helicopter, the doors wouldn't shut, the wind came in and it rattled like hell," he said of the chopper ride. "But we made it."

Punters applauded as Barber, Nicholls and Findlay clambered from their bone-shaking transport – which had gone down well given it was painted in the national colours of Wales. "I was so cold I marched straight into the restaurant and devoured two of the racecourse's biggest beef pies," Harry said. "I needed heat. When we arrived, Denman was 1/9. He started the race 1/12. Nowadays, that would be 1/25 in the same race."

"Paul Barber and I were in the paddock before the race and Denman looked magnificent," Harry said. Paul Barber didn't look quite so well. "He heard me having £360,000 on Denman to win £33,000 and thought I was stark-raving mad," Harry said. "He couldn't get his head around it and kept saying: 'Harry, Harry, slow down, slow down.'

"I said: 'Leave me out, Paul. This is the greatest gift of all time.' So it proved, Denman won by 17 lengths, and if Christian Williams had pushed him out, it would have been 70. It was, and always will be, the easiest £33,000 I've ever won."

Bangor-on-Dee was a little cherry on top because Denman's demolition job in the Challow Hurdle had guaranteed him starting as hot favourite for his championship race at the Cheltenham Festival – the Royal and Sun Alliance Novice Hurdle over two miles and five furlongs.

"Before that run, there was no target for him, and we didn't know how good he was, so there were no ante-post wagers before the race, and therefore no financial pressure, " Harry said. "But in the pre-paddock and then main paddock before the race, it suddenly dawned on me why they called it the Sport of Kings.

"I was pretty certain this kind of feeling would be a one-off, and I was soaking it up. I stood there thinking: 'Win or lose, I won't get this feeling again, there won't be another Denman.' Of course, I hoped we'd win, because I couldn't bring myself to think I'd ever have another favorite at Cheltenham, but it still wasn't my place. I wasn't really wealthy and I wasn't going to buy hundreds of horses, so it felt like a bit of a one-off.

"The buzz of being closely involved with a potential champion at Cheltenham was unreal, and very different. Even Kay, who wouldn't cross the road to go racing, knew that Cheltenham had a unique atmosphere in sport. The major reason for that was that it had the most knowledgeable crowd on the planet.

"Royal Ascot, World Cup Finals or Wimbledon, every other event had a fair percentage of people in the crowd who didn't know that much about what they were watching, but that number was almost nil at Cheltenham. Even in the old days, without all the TV screens, if a fancied runner made a bad mistake out in the country, the response from the crowd would be amazing. Everyone knew exactly what was going on."

There was an appreciative roar as Denman's jockey Ruby Walsh positioned the favourite perfectly to take up the running as the field went out into the country, pile on the pressure and make the race a true test of stamina. As they passed in front of the stands, though, it became clear that Walsh was holding

Denman up in fourth or fifth place, and those ahead of him weren't exactly overexerting themselves.

"I felt sick in my stomach and just couldn't work out what he [Walsh] was trying to do," Harry said. "His tactics were playing straight into the hands of a speedier type of horse doing us for toe in the later stages. And that is exactly what happened."

Indeed, Nicanor challenged Denman before the last and beat him by two-and-a half lengths. "I'm as certain now as I was on the day that had he been ridden more aggressively, the result would have been very different. I was pissed off with the ride Ruby gave him because we shouldn't have lost, and if we did, it should have been from a length and a half in front, getting caught. After the race, I kept my counsel, otherwise I'd have been castrated."

Paul Barber knew exactly what his partner was thinking, placed his arm on his shoulder and said: "Think of the way he got up and jumped the last when he was already beaten, and I'll tell you now, he'll win the Royal and Sun Alliance Chase next year."

Harry knew that Barber didn't make extravagant predictions, and as usual when he spoke, he listened carefully to every word. The dairy farmer had just sown the seed that would win Harry well over £1 million, 12 months later.

***

Walking out of the racecourse that night, Harry worked out that his mum was 1/2 to never have a winner at Cheltenham. He could not have been more wrong. Less than 48 hours later, Desert Quest won the Vincent O'Brien County Handicap

Hurdle, and Harry was looking down among a cheering crowd as Margaret collected the trophy from the late trainer's wife, Jaqueline. He couldn't stop laughing when thinking of how he'd met the man who sold him the horse.

When Harry was in his early 20s, he regarded David Loder as the most prodigious trainer of early-type two-year-olds that ever lived. It seemed that the horses would jump out of the stalls and know exactly what they were doing all the time. "He was the ultimate punter's pal of his generation," Harry said. "I'd been all over the country betting his hotpots, more often than not first time out, but I'd never met the man himself."

In 1999, Harry was reading the travel pages of a Sunday newspaper that waxed lyrical about a new hotel that had opened in Dubai. The description was of a spectacular edifice like nothing the writer had ever seen. Harry had no idea where Dubai was but when he read that it housed the first seven-star hotel in the world, he was on to his travel agents. Next evening, he and Jim O'Rourke were checking into the Burj Al Arab. The first thing the pair realised was that there wasn't much to do in Dubai. But the hotel was stunning.

"As it had only just opened, and they were charging £1,000 a night for the rooms, we wondered if we were the only people staying there," Harry said.

But there was at least one other guest – David Loder.

At the time, Loder was training horses from his base in Newmarket for Sheikh Mohammed, who would become head of the Al Maktoum family, the ruler of Dubai, a leading bloodstock authority and founder of the Godolphin racing enterprise. Loder's friend, mentor and boss as a young boy, Anthony Fortescue-Thomas, was breaking in around 100 yearlings for the Sheikh at nearby stables before sending them on to his protégé to train. Loder was a regular visitor to Dubai, checking on the horses, and knew every one of them long before they arrived in Suffolk.

He would also be in the Burj Al Arab spa early each evening – "Like clockwork, earplugs in, swimming cap on, 20 lengths in the pool and then a lie down before taking a steam," Harry said. "Nobody has been born that liked a steam or Turkish bath more than Jim and me. We were never out of the spa area, it was the dog's bollocks.

"We were grafting David Loder for three days, but no matter what we said, he was stony-faced and never uttered a word. But on the fourth day, I said something that cracked him up. We were in. As he said that night: 'Why would I want to strike up a conversation with a couple of London spivs?' He told us some great stories and we became pals."

When, some five years later, Loder heard that Harry was keen to buy a few jump horses, he rang to say that if he was serious, he should come to the Moulton Paddock yard in Newmarket and look at a cracking four-year-old from the Flat who would, in Loder's estimation, make a brilliant hurdler.

By co-incidence, Harry had become friends with Fortescue-Thomas through Richard Barber, Paul's brother. He had never bought a horse on his own without Anthony going over them first with both hands and eyes, and there was an instant rapport with Desert Quest. "I agreed a price of £100,000 with David, but there was a stipulation," Harry said. "I had over £200,000 on Roger Federer to win the US Open that weekend. If the Fed won, the horse was mine; if not, he could sell him to somebody else.

"As we were on our way out of the stables, Loder suddenly

said: 'We'll throw in this Presenting horse for £30,000 as well if you'd like him.' I'd have been 66/1 to bother to get Anthony to look at him if it wasn't for the fact that he was out of Presenting, a horse Paul Barber loved. When he'd had a look at the second horse, Anthony said: 'We can't possibly leave without him.'"

Four days later, Federer beat the American Andre Agassi 6-3, 2-6, 7-6, 6-1, in New York. Harry signed a cheque for £130,000 and both horses were on their way to Ditcheat. HereComesTheTruth was the Presenting horse, and within two minutes of him striding from the box at the Barber household, the boss was darting into his kitchen to pick up the phone and transfer £15,000 to Harry's account.

Harry backed Denman to win the 2007 Royal and Sun Alliance Chase at Cheltenham to get himself over £250,000, all at 10/1 and 8/1, before the horse had jumped a fence in public. His first novice chase was at Exeter on October 31, 2006, where Penzance was a worthy opponent, and both horses had been jumping well at a decent pace when they approached the fourth last. It is not the best track for viewing options, but Harry had a good pitch near the winning line with trusty binoculars to hand.

Penzance sailed the fence while Denman missed a stride, never took off and ploughed through four foot of birch. The surprise was not that he stayed on his feet, as he had landed on all fours, but that he didn't lose any ground on his opponent. Harry believed it must have been an optical illusion. A shuddering mistake like that and a horse would tend to lose at least four lengths, but within two strides, Denman was level again.

Surely no horse could smash through a fence at such force and it not even put him off his stride? "I laid the binoculars down and said: 'Fuck me, he's a tank,'" Harry said. "Denman bolted up. There are very few things in racing that happen like that, and when you see it, you know. From that moment, he was 'The Tank', full of bravado, braggadocio, a real man of a horse. A fucking monster – Andrew Thornton was right. I thought to myself: 'This horse will never get beat.'"

And for an awful long time – including in the biggest race of his life, the crème de la crème of the National Hunt calendar – Harry was right.

***

The famed Irish owner and punter JP McManus took Denman on with Don't Push It in his next novice chase at Cheltenham. Never had so much money changed hands in a race outside the March festival, as both sets of connections kept piling in. "JP knew he would get a value price by taking us on with a good horse, and he brought out the heavy artillery," Harry said. "The two horses had a belter of a race, with AP McCoy doing all he could to get his man the money, but Denman rallied on the run-in to win by three-quarters of a length. Everybody there that day knew they had just seen two really good horses."

Denman won his next two novice chases, both at Newbury, by a combined total of 48 lengths, and went to Cheltenham for the race Paul Barber said he would win as a red-hot 6/5 favourite. Walsh, now on Denman's back for the sixth time, rode a confident and aggressive race, and after getting the better of a protracted mid-race duel with Aces Four, moved smoothly ahead of the field four from home and ended up 10 lengths clear of the Irish contender, Snowy Morning. Harry had made his million.

The bookies immediately installed Denman as 4/1 second

favourite behind his stablemate and 2007 Gold Cup winner, Kauto Star, for the 2008 version. But everyone was talking about The Tank.

Denman would run twice more in 2007, first in the Hennessy Cognac Gold Cup at Newbury on December 1. In the build-up to the race at the testing Berkshire course, there was hesitation on the part of Paul Barber as to whether Denman should run. Newbury on Hennessy day could be hugely punishing. Barber's horses had been hurt there before and he was worried. It provoked an intense discussion.

Harry's pal Frank Harvey made a special case on Denman's behalf. "The Hennessy was the natural target for the horse, and having won the race twice on Broadheath and Playschool, I knew Paul Nicholls was fully aware of the importance of the race for a progressive young chaser," Frank said. "Horses like Arkle, Mill House, Burrough Hill Lad and Bregawn had all completed the double of Hennessy and Gold Cup. I argued all the pros to Harry. He took notes, flew to Ditcheat with my stats dossier and put it to the two Pauls. I couldn't have been happier when he called later that night and said it was all systems go."

Harry said: "All the lads thought Denman was the ideal horse to carry a lot of weight, because that's what a good horse did in the Hennessy, gave a lot of weight to inferior horses."

Denman, under 11st 12lbs, would indeed give up almost a stone to his rivals, and Sam Thomas – who had ridden him only once – was entrusted with the journey after Walsh had dislocated his shoulder in a fall two weeks earlier. Though sent off at odds of 5/1 second favourite, Denman leapt clear at the water jump and pounded through the ground to win by 11 lengths from Dream Alliance, who was carrying a full 18lbs less. It was one of those 'pinch yourself to make sure it was true' performances. Denman was now 7/4 joint favourite for the Gold Cup with Kauto Star.

Denman completed the year with a four-length victory at Leopardstown in Ireland with Walsh in the saddle, and began 2008 with a field-demolishing 20-length success at Newbury when reunited with Sam Thomas. Walsh was the No.1 jockey in the Nicholls yard and said he would remain loyal to Kauto Star, who he had ridden to Gold Cup victory the previous year, for the reprise.

The responsibility for guiding Denman on the most important journey of his life would therefore fall to Thomas, the 23-year-old Welshman.

***

The writer Donald McRae spent a day at the Ditcheat HQ where Kauto Star and Denman were next-stable neighbours for a feature in *The Guardian*. Lucinda Gould, the stable lass who looked after Denman, said the horses were 'almost like brothers.' She added: "We all know how different they are as horses, but the strange thing is they could hardly be closer when they're here. If Denman was a person, he'd be a Guinness-drinking, Irish rugby player whose bottom stuck out of his jeans. He's a bit of a lad. But Kauto is a real French poseur. He only has to see a camera to pull a pose."

The width of the wall separating their respective stables was the measurement that divided Kauto Star and Denman in the minds of those captivated by the feverish build-up to the high watermark of the 2008 Festival. The race was far too close to call with any degree of certainty.

HORSES FOR COURSES

Harry Findlay and Clive Smith, Kauto Star's owner, engaged in stage-managed banter for the cameras, insisting that if their horse didn't win, they wanted it to be the other's that prevailed. It was all very nice, but all rather contrived. Who was going to win – Guinness or Chablis?

Harry, as usual, was a magnet for the media. They doted on his every emotive word. The talk in National Hunt racing was of nothing else. Harry told Chris McGrath of *The Independent*: "I've said all along that over three-and-a-quarter miles, there'll be no excuses from us, even on good ground. Over three miles, I think Kauto would be a good thing, even round Cheltenham. But there's still a doubt about him truly staying in the Gold Cup. If Kauto comes off the bridle at any stage, we've won. If you're behind us and you come off the bridle, you're done for."

McGrath wrote: "Such theatrical exclamations have, admittedly, made some world-weary folk on the racing circuit tire of the Denman circus. But Charles Dickens would not be so prudish. He would sit down, go back over his oeuvre, and ask himself whether he ever stretched a character quite so tautly between reality and caricature."

Something had to give in the top-of-the-chart race. Denman had only lost once in 14 outings, at the 2006 Royal and Sun Alliance Novice Hurdle at Cheltenham. In his previous ten races since October 2006, Kauto Star had been beaten once, losing out by one-and-a-half lengths to the grey Monet's Garden at Aintree.

There were ten other horses in the Gold Cup field, but only two were focusing debate in bookmakers' establishments and snug bars across Britain and way beyond. Millions was being wagered on them. Kauto Star was the 10/11 favourite. Denman drifted slightly on the day and would come under starter's orders at a little after 3.30pm at odds of 9/4.

As it turned out, there would be just three horses in contention across the three miles, two-and-a-half furlongs of the race over its 22 fences – the two noted participants and another of Nicholls' horses, the grey Neptune Collonges.

In the early stages of the race, Neptune Collonges set a good, steady pace, exactly the way Denman's associates had hoped the challenge would evolve. Thomas settled Denman in Neptune Collonges' hoof prints and was never more than a couple of lengths adrift. When the field – now widely stretched – strode past the stands with one circuit to go, Denman had pressed ahead uncompromisingly. With each of his giant leaps, an equally massive roar erupted from the stands.

As the contenders reached the brow of the hill before entering the home straight for the final time, Ruby Walsh had already gone for his whip on Kauto Star. He may as well have raised a white flag. The gap between the pair could not be breached.

At the last of the fences, Denman was clearly a very tired horse, but by then he was clear by ten lengths and his race had been run. Thomas rode him out majestically to land the Gold Cup from Kauto Star, who held off Neptune Collonges to finish second, seven lengths adrift of the horse from the next-door stable.

***

Jerry Desmond, a former chairman of the Irish Coursing Club, was the first to grab Harry by the arm as he made his way to the merry, heady throng of the winners' enclosure. "I'd never heard Jerry swear before," Harry said. "But he just looked at me and said: 'Oh my God, Harry. You've only gone and won the fucking Gold Cup.'

"It was if something mystical had happened. I said: 'Jerry, you and I both know Denman would have to win 12 Gold Cups for it to be half as good as the Big Fella winning the Irish coursing Derby.' I'll never forget the look on his face because he knew I meant it. Jerry sadly passed away in 2015, but not before he stood solidly behind me in print after my warning off in 2010."

Harry's phone rang and it was June Bowler, with whom he'd dallied at bookmaking in the failed venture in Marlow when he was a teenager. "It was the best phone call I've ever had in my life which came right out of the blue. Sadly, June was gravely ill and didn't have long left to live, but she just called to say she had watched every race and read every interview. I was so happy to get the chance to talk to her. I told her Jim O'Rourke and I hadn't changed a bit, we're exactly the same people. She said she knew that and I told her I thought about her all the time. She was the best."

The celebrations were about to get into full swing. Paul Barber had owned a Gold Cup winner before – See More Business in 1999 – so both he and wife, Marianne, had experienced the emotion of such a triumph. Paul Nicholls trained See More Business and Kauto Star to their successes, so the acclaim wasn't a shock to his system. For Harry The Gambler, Harry The Dog, Harry the Outsider, Harry who often felt uncomfortable amid the racing hierarchy, this was something very new. He reacted the way most people in his position would react.

"Harry was ready to go off, bang!" Paul Barber said. "I'd never seen him in such a state as he got himself into that day.

He'd been shoveling money on Denman, day after day, more and more, and telling everybody else to do the same thing."

"Harry took the Gold Cup down to his box near the last fence, which was via the Guinness Grandstand. It was so crowded around him, he had security running around in circles. I let him enjoy it. I went around with him. There were people from all walks of life around him and there he was, brandishing the cup."

Even those whose betting slips were torn and scattered across the fields and car parks of Cheltenham could not help but be moved by the Denman story. Harry's box teemed with people. Kay feared at one stage that there might be too many for the foundations to take. "We were in one of those metal boxes built one on top of the other, and they had to put security on the door because so many people were queuing up outside to come and have a drink with Harry," she said.

"They were scared the whole lot was going to collapse. We had to have our own bouncers on the door, so when two punters left, two more went in. That's what Harry was like, all for the ordinary man and punter."

These were, indeed, the characters Harry felt happiest to be with and to see happy. If there were those in the racing establishment who baulked at a gambler standing in their midst shouting the odds, that was their problem. All he knew was that Denman, a horse loved by the working-class racing follower, had delivered, and he had played a small part.

"People asked me many times if I was a proud to own a horse like Denman," he said. "It wasn't about pride. That would be the kind of thing you'd feel if your son played for the All Blacks, or your daughter worked in a science lab and helped find a cure for cancer. That's pride."

But Harry was still regarded by many as the brash interloper. "To make matters easier for myself, I'd deliberately tell people I was a know-nothing about horses, but looking back, as a kid, I really loved horses like Gay George, Panto Prince and Sabin du Loir. I loved it when Burrough Hill Lad won the Hennessy, watching him four out knowing he would shit in off top weight. I thought I'd never see a better weight-giving performance than Burrough Hill Lad that day. Eight years later, my mum owned the winner, giving away 10lb more."

The supreme effort Denman put into his Gold Cup success was evident, and what was even more remarkable, the horse had done it with a weakened heart. Paul Barber described the 2008 race as: "The biggest Gold Cup of modern times. It was *the* race. But, by God, he was knackered at the finish. We discovered he had a fibrillating heart. He had to go to Newmarket to be taken care of, and I don't think he was ever quite as good after that. It took a lot out of him.

"But he still finished second in three further Gold Cups [in 2009 to Kauto Star, 2010 to Imperial Commander and 2011 to Long Run]. And he won another Hennessy [in 2009, defeating What a Friend], carrying the highest weight ever. He was a good horse, a very good horse."

Harry went one better, as was his wont. "He was the best horse ever. He had his heart problem, and it was our fault because when he won the Gold Cup, I think his heart burst in that race after the third last, otherwise, I promise you, he'd have beaten Kauto Star by at least 40 lengths. If you think I'm mad, or exaggerating, just ask Lester Piggott when you next see him at the races. Talking to the great man, I've no doubt he was Denman's biggest fan of all time. It was scary listening to just how good he thought the horse would have been and how fast he really thought he was. But, like the legendary AP McCoy said, he was probably never the same again after the 2008 Gold Cup."

For 48 hours after Denman's success, a rosy glow had descended upon the connections. The weekend papers were full of acclamation and support, and the Findlay-Barber 'Odd Couple' act was the talk of every racing enterprise and betting shop dialogue. But an article in the Monday, March 17 edition of the *Irish Independent* would land with a bone-jarring thud.

Vincent Hogan, the writer, laced into Harry in no uncertain terms. The headline was: 'Harry's Sick Game'. It described him as a 'wide-boy' ex-criminal. Hogan wrote: "The multi-millionaire men of the people stroll amidst the great unwashed, dispensing Papal waves, smirking enigmatically at all requests for profit-making wisdom. It is as if they have gathered in Gloucestershire on a humanitarian errand. Mostly, to be fair, they have the grace not to flout their well-being. JP [McManus] certainly doesn't.

"Harry, though, prefers to do things differently. He is a vulgar example of noisy money, the real-life manifestation of Harry Enfield's loathsome 'Loadsamoney' character. Harry name-drops. He trash-talks. He brags. He is a snake-oil salesman parachuted into the tweedy set….it felt at times as if the Festival itself was, somehow, no more than a piffling adjunct to Harry's West End show…..the so-called rags-to-riches 'I was surviving without thieving until I was 20,' fairy tale."

Harry was mainly concerned what Don Cuddy, the greyhound trainer, would think about the article. It wasn't long before Don was on the phone, raging about it. Vincent Hogan was a decent hurler in his time but he had neither met nor knew Harry, so what – or who – possibly inspired such a vitriolic piece? Harry's friends were aghast. Jim O'Rourke for one.

"I don't know if people felt threatened by Harry because he was better than them. Harry had class in abundance. Envy is rife in life and even worse amongst gamblers, but why did people go to such lengths to try to bring him down?" Jim said.

"He even copped serious abuse in Timeform's annual *Chasers & Hurdlers* book that ordinarily wouldn't even comment on owners. The *Irish Independent* piece was actually printed twice in the same paper on St Patrick's Day, but Harry made them pay for their mistake by winning significant damages out of court."

Frank Harvey was incensed, too, and the letters pages of the *Independent* were filled with notes from those defending Harry. "It was humbling to read the many protestations to the article from people either side of the water," Frank said.

Harry shrugged his shoulders: "You didn't need to be Colombo to work out who was behind the article, and when we found out and told Paul Barber, he said that we should name one of our unraced four-year-olds after him. We called the horse 'The Begrudger'."

***

Denman continued to recuperate. Dan Skelton, an assistant trainer to Nicholls, told Donald McRae for *The Guardian* about the sense of nervousness everyone felt as Denman suffered and struggled. "It could be quite awe-inspiring to be alone with them, and normally you'd never catch Denman lying down," he said. "But after the 2008 Gold Cup, he lay down every night for three weeks. It was a sure sign of how much the race took out of him. He poured everything into winning."

The heart treatment would begin a few weeks later. Paul Barber described it as like resetting a watch – using a prescribed poison every half-hour to boost his heart. "When he came back from that treatment, you could tell it hit him for six," Skelton told McRae. "People didn't realise how close we came to pulling up the stumps on him. But he was so tough and gritty that in the 2009 Gold Cup, he finished second to Kauto. Most horses would never finish second in the Gold Cup after the best run of their career. But Denman did it on the back one of his worst preparations."

Indeed, after the 2008 Gold Cup and the heart scares, Denman had not run again until Kempton Park in February 2009, almost a year on from his Cheltenham triumph. The race was regarded as the stepping stone towards a reunion with his stablemate Kauto Star in the Gold Cup, but at Kempton, Denman trailed off 23 lengths behind Madison Du Berlais.

Was Denman in good enough shape for a respectable defence of his Cheltenham crown? Harry didn't want him to be exposed. He said as much when speaking at a pre-Cheltenham evening at Exeter racecourse a few days before the race. Paul Nicholls was on the stage with him along with a couple of jockeys.

"I was asked by the punters what I thought of Denman's chances, and when I said I didn't want him to run, Nicholls' head nearly exploded," Harry said. "Paul Barber was back in the pub in Ditcheat and when I went in later in the evening, he wondered how the session had gone. 'What did you say about Denman?' he asked. I said I told them the truth and I didn't want him to run. He pissed himself laughing and thought I was joking. Nicholls was impressed how I'd dodged the bullet."

Kauto Star would win the rematch in 2009 by 13 lengths. Both Harry and Nicholls had told everyone he was a good thing.

Less than a month later, in his next race at Aintree, the famous Grand National course, Denman fell. He had never fallen before. The course was stunned into silence. Before he knew what he was doing, Harry dashed from his position at the back of the stands and was in a huddle around the horse.

"Nicholls came flying from nowhere and everyone was panicking because there was a lot of blood flying out from one of the veins in Denman's leg, and though I'm not squeamish, it wasn't a great place to be," Harry said. "Nicholls told us not to panic, that he knew where the bleeding was coming from and exactly what to do. He was right on it.

"He assured everybody that it wasn't a serious injury as he worked with the vet. It was a stressful environment but he calmed everyone down and seemed to work out what the problem was even before the vet did. He couldn't have impressed me any more than he did that day. He had one of his superstar horses lying on the ground, pumping out blood, and he didn't turn a hair. Total professional.

"He was also the best trainer by a mile for a stable visit, whether you took along a few youngsters or another trainer − and I took plenty of those − he was always willing to engage with them. He would explain everything. If I'd been an assistant to Don Cuddy, the greatest greyhound trainer of all, and I'd told other trainers or their staff the kind of things Nicholls openly told everyone, Cuddy would have lowered me into a meat mincer head first. But Nicholls couldn't help himself.

"He got just as much of a buzz out of racing as any punter would without having a bet. His enthusiasm for his horses while they worked in the mornings was infectious. He kept nothing to himself. Make no mistake, Dan Skelton and Harry Fry are both class acts who would have made it on their own, but what they learned at Ditcheat was priceless and a massive advantage to their respective careers."

***

AP McCoy rode Denman three times and never won on him. "Yes, he was a tank, but he seemed a big, gentle horse at the same time," the imperious 20-time Champion Jockey said. "When he beat Kauto Star in the 2008 Gold Cup, he was taking on a really good horse in his prime. Denman was probably the perfect Gold Cup horse, so much courage and stamina in abundance – he won two Hennessys carrying huge weights.

"The first time I rode him, at Newbury in 2010, I fell off. I can't remember exactly what happened, but whenever you ended up on your arse, you could dress it up as much as you liked, but it was one of my more embarrassing days."

AP would be engaged to ride Denman the following month, at the 2010 Gold Cup, as the horse was urged once more to try to land the biggest prize. On the eve of the race, Harry sent him a text message that simply read: 'Tora! Tora! Tora!' He re-sent it in the morning. Paul Nicholls' view was that the jockey should be more conservative.

Harry had AP to himself in the paddock before the race and made the most of his final opportunity to try to convince him to be more aggressive. "But just as he was about to be placed in the saddle, Nicholls appeared from nowhere, grabbed him by the right arm, looked him straight in the eye and said: 'Whatever you do, champ, don't be too brave.'

"To me it was like Dwight Eisenhower going up to General Patton on the eve of the Battle of the Bulge urging him to go easy with the tanks."

Denman was beaten into second place again, overtaken two out by Imperial Commander. McCoy worried that Denman might fall away from the leader as they came up the hill and was amazed at the horse's resilience. "It's a shame AP never had eyes in the back of his head and therefore knew that Kauto Star was beaten after five fences," Harry said. "He would have upped the tempo of the race for sure and given Denman the chance to go at his pace. He was The Tank, but he was a fast one and very much had his own cadence. Ask Ollie Magern, a tough front-running chaser, about him. They went toe-to-toe over half a dozen fences at Newbury, when Denman was at his fastest beat and in his best mood. Denman was lethal around Newbury.

"To win at the very highest level in sport is akin to winning a war. In battle you have to use all your weapons, and I don't believe we did that Gold Cup day and left ourselves vulnerable to Imperial Commander's turn of foot."

McCoy said he thought he had given Denman a good run. "I'd say that in 2008, he left his heart at Cheltenham when he beat Kauto Star. He emptied the tank that day. I think it almost killed him, even if he went on to win another Hennessy. No one can argue that Denman wasn't a phenomenal horse. He was one of the greatest of chasers."

McCoy was full of admiration for Harry the horse man,

but as for his betting propensities, even the bravest jockey of them all said he could never be *that* brave. "To experience the highs and the lows Harry has, that takes something different," he said. "It can't have been good for his heart, either. At least when you're riding a horse in a big race, you're in semi control. When you have £250,000 on a horse you've no control over, your destiny is in someone else's hands. I wouldn't have had the bottle for that. I wouldn't have minded if I was backing myself, but to be putting it on someone else, that takes big balls does that.

"Yes, Harry ruffled feathers, but I treated everyone as I saw them and how I'd expect them to treat me. There was room for all kinds of characters in racing. I always found Harry very interesting, respectful and liked him because we shared a love of all sports. The game needed people like him, it was better off with people like him. He had his view and he backed his view."

Harry might have been courageous when it came to backing his own beliefs with real hard cash, but he would watch jump jockeys go about their business in a state of absolute awe. He saw them ride, fall, leap back in the saddle, sweat, curse, cry and wretch, but he never saw one of them turn his back on a challenge. McCoy was the epitome of his craft.

"Everyone knew about AP – a legend, the toughest man in the world, and make no mistake. I saw him get kicked in the face one day and I would have bet 20 to win 1 he wouldn't ride in the next race, but he came out looking like the Elephant Man with fucking tape all over his face. I'd have been crying for my mum for a year, but that lunatic was out on another horse half an hour later.

"AP once told me that he'd smashed his hand so badly, if he'd had a pair of nail scissors with him, he could have snipped it off. He'd explained to me that he always knew that within 45 seconds the medics would be there, and he'd trained himself to tolerate the pain for that long.

"I remember Christian Williams, the first jockey to ride Denman for us, falling off Beshabar, my mum's horse, one day. He'd been really cut up by a horse that landed behind him, the skin was coming off his arm, it was one of the worst breaks ever, but he was looking up at me, saying: 'Harry, Harry, he would have won, he would have won,' as they administered the gas and morphine. God, they're brave bastards."

12

ASIAN HANDICAP

Harry Findlay beat Tony Bloom at pitch and putt golf in San Diego, rooftop tennis at the Crown Towers in Melbourne and one round of the old TV show *Blockbusters* in Terry Harrison's bookmaker shop in Brighton. For Harry, they were moments to savour because Tony Bloom didn't lose. Not to anyone.

Neither man could have anticipated as they first shook hands in 1996, when Harry inveigled Bloom's ticketless father, Ron, into Hove cricket ground, that two such distinct people, each possessing a rare mathematical talent, were embarking on a partnership that would be truly transformational.

From Camden to Singapore and Plumpton to Las Vegas, they worked to mutual benefit, despite the occasional and, ultimately, partnership-fracturing row. When the split came, few were totally surprised, for the pair was chalk and cheese personality-wise; the full frontal, stand-up, tell-it-as-it-is Harry Findlay, and the quiet, astute, private to the point of reclusive Tony Bloom.

The pivotal element in their relationship was not the racing colours they shared with limited success until the falling out, but the Asian Handicap, a dream system that required people with gifted minds to understand, appreciate and activate. When Bloom discovered it, he knew the one person who was vital to build the edifice higher and higher. Nobody else but Tony Bloom would have picked Harry Findlay.

It was an imperative because if he tempted Harry to become part of developing the project, Bloom would also benefit from the expertise of the shrewdest of football betting minds – Harry's mentor, 'Scotch' Tommy Bradley.

Tony and Harry may have been from different ends of the spectrum as people, but the betting bug had bitten both from an early age. In his book, *Gambling*, published in 2006, former England cricket captain turned chief cricket correspondent of *The Times*, Mike Atherton, wrote that Bloom would use a fake ID to get into betting shops when he was 15 – the same age Harry was when his mum was trying to get him banned from all similar establishments in High Wycombe.

Tony Bloom studied mathematics at Manchester University, joined the accountancy firm Ernst & Young, and worked as an options trader on the London Stock Exchange before abandoning that career to utilise a formidable mathematical intellect in the cold-blooded world of professional gambling. He told Atherton: "I believe in betting aggressively, and occasionally, to win big, you have to risk losing."

The poker tables of the world were the public theatres where Bloom demonstrated powers of concentration, decisiveness and strategic thinking that placed him at the highest peak of the gaming mountain. *The Guardian's* Victoria Coren wrote in 2010: "The Finn, Patrik Antonius [who by 2017 had live tournament winnings of $7 million], is a brilliant pro player rightly respected by poker fans around the world, many of whom may never have heard of Tony Bloom.

"But if tournament winnings [the flawed yet standard measure of success in poker] were divided among the number of tournaments played, the low-key Lizard would probably turn out to be the biggest winner in the world. He is a phenomenon, and he's not even a full-time player."

Bloom would much rather have had a discreet veil pulled across all of his endeavours, but the poker was out there, in full view of the world. He could not hide. 'Starlizard' – a company in which he had an enormous stake – became one of the most successful trading platforms in the world because so few people knew how it did what it did, and those who did know, would never tell.

In 2016, the magazine *Business Insider* published an article devoted to Starlizard, formed ten years earlier and whose name combined the power of its 'Star' system – in which each employee had a stake – with Bloom's 'Lizard' moniker. Starlizard employed some of the sharpest brains in betting to advise Bloom how to make subtle, transformative gains from the Asian Handicap system on football across the world.

Writer Oscar Williams-Grut sought to explain the defining modus operandi of Starlizard and the talent that defined it. Clearly, secrecy was an overarching necessity. The article contained an enormous amount of detail, but former employees spoke on the guarantee of anonymity. No current worker at the company's headquarters in Camden, North London, was quoted. They had too much to lose.

"Starlizard treats gambling the way hedge funds treat stocks. It is a consultancy that offers proprietary odds analysis to rich clients looking to make smart, high-stakes bets. These high rollers then use its internally generated odds to identify the 'value' bets – instances in which the retail bookmaking market has underestimated or overestimated a team. In these cases, the risk-reward ratio is swayed in the bettor's favour.

"It specialises in estimates tailored to the Asian Handicap market – Bloom's favourite – by calculating what it sees as the most likely scoreline for any given football match. This is crucial as the handicap rests on the pre-match favourite scoring a certain number of goals. Starlizard allowed Bloom's syndicate to make cold, calculated decisions about where to stake cash, separating the decision-making from the money and making it as mathematical as possible – no gut feelings."

Starlizard was making its name and revenues of almost £15 million in fees from high-rolling clients because it was a one-of-its-kind company that, more than anything, required Tony Bloom keeping a steady, defining hand on the tiller – and to stay one step ahead of the game.

What was the 'Asian Handicap' everyone was getting so worked up about? Its origins were traced to late 1998 when American journalist and gaming expert Joe Saumarez Smith took a telephone call from Joseph Phan, a bookmaker from Indonesia, who was setting up the first online betting site in Asia. The special offering of the site was to be a system they named hang cheng.

In an interview for Bet Asia, Saumarez Smith, said: "Mr Phan explained to me how it worked, and I thought it sounded like a handicap system. No one in Europe had heard about this way of betting, with the possible exception of a few people who worked for Victor Chandler, such as Tony Bloom. I emailed Phan saying I thought 'Asian Handicap' was the best way of describing the system, and the next thing I knew, it was all over his website."

Saumarez Smith was correct in assuming that, through their network of intelligence, Victor Chandler was on the case and Bloom was already into his stride, devouring the intricacies of the methodology and sensing it could become a gambling phenomenon – with him as its dominant force.

It was crucial that as few people as possible discovered what was happening and got in on the act before Bloom had it all worked out. Harry said: "Tony and Victor Chandler did it on their own because you keep a golden nest-egg to yourself. You don't put it on the front page of the fucking papers."

But the two people he had to let in on the secret were Harry and, through him, Bradley, who, in his 70s, was regarded as the sage of football bettors. "Tommy was old school from the Glasgow district of Govan, Sir Alex Ferguson's hometown, and was tight as fuck," Harry said. "He'd been a bookmaker in the shipworks, then became a punter. Tony knew I was mustard on football, and with Tommy on board, he would have the best possible three-way algorithm for the [English] Premier League."

When Tony Bloom rang Harry, he asked: "Do you know what the Asian Handicap is?" Harry said he'd never heard of it. Within 30 seconds of Tony starting to explain it down the phone, Harry had it sorted in his head. Like minds thought alike. "I got it straight away. We started working on it two days later," he said.

If the Asian Handicap was a breeze for people as mathematically adroit as Tony Bloom and Harry Findlay to understand and thus exploit, it required explanation for the non-genius types. The fundamental essence of the Handicap was: -0.5 [minus half a goal] meant the team you were backing just had to win the game, and if you were backing +0.5, your team only needed to draw the game or better for you to win. -1 [minus a goal] meant your team needed to win by two goals for you to win, but if they won by a single goal, it would be a no bet [and your stake returned]. +1 meant a draw or better to win the bet, but if you lost by a single goal, once again, it would be a no bet.

"Over time I realised that, on the maths, Lizard was right ever so slightly more than Tommy and I," Harry said. "When it came to the handicap in the early days, if we wanted to have £20k on Chelsea at home to a good team – Manchester United, for argument's sake – we'd be inclined to back them draw, lose half – i.e. a punter would lose 50% of the stake if the match was a draw, which was classified as -0.25 on the Asian Handicap system. Lizard invariably would go for the bigger price and back them -0.5 – i.e. Chelsea had to win the game.

"The enticing 'draw and you get half your money back' element would often draw us in, but Lizard knew where the best value was nine times out of ten, regardless of what the handicap was. Like his mum once said to me: "No one beats my Tony at maths."

The partnership between Tony and Harry on the Asian Handicap had started before the 1998 World Cup, at a time when both were out of form. Harry owed Tony 'a nice few quid' and initially found the whole Handicap enterprise very stressful, not least in that he was living with Kay's parents at the time and 'didn't have a pot to piss in.'

Every Friday night, Bloom would ring for the next day's prices from Harry and, through him, Tommy. As the bets mounted and the need for accuracy intensified, Harry was starting to feel the heat. Bloom never wavered. "All these £5k and £10k bets with no money of my own were piling on the pressure," Harry admitted. "Tony just said: 'We're certainties to win, they can't beat us. Keep positive, don't worry, you'll be all right, just keep going, I've got you covered.'"

***

The buds that would flower all over Tony Bloom's world were planted in 1998 when the French football team took its nation by storm and won the football World Cup staged on home soil. The previous year had not been Harry's best, and Bloom was more than happy for him to sign over his home in Sheffield for its full £90,000 valuation in order to give Harry a significant betting stake for the Finals.

After early £25,000 wagers on Tunisia +1.5 against England (Tunisia lost 2-0) and on USA +1.5 against Germany (USA lost 2-0), Harry was behind the eight-ball, and the next big play (£30,000) was his first-round nap – South Africa +0.5 against Denmark, who only needed a draw to qualify.

In the Findlay household, the atmosphere was so intense as the match kicked off that Kay decided to take Jade out for the afternoon, so they wouldn't have to endure Harry going through his agonies. But before they had changed for a long walk and reached the front door – only 12 minutes into the match – the Danes had taken the lead. The silence was palpable.

Harry was increasingly desolate as South Africa dominated the remainder of the first half but failed to score. Then, six minutes into the second half, their striker Benni McCarthy was one-on-one with the great Danish goalkeeper Peter Schmeichel. "I knew in my heart of hearts he'd duff the fucking shot after such a great build-up, and I was spot-on," Harry said. "But it worked a treat because his toe-poke went straight between Schmeichel's legs."

Alone on his sofa, Harry started to clap. He clapped so long that he felt a tingle spreading up both his arms, sensing that this was a turning point in his life. Fifteen minutes later, the Danes were reduced to 10 men and Harry's money was safe. The match finished 1-1. Three weeks later and Harry had won a massive share of £2 million.

***

Before kick-off in the World Cup final between France and Brazil on July 12, 1998, Harry Findlay had turned his £90,000 stake into a pretty £1.5 million. He then decided to have his biggest individual bet of the tournament – £300,000 on France +0.5 at even money. When the handicap remained the same at half-time, he had another £200,000 on the French.

Harry was not the only one with such a firm opinion on French title prospects. Bloom, who was in charge of football affairs at the Victor Chandler offices in Gibraltar, advised the firm to bet their entire profit from the competition on the French +0.5 in the final (i.e. France or the draw in 90 minutes). France, who led 2-0 at half-time, won 3-0, and Bloom became the most feted man in betting circles.

In the *Business Insider* article, Williams-Grut wrote: "A former Starlizard employee described his success in the World Cup as the founding myth of Bloom's career. No one knew the exact amount staked or how much Victor Chandler won. The company later became Bet Victor, one of the UK's better-known online gambling brands. Emboldened by his success at Victor Chandler, Bloom went on to set up Premier Bet in 2001, an early online bookmaker that took bets under the Asian Handicap system."

In the early throes of the Bloom-Findlay-Bradley partnership, Harry was allowed to bet up to £60,000 on the outcome of any single English Premier League match over a weekend.

"Tony and his company would never bet until the Saturday because they'd bet so big that they didn't want the money affecting the prices until the day of the game," Harry said. "But I had a special deal and was allowed to have up to £20k on the Thursday, £20k on the Friday and £20k on the Saturday. £60,000 was my limit on any game.

"So, if on Thursday morning, Tottenham's centre-half broke his ankle, I could have my £20k on the other team right then. Everyone else had to wait until Saturday. I had the best deal in the world because of the help I was to Tony.

"The Lizard might have rubbed you up the wrong way sometimes by deliberately contradicting your thoughts or opinions, but that was his way of getting information quickly. I loved that deal. £60k was a fucking big bet. On Saturday, there were 10 games in the league and I reckon that, on average, in the first couple of years, I'd have a £60k bet, a £50k bet, two £30k and a couple of £20k bets, and I'd be on eight or nine matches out of the ten. That was my wages, my treat.

"Even from the early stages, Tony was always improving the model. And over a period of time, I could tell he was becoming less interested in the prices Tommy and I had for the games, so that when Matthew Benham [who became the owner of Brentford FC] joined the firm, we were more or less a second thought. Our influence on what bets the company was having was clearly waning. Tony had taken it to a different level."

Indeed he had. Bloom had squeezed every last bit out of Harry and Tommy's expertise on football and was becoming increasingly clear in his own mind of the correct odds. He was honing his system to perfection – backed by an innate understanding of how to assimilate and weigh information quickly. What Harry and Tommy were able to contribute was becoming a lot less valuable to him.

Tony Bloom hallmarked the sophisticated algorithms required to dominate the gambling world. He had been the first off the mark understanding the Asian Handicap and was building a framework that no one could better, especially when no one knew exactly how he had done it.

He was the ultimate at disseminating information, putting that information into odds, and that those odds were accurate to a tee. That was why he was becoming the most successful sports bettor out there.

***

The 'Star' prefix of the name Starlizard was the structure on which the company based its entire ethos – everyone who worked there should feel as if they were a part of the furniture. It evoked enormous loyalty.

In 2006, the year Starlizard was formed, Harry and Kay were among those invited onto a boat Tony Bloom hired for a few days of sun and fun on the Mediterranean, where family, friends and work colleagues – almost 100 of them – were treated to unabashed luxury. No expense was spared and no one was expected to pay for anything.

The summer World Cup Finals were on and Harry regaled all on board about the 'three best bets of all time' in the quarter-final. "The day of all days," he told them. The handicaps were Portugal v England [Portugal +0.25, draw win half], Argentina v Germany [Argentina +0.25] and France v Brazil [France +0.5]. When the group disembarked for a night in Barcelona – Harry's favourite European city – anyone who had taken his advice had far bulkier wallets. It had, by some way, been Harry's biggest-ever winning day.

By this time, Harry was on a remarkable £10,000 a 'star' from Tony – his share of a designated bet. From Bloom to the broom-handlers, a lot of the people in the company won money betting when Tony's own bets were successful. "Even as the cleaners were mopping up at night, they were winning, and they were always getting on at the right price," Harry said.

A single 'star' was a mythical figure, and though Harry was as close to Bloom as anyone in the early days, even he didn't know precisely how much a 'star' was worth. "If I was guessing, it would be between £400,000 and £600,000. It could have been £300,000, but equally, knowing the Lizard, £750,000 was more likely," he said.

"What was important was how the 'stars' were split up. I always thought Tony kept about 50%, or just over, and the rest would be shared. I was on £10,000, and I'm sure there were three or four guys getting a bigger slice of the action than me. But, crucially, most people at the company had a piece of the pie and, on a regular basis, knew what it felt like to win.

"Incredibly, I had the winnings from my own bets, plus £10,000 from every star that Tony put on. It was massive. No one who worked for him was allowed to bet with anyone else, and apart from their wages, they all got a bit of the star, so when the bets were going well, they all did well."

But, because he was succeeding on such delicate margins, even someone as successful as Bloom had to cut his cloth. A couple of years after Starlizard was formed, during the time Harry was the darling of National Hunt racing as Denman was ridden to glory in the 2008 Cheltenham Gold Cup, Tony Bloom called to tell him that everyone involved would be taking a hit.

"I knew it was coming because some of those who had been on £2k a 'star' were getting cut back to £1k and had started screaming," Harry said. "Tony rang and said: 'Harry, sorry mate, I'm cutting you back to £5k a star.' I'd have been wasting my breath trying to get it any higher, so I went for a different tactic. I said: 'Okay, but instead, I'll go down from £10k to £2k, and it's for life.' Straight away he said: 'Yes.'"

It was, for Harry, akin to a lifetime's security and a real masterstroke.

***

Harry's persuasive manner and enthusiasm for the racehorse industry encouraged Tony Bloom to become more deeply engaged in equine pastimes. There had been a fleeting and successful liaison in the summer of 2002 when Tony asked Harry if he could find him the right horse and trainer to win his grandfather's memorial race run annually in the summer at Brighton. Harry, top trainer Dandy Nicholls, and the horse Compton Arrow, obliged by the shortest of short heads.

Tony was not usually one for distractions – not with a huge gaming empire to help take care of and poker competitions to harness his competitive edge – but the thought of owning a few outstanding horses had a certain appeal. "And I was good at talking him into things," Harry said.

The Findlay-Bloom purple and white colours did make the occasional generous splash, largely thanks to one horse. The summer of 2009 was the sunniest of their racing association. In June that year, High Standing – purchased for £55,000 – won the prestigious Wokingham at Royal Ascot, after which the cameras once more pursued Harry for instant comment. It was, after all, his first victory at the Royal meeting.

Maybe the cracks in the partnership had begun to form when Clare Balding asked if this was Harry's best racing moment of the year. "Saxby winning a seller at Thirsk for Mick Channon four days ago was a lot better," Harry replied.

Before too long, the sun had indeed set on Bloom and Findlay as a racing team. Harry told Greg Wood of *The Guardian* in September: "Tony has businesses to run, and he's got a big commitment to Brighton and Hove Albion FC [Bloom had become chairman in May 2009, two years sooner than Harry prophesied to his father, Ron, it would happen]. He's more interested in having a horse or two for big meetings like Royal Ascot. For me, it's a full-time thing, and the big enjoyment is having horses running all the time."

The pair had 42 horses on the Flat in the 2009 season. High Standing was their biggest earner at around £150,000. They had a few more decent winners, but they were few and far between for Bloom's liking. The granite accountants he employed soon worked out that this was not a deal that worked to his benefit.

It hadn't helped the smooth running of the operation that Bloom brought Graham Doyle in to look after his interests, because Doyle and Harry were at loggerheads straight away. "I'd never done it before in my life, but when Graham sent me a text he'd meant to send to Tony, I went to find him at the champagne bar at the top of the new main stand at Ascot and dragged him down to the entrance where I took off my jacket, rolled up my sleeves and challenged him to a duel," Harry said. "Two days later, in the Camden office, Lizard screamed at me, no more money and no more horses."

Each man would take a share of the blame when the partnership finally crumbled. Bloom, who barely put a foot wrong in the gambling arena or at the poker table, ought to have resisted the temptation to join forces with Harry this time. For once, the Lizard should have said 'no', but didn't, and he knew it.

It was a source of regret, but there came a time when he needed to put kinship to one side, own the odd horse rather than 40, and become less attached to a world not reliant on his mathematical talents.

Harry said: "I was stuck because the deal was that I gave Tony half of all my good horses, apart from Denman. I had about £2 million of bloodstock, the Lizard had a half share of those, and he paid for all the yearlings, which turned out to be a right bad deal for him. However much you thought they were going to cost, they cost more, and we had 30 to 40 horses together, trained by all different people, which was another big drain on the money."

Watching from afar as the parting became increasingly inevitable was Eamonn Willmott, Harry's school friend, gambling inspiration and, as irony would have it, now the manager of Horses First Racing Ltd, in which both Tony Bloom and Harry owned shares.

"Harry knew Tony when he was very young, before he'd made any real money at all," Eamonn said. "On one level, Tony really liked Harry because Harry helped him massively in so many ways, especially outside gambling. They had an intricate relationship. Tony didn't speak to many people and valued very few opinions. He was self-made, a proper serious, unusual genius, who very quickly surrounded himself with some of the best football brains in Britain, but when it came to Federer-Nadal on a Sunday afternoon, there was only one person he'd ring."

For eight years, Harry had attended the first week of every Grand Slam tennis tournament and, for more than twice that time, tennis was his biggest winner. "But since 2013, I hardly touched it because computers and syndicates run the markets, and they have no weaknesses," he said. "Most human beings wouldn't dream of betting anything at 1/12, whereas I used to do it all the time, but that advantage has gone. Every time I fancy a good thing on the tennis, I cannot believe how short they are, and I know I couldn't make the game pay any more. It's the same with the horses. I'm betting them as much as ever but so rarely do I get involved with the really short odds-on pokes. All the real good things get hammered in the betting and any value is now marginal at best. In the late '70s, I bet Dramatist at 4/7 and 8/15 in a novice chase over two miles, five furlongs at Newbury. Exactly the same race today and he'd go off at 2/9!

"To win at gambling, you have to have the ability to adapt, and nobody does that better than the Lizard. He finds a way to make any game pay. He just adapts to the markets and ultimately implements his own system. He owns half of Brighton and more then three quarters of Camden Town, and it won't stop there."

But, in 2009, Harry had overindulged the number of horses he owned with Tony and paid too little heed to how much each one cost. When a meeting was called in London to discuss the details of the severance, two people regarded for their mathematical quick-wittedness were more than £2 million apart in their assessment of how much Harry had overspent.

Bloom's bookkeepers – Harry also had a particularly fraught relationship with Adam Franks, his leading accountant – produced figures asserting that their boss was owed £3.8 million. Harry believed it to be £1.7 million and argued his corner. Voices were raised in the ensuing debate. And when Tony said: "What are you going to do now?" Harry saw red. "I'm going to get a window-cleaning round, what the fuck do you think I'm going to do?"

"Tony said I didn't realise how much I was spending," said Harry. "And he was probably right. But even if I did owe him

£3.8 million, we both knew we were going to carry on winning. I never enjoyed gambling as much if I wasn't under a bit of pressure, because that's the way I lived my life. I shouldn't have taken the high road. We could have sorted it out. He made me sign the house in Bath over as well as my £1 million shares in Horses First Racing, so he got his money. By a sheer act of God at the solicitors, I managed to salvage half of the money from the sale of the house."

Jim O'Rourke, Harry's long-standing friend, had seen the split coming. "There'd have been people bending Tony's ear about Harry," he said. "That's the way it was. They all knew Harry was his partner, they'd have seen the way Harry lived his life, first class, and resented it.

"We used to call it the helicopter syndrome. Lizard, his family and friends would turn up after the first race, pouring with sweat after spending three hours on the M25 when nine times out of ten, Harry had landed half an hour before the meeting in one of Westland's finest.

"But every time he was on TV, Harry helped build Tony's reputation. Harry introduced some of the very best people into Tony's firm, and they're all made for life. Why would either of them want to fall out?"

One lunchtime, at Nobu in Melbourne, and in sheer exasperation, Harry screamed at Tony: "Listen, just tell me eye-to-eye, do you think in any way I deliberately got the figure too high or tried to fuck you? He said: 'Oh no, you're 100% honest, I don't doubt it for a second, you just spent far too much money.' He was right, but at that moment, I'd rather he believed that I'd fucked him. I'd have felt better about it."

Ultimately, it wasn't the way either man would have wanted

the partnership to end. On the train home on the evening of the split, Harry was quietly seething. "I was in my office late that night with Big Fella Thanks curled up at my feet. I calculated I'd done over £5 million and that my £2k star for life deal was over. It probably cost me over £10 million in the end. I knew more than anyone how much the stars were worth, but shit happens and it's only money. To be honest, my mum and I were both more disappointed that he never said or did anything when the BHA went after me. If the roles had been reversed, Tony knows exactly what I'd have done. But, as he said at the time – 'It's not just about me any more.'

"For such a private man, what he has achieved with Brighton and Hove Albion is remarkable. I was at the Goldstone Ground for the last few games there and knew how badly the football club situation affected the whole town. There will never be another chairman like Tony Bloom, and you don't need to be Einstein to work out who told him to go on the train or coach with the fans to away games.

"I think the team over-performed last season and could easily be fancied to go straight back down. But the betting market says differently because of one man, and they're right. With Tony in charge, it's most unlikely to happen. It's not just about what he's done so far for the club, it's what he and his son Joshua are going to do in the future. There will never be a better time to be a Brighton fan and that's exactly what I told Greg Wood of *The Guardian* ten years ago when he cockily asked me: 'Oi, what about your mate, the poker player, he's just taken over my team!'

"Tony hasn't got more than a handful of horses now, but they're all well bought and placed. As always with the horses, I just do exactly what Glen tells me – selections and stakes. But I always double my bet if we're on one of the Lizard's horses.

"I haven't spoken to him since our split, but even now, if Tony was stuck on a desert island and his life depended on it, a football match was on, he had three calls to make at half-time, and getting it right was his only hope of rescue, I'd bet big odds-on I'd be one of those calls."

13

WARNING OFF

Gullible Gordon ran in the Dartmouth Term of '65' England Expects Amateurs Riders' Novices' Hurdle at Exeter on October 21, 2008. The joint owners of the chestnut were Paul Barber and Margaret Findlay, Harry's mother. To all intents and purposes, Harry was considered the joint owner, certainly as far as the betting world was concerned. He'd named the horse after his younger brother.

"If Gordon came home from work with £100 on a Friday night, it would take me less than five minutes to get at least half of it from him for my weekend's punting," Harry said.

Producer Stewart Mitchell made a film in 1997 about Harry called *Stood For This Massive*, which won awards all over Europe and quickly found its way onto BBC2. Gordon and some pals were watching it at home when Harry was talking about what it's like as a kid when you've got no money and you're dying for a bet. He went on to mention stealing some of his brother's LPs to fund his habit. As Gordon watched open-mouthed, the penny finally dropped as he said: "I wondered where all my Genesis albums went."

Harry had £80,000 on Gullible Gordon at Exeter. As he walked into the paddock before the race to speak to the trainer and jockey, he heard Paul Nicholls tell Will Biddick to hold the horse up in fourth or fifth place.

"I nearly had a heart attack," Harry said. "Bloody hell, Paul. He's a three-mile chaser, surely he's got to try and make all."

Harry had no chance of getting his way and planned to cut his bet in half, but only managed to dump nearly £18,000 of it before the off. Gullible Gordon finished sixth. That's exactly what he told British Horseracing Association investigators Mark Phillips and John Burgess when they turned up at his Rowas Lodge home in Bath just over a year later. The only other thing they were worried about was Harry laying Denman for £121 by mistake in the ante-post market for the 2008 Gold Cup, but as he backed him for four times as much seconds later and was a net backer of more than £40,000 overall, it was deemed irrelevant.

It was Harry who told the investigators: "If you're worried about me laying Gullible Gordon, you might as well nick me for Glen [Gill] laying him in-running the other day at Chepstow, but as I had £64,000 on him before the race, and effectively had only given away £5,000 in hedging money over the last half a mile [the horse came into the home straight 20 lengths clear and won easing up], I really was only joking."

WARNING OFF

The Rules of Racing did not permit lay betting against a horse – 'whether by an owner or a person who played an active part in managing it, if in joint ownership, or by a 'service provider' to its owner.' The BHA decided to appoint a panel to look into the case. On June 11, 2010, their verdict was issued: "We impose a disqualification of six months to come into effect Friday, June 11, 2010, until December 10, 2010, inclusive."

***

The evening he was warned off, Harry Findlay dined with the Sangsters and Brian Meehan, their trainer, at the Outside Chance at Manton, in Marlborough, Wiltshire. It was the young Sam Sangster – 'after a few pints' – who stood up at the table and offered to run all Harry and Margaret's horses in his name and colours that had been his mother's, the exact invert of the green and blue Sangster silks made famous by his father Robert, the thoroughbred owner whose horses won 27 European Classics, including two Epsom Derbys. It was in these classic shades that Maggie's Bergo won the Queen Alexandra Stakes on the final day of Royal Ascot.

"Sam said: "Within days of that dinner, I had runners from all over, from Ann Duffield and George Baker – it was extremely exciting. But the icing on the cake was the mighty Bergo, my first-ever runner at Royal Ascot, turning into the straight. They were never going to catch him. Hand on heart, I can say it is my favourite day in racing and Harry was the man behind it."

Harry described trying to watch Bergo on television at home as one of the most bittersweet moments of his life, but it was the only time he had wanted a horse to win a race so much that he closed his eyes for the final 200 yards. The horse's victory guaranteed Ryan Moore, the jockey, the winner he needed to claim the prestigious Ritz Club Trophy for top jockey at the meeting.

Sam's brother Guy, said of Harry: "I was fascinated by him before we met, and when I finally did, I recall saying: 'My name's Guy Sangster and I don't buy racehorses.' The following season, Harry and I had a string of a dozen together with trainer Brian Meehan at Manton. That says all you need to know about Harry, although my brother Adam, who lives in Melbourne, assures me that Harry should have been an Australian."

Meehan added: "Harry and I bought horses together for two years. He was a great talker and didn't mind asking anyone what they thought a horse was worth. If any horses were on both of our final lists, we'd decide on our price and try to buy every one that went for less. We bought some lovely yearlings and had plenty of success, but the best horse I trained for Harry was bought, initially, by John Best. He was a two-year-old Dubawi colt and Harry named him Titus Mills after his daughter Ella's headmaster. After winning his first two races at Ascot and Goodwood, I thought he was potentially one of the nicest horses I've trained, but sadly he broke down when travelling like a winner just after halfway in the Racing Post Trophy at Doncaster in 2010."

By the time Harry had arrived at Manton, news of his warning off was starting to spread like wildfire. Harry had helped fan the flames by inviting himself onto Matt Chapman's programme *At The Races* the afternoon of the hearing. Chapman was astonished. "Harry had worked out that the BHA was coming after him and cleverly arranged to be interviewed," he said.

"He told everyone live on air that he'd been warned off,

before the BHA announced it. Even in the worst of times, he was ahead of the game. There is a real sense that sometimes those in power are simply out to get certain people. What happened to Harry had echoes in the Kieren Fallon witch-hunt [the Irish jockey was exonerated on charges of race-fixing and trying to defraud the internet in the early 2000s], but Harry came through it eventually. I hope he's not the last of his kind."

Harry had a couple of two-years-olds with the shrewd Eve Houghton-Johnson at the time of the warning off. Something or someone must have spooked her because she wouldn't speak to him about the horses over the phone. He wrote her a letter saying that, in the circumstances, it would be best if she kept the horses herself. Under pressure, it was a good move because, three months later, Eve did call Harry to say that one of them, Dew Reward, was a certainty in the 3.30 at Bath. He won by half a length from Fly By White.

The Sangsters aside, there was encouragement from others in the racing community. Margaret Findlay, interviewed by Alan Lee of *The Times*, said: "Tim Vaughan and Ferdy Murphy [two top trainers] have been vociferous in their support, not only condemning the fact that Harry was charged, but pointing the finger of blame at the BHA's Paul Roy, Nic Coward and Paul Scotney, a man who, in my opinion, knows less about betting than I do, despite being their head of security.

"We've had horses at Ditcheat for eight or nine years and many people there will know just how honest and straight Harry is with his gambling. Yet the support from the place where Gullible Gordon was trained has simply not been loud enough nor strong enough."

HARRY FINDLAY

***

Harry Findlay had a fondness for naming his horses after the special characters that had influenced his sporting life. One of these, Stefanki, was so called after tennis coach Larry Stefanki, who helped nurture such talents as John McEnroe, Tim Henman and Andy Roddick. When they bumped into each other on the tennis circuit, Larry acknowledged Harry and they chatted about all sorts. Larry called him 'The Tennis Gambler'.

On the day of the appeal into his warning off – July 14, 2010, – Stefanki was running at Lingfield Park. Before the George Baker-trained 6/4 favourite entered the stalls for his six-furlong dash, his owner learned that his six-month disqualification from anything to do with racing had been reduced to a niggardly fine of £4,500. Stefanki won by three-and-three-quarter lengths. Shit in, as Harry would say. But Harry couldn't have cared less.

Roderick Moore, the eminent barrister, had been one of six people to offer pro bono to represent Harry at the appeal – but his was the only proposal to arrive via a letter in the *Racing Post*, so sure was he that Harry had a watertight case. Moore's associate Daryl Cowan spoke on the steps outside the offices where the appeal was heard. Listening to him, Harry felt the tears rising.

"I'm delighted and, frankly, relieved both for our client and for racing," Cowan said. "A disqualification was plainly wrong and the appeal board, to their great credit, agreed. Harry's main concern throughout has been to clear his name. While most people within the racing industry recognised he was in no way dishonest, he was distraught that the general public, who may have a lesser understanding of the way in which betting operates, might think of him as dishonest in some way.

"He is very grateful to the appeal board for making it clear, in no uncertain terms, that this was not a case of corruption and that it felt justified [...] in expressing [its] own clear view that Mr Findlay should not have been disqualified."

Jim O'Rourke rang Harry that evening to offer his congratulations on the outcome of the appeal and to tell him – if he didn't know already – that Stefanki had prevailed. "It meant nothing to him that he'd won the appeal and nothing that the horse had won the race," Jim said. "He was a broken man."

The pieces would take a long time to be put back together. Harry said: "The day I got warned off, Betfair had run a piece on the front page of the *Racing Post* saying the verdict was wrong and they still wanted to do business with me because I was one of the straightest punters on the planet. I was always in constant contact with their integrity team. I had my card marked over six months earlier that the BHA were looking into a Paul Nicholls owner, and for the life of me I couldn't work out who it was, but I knew it couldn't be me. One of the top racing journalists in the country, Lydia Hislop, once wrote: 'Harry Findlay doesn't use his horses as vessels to bet with.'"

To Harry, that was like praise from Caesar. "I spent my time as an owner trying to prove that you could do it straight, and yet they came after me," he said. "It was beyond bizarre and simply the biggest trumped up charge of all time."

When the BHA sent Harry their case file – *An Inquiry Concerning Harry Findlay* – he read the summary over and over again and his eyes kept returning to points 15 and 16. The BHA had brought a case against Anthony Ramsden and Robert Owen, and attempted to draw a parallel between that and the one against Harry.

The BHA said: "Laying to lose when such laying is part of an overall back position was recognised as a breach of the rules by the Disciplinary Panel in the [Ramsden and Owen] Inquiry and the betting on the horse, Mickmacmagoole, in April 2007, even before the old rules were amended to make this expressly clear."

Point 15 in the Findlay Inquiry stated: "The lay bets made by Ramsden and Owen were designed simply to ensure that the price of the horse did not contract, so that good odds would be available when they came back to it. The amounts laid by Ramsden and Owen were small in absolute terms [between £27 and £417] and insignificant when compared to the amounts to which they had backed their horse [between 0.2% and 2%] and were never intended to provide any significant return should the horse not win. There is no suggestion in the report of the Inquiry that the bets were informed by any inside information casting doubt on the chances of the horse."

The following point, No.16, read: "By contrast, the lay bets made by or on behalf of Mr Findlay were large in absolute terms and were intended to provide very substantial hedging positions for the back bets already placed, constituting around 22% and 50% of the back bets respectively."

Harry was amazed. "I nearly pissed myself at the stupidity of it," he said. "I immediately phoned the BHA and explained why point 15 was deception and 16 was clearly not deception, and the girl there got it straight away. She said she'd speak to somebody else and get back to me. Within 20 minutes, she called back and told me to take 15 and 16 out of the file. And people wondered why I turned up at the hearing without a lawyer."

When the case was formally heard, both points 15 and 16 had been removed from the ledger. "And they still warned me off for six months," Harry said.

The chairman of the appeal board, Sir Roger Buckley, talked in his summation about a 'gambler's instinct.' The moment Sir Roger used that phrase, Harry knew he had found a kindred spirit. The board's verdict was so contrary to the original outcome, it raised obvious concerns about whether the case should have been brought in the first place. Why had it been pushed so hard? Had there been a concerted effort in horse racing to try to bring down a person that some in the sport perceived as boorish and akin to a Catherine Wheel on a loose nail?

Harry said: "When the BHA investigators initially came to see me, it was because they were worried about me laying Denman for £121 when they knew full well it was a genuine mistake because I had £400 back on him to win, literally seconds later, and was just topping up on him in an ante-post market. It was actually me who mentioned the Gullible Gordon race to them, so the whole investigation was truly farcical.

"I clearly remember what also happened that day. I said to them [the BHA investigators, John Burgess and Mark Phillips] that I had horses with 12 different trainers, and as the rule stated, you mustn't lay any horses from any yard where you were an existing owner. I asked: 'What should I do, would you just like me to stop laying altogether? It was no problem for me; over 95% of my horse business was betting them anyway, not laying them, and like everybody else, nobody got fat laying horses.

"They [Burgess and Phillips] gave me permission to carry on. In fact, I remember us all pissing ourselves laughing because

Mark Phillips told us I was over £700,000 behind laying Paul Nicholls' horses! I couldn't have been more professional or diligent and even rang my man at Betfair, Andy Riddell, and their lawyer, Martin Cruddace, while the investigators were still in my office to confirm it.

"The day after I said in the press that I had been given permission, I was lambasted as a liar on the front page of the *Racing Post* by the BHA chairman, Paul Roy. He was not just a very wealthy and powerful man but, in my eyes, a bully who took plenty of stopping. Finding friends in the racing industry at that time was almost impossible, but one man did step up to the plate – the late, great Alan Lee of *The Times* who, after watching Mr Roy have a winner at Royal Ascot that month, described him as looking more like a dead man walking than someone who had just won a Group 1 race. I fucking loved that."

Within 24 hours of being warned off, Harry's mobile phone buzzed. At the other end of the line was Barney Curley, the Irish gambler who had masterminded what went down in racing folklore as the most notorious betting coup of all time, the 'Yellow Sam' affair at Bellewstown, Ireland, in June 1975, when, by intricate ploy and extraordinary connivance, he ransacked the entire bookmaking setup on the course and won over £300,000 on a single race. At 2017 values, it would have been worth over £1.8 million. Curley remained a figure of enormous respect, influence and intrigue. He had never rung Harry before.

Harry said: "Straight away, Barney told me not to worry, that everything would be sorted and that me and Mum would be able to go to Royal Ascot the following week and watch our horse Bergo run in the Queen Alexandra Stakes. He told me the warning off would be annulled. All I had to do was get the train to London the following day, meet with him and Paul Roy and everything could be worked out."

Harry's reply to Curley was succinct: "You can tell Paul Roy to fuck off." As far as he was concerned, the damage had been done.

Many folk who lived and breathed racing – or simply loved a punt on it – were aghast at the warning off and concurred that justice of a kind had been served when the appeals panel distilled the disqualification into a fine.

Clare Balding, who would willingly pursue Harry for that one special quote to make all the difference to her broadcasts, couldn't believe that she might not interview such a figure on a British racecourse again.

"When Harry said he wouldn't come racing again, it was a huge loss to the colour of the sport," she said. "The passion he had for his horses and dogs wasn't a business for him, it was following something he adored, and when he had money and could afford to, it was what he wanted to spend it on.

"Harry and Barney Curley were alike in that they didn't fit the racing pattern. They played by the rules but they made their own rules sometimes. Harry shouldn't have been cast out. I didn't think he'd done anything wrong.

"For me, Denman was one of the greatest horses ever. I loved him and his attitude. There was a fair amount of Harry's personality reflected in him; it just seemed right that he would own a horse that was so gutsy and did things that other horses couldn't or wouldn't do."

Paul Barber, with whom Harry had enjoyed so much remarkable success in racehorse ownership, was shocked at the initial sentence. In the *Racing Post* on July 6, 2010, he said: "I feel

Harry has been victimised – nobody realises how badly he has taken this. He feels his good name has been ruined by very poor decisions from the BHA, and I agree. I think what the BHA has done is unbelievable and I wish Harry well with his appeal."

The passing of the years had done nothing to minimise Barber's support for his partner: "We didn't know an awful lot about the case initially, but we knew Harry was an honourable man," Barber said in 2017. "He kept saying he would turn it [the initial decision] over. I didn't think that he would, but he bloody did. I'm certain a lot of people in racing didn't realise that he had turned it over. The press weren't particularly good to him at the time."

There were those who knew the industry and worried that Harry had been served up as a scapegoat. Philip Davies, the Conservative Member of Parliament for Shipley in West Yorkshire, had been raised in nearby Doncaster, where his parents ran a family bookmaker. Davies had long been an ardent punter and a man given to speaking his mind, both inside the confines of Westminster and beyond.

The MP was typically forthright. "Horse racing people had always been a bit sniffy about gamblers but failed to acknowledge that without gambling, horse racing wasn't a sport," he said. "They [the executives] were quite happy to take all the levy money from gambling, all the picture rights money from gamblers – £180 million or so a year. These were the same people who wouldn't accept that, without gambling, they had a sport that was worth nothing. Harry epitomised exactly what the hierarchy hated about gambling, but what gamblers loved about it."

"I suspect that in terms of skullduggery in horse racing, there were far worse examples than Harry who are probably still among the training ranks. The authorities didn't have to like Harry, you couldn't dictate to people who they could like and not like, but that wasn't an excuse for them to punish him the way they did. There were lots of powerful people in the establishment who, for whatever reason, didn't like Harry and thought he was bad for the sport."

Davies was concerned, too, about the veracity of the rule itself. "I'd had a row with Nic Coward [then BHA chief executive] at York races when he hadn't been long in the job, and I said to him, pretty forcibly, that the rule was absolutely ludicrous," he said. "It was obvious to me that Nic Coward knew nothing about racing and even less about betting.

"Stopping horses from winning was a scandal, and the BHA was right to tackle people who were using Betfair for crooked reasons. But I said to Coward he couldn't have this blanket ban on laying horses, and gave him two examples why.

"First, if I placed a massive bet, got a bit nervous and wanted to lay a bit off, why should that be a crime? If there was an audit trail to prove I was a net backer, then that shouldn't be an offence.

"Second, say I had owned the Derby winner Authorise. The previous year I had backed it at 33/1 and it shot to favourite: a) I'd had a massive ante-post bet at 33/1 and now it's even money. Anyone sensible would want to lay some of that off, it just made financial sense; b) I'd got huge prize money at stake from the horse winning, I'd got the breeding rights for millions of pounds – were you really going to warn me off if I laid Authorise to cover my ante-post bet from last year? Is that what you were saying?

"It was nutty, it made no sense whatsoever, but that was the rule they introduced.

"Then there was the punishment. It was an offence, so they could say – 'Well everyone knew it was there, they knew what the rules are, and that's it.' But you had to draw a distinction between people doing it for financial gain and those who wanted to get back some of their investment. Not to differentiate between the two and basically take away the whole of Harry's racing life, was totally wrong."

Bearing that injustice in mind, Davies wrote to Paul Roy, a letter he copied to the *Racing Post*, stating his opinion that Harry Findlay had done more to promote racing than the BHA had in its entire existence. The response from the chairman was immediate.

"I'd just finished a constituency surgery and was in the car when the mobile phone rang," Davies said. "It was Andy Stewart [a BHA executive], someone I got on well with. It was rare for him to ring out of the blue. He said he was at Ascot races with Paul Roy, who wanted a word. He apologised in advance for what was going to happen.

"I don't think I said a word in the entire ten-minute call. Mr Roy was going spare at me. He was rather abusive. When he hung up, I got a follow-up message from Andy Stewart saying again he was really sorry."

It was clear to Davies that his insistence that Findlay was a powerful force for good in the sport had struck a raw nerve with the BHA hierarchy. "But Harry got racing on the front page instead of eight pages from the back," the MP said.

"When Denman won the 2007 Royal Sun and Alliance Chase, and Harry won £1 million in ante-post bets, virtually every front page had a picture of 'The Man Who Won A Million.' You couldn't buy publicity like that for horse racing. I'm sure more people followed Denman from that moment, and as a result, every betting shop punter had a real admiration for Harry. They wanted to be him.

"He had been a larger than life character with the strong opinions that marked out gamblers. By their very nature they had to be opinionated, because that was what they made their financial decisions on. Harry was great company, he wore his heart on his sleeve and he would tell you exactly what he thought, whether it was politically correct or not. Usually it wasn't."

Sir Mark Prescott, one of the most famous and respected trainers in the country, concurred with Davies' viewpoint. He had been a first-hand witness to how much Harry enhanced racing, be it involving horses or dogs. Sir Mark, too, sensed an injustice.

"Harry was the victim of a new rule that nobody understood, or how it was supposed to work," he said. "I don't think the BHA thought it through carefully enough, it was brought out in a hurry, as a knee-jerk reaction to the changes in the betting game.

"The BHA was frightened of the consequences, the internet was coming up fast, a hasty rule was conceived and I don't think anyone felt it would be so literally applied because he [Harry] could show he had backed it [Gullible Gordon] to win. I think everybody felt that he was the victim of a rule that hadn't been tinkered enough to catch the people it was supposed to catch.

"Harry was the unlucky stool pigeon who took the fall, if that isn't mixing my metaphors. That it hurt his good name really stuck in his craw. I was surprised how that aspect of the ruling hurt him rather than its practicality, but it showed what a good man he is. The game had always leant itself to big characters, and in the current internet age, there hadn't been the room for those sort of people. Well there was, but they had to make it for themselves."

AP McCoy, the greatest of jump jockeys, placed the affair into a defining context when he said that Harry's warning off was: "A decision taken by those who obviously had no understanding of racing and racing people."

Barney Curley was even more equivocal. He said: "Harry had become too dangerous for a lot of people in racing. They had to crush him. The bottom line was instead of going after him, they should have asked him to run the Tote."

***

In an article in the *Irish Independent* three months after the appeal was heard, Mark Phillips, one of the two original BHA investigators, discussed the issue of laying horses from yards where an owner had them in training. It became another profound exoneration of Harry's position.

"It was not against the rules, and obviously I knew what his [Harry's] profit and loss account was from laying horses from these yards," Phillips said. "I didn't have a problem with it. One of the main things, for me, in Harry's case was that Betfair didn't close his account. When people were warned off, their accounts were closed. They didn't do it because they saw this for what it was. The fact that they continued to let him bet was a big thing."

Phillips further endorsed Harry's recollection of the conversation he had with him and Burgess at his home in 2009. "Harry said to me: 'If you want, I won't lay horses full stop.' But I said that wasn't necessary. His point was that he had horses in so many yards, if we didn't want him to lay horses from those yards, he wouldn't lay horses at all. I remember he offered that and I said it wasn't necessary. So that, I suppose, was what Harry was taking as permission."

Julian Snow, eminent barrister-at-law, former real tennis champion, one-time professional punter and possessed one of the shrewdest of minds, recognised the travesty of the case: "The idea that Harry would be involved in anything corrupt was absurd," he said. "People like Harry and I wanted everything to be on the level. And anyway, the first time you bet on a fixed match or fixed race, you might win money, but the next time you rang up, people would say: 'Fuck off, go away.'

"He laid his own horse, but only after he'd backed it for much more. The point of it [the rule] was to avoid people profiting from inside information when their horse wasn't fancied, and he was doing the opposite, his net position was he wanted it to win, he was fancying it and laying off some of his bet like any gambler or trader would. That didn't mean he didn't want it to win – he was indulging in good business."

Reaction to the warning off was widespread, as was expected – headlines every hour on the hour on Sky Sports News and BBC Five Live. Jim O'Rourke said: "What did the public think he'd been up to? How would anyone feel? To Harry, his reputation was everything, and it was ruined."

Indeed, the coverage given to his success in winning the appeal was minimal by comparison to the initial story – the old '*Sun* apology' standard. The residual damage of the front and back page news of a six-month ban from all things racing was hardly commensurate with the small-print 'success' of the appeal buried away on an inside page when Harry's disqualification was reduced to a small fine.

The media coverage was mixed and, on occasion, tremendously hostile. On the day of the successful appeal, Racing UK was transmitting live. O'Rourke shuddered when he recalled the coverage. "The presenter Alex Steedman heard the outcome on his earpiece," Jim said. "He said: 'Wonderful news, we've just heard from London that Harry Findlay has won his appeal, da de da.' He turned to his co-presenter, Jonathan Neesom, and said: 'Isn't that great news?'

"The response was: 'It's an absolute disgrace and once again shows what loud, lairy, rich men can do when they ride up to London town in their flash horses and carriages with their wealthy barristers in tow.' Alex looked at him like he was fucking mad.

"To the best of my knowledge, Harry had neither met, nor spent any time with Neesom or David Yates, the *Daily Mirror* correspondent, who once said on TV: 'If I hear his name once more, I'll throw up in the bin.' Where the fuck did that come from? And while we're at it, please name one other owner who would have been talked of like that?

"But, as I often said to Harry: 'Never forget how much pain your success inflicts on certain people.' There were those who couldn't handle somebody who could go on the internet and win millions on their talent alone. They couldn't comprehend that, especially because they'd love to do it, everyone would love to do it.

"After four years of Betfair, Harry was over £5 million in profit but, incredibly, had also paid over £4.5 million in commission – all at 2% – because he was playing in so many markets. He was the ultimate Betfairian and believed he did so much for the company. He felt betrayed when they eventually bowed to Paul Roy's pressure and will never forgive them.

"It's common knowledge that Harry managed to hold Betfair

over for nearly a million primarily because he wore it as a badge of honour and liked talking about it. How could you put a price on somebody's integrity? Betfair knew 100% that Harry had done nothing wrong and sold him down the river despite everything he'd done for them. Harry's racing partner Glen Gill always had a 20% share of his Betfair business, and with all that happened, he insisted on paying his share, so Harry received a near £200,000 cash bonus."

There were significant media defenders of Harry's position, as in the case with the much-respected Greg Wood, the racing correspondent of *The Guardian*. On July 15, on his Twitter feed, he wrote: "Who pushed for Harry Findlay to be charged? Will he/she/they resign?"

The first and final paragraphs of Wood's article the following day emphasised his disquiet. "Had the original hearing come to the same, correct conclusion that Findlay's offence warranted just a stiff fine, the racing world would have moved on by now.

"Instead, a high-profile owner who has invested huge sums into the sport has had his reputation maligned, been subjected to what the board described as the 'considerable stigma' of disqualification and has spent the last month wondering whether sanity would ever prevail. He [Harry] has now given up most of his horses and suggests he may emigrate to Australia. Given his treatment, who would blame him?

"This case has, eventually, reached the right conclusion. With owners likely to be in increasingly short supply in future, however, a rule book that does not treat them like murderers for a relatively minor offence might be a good idea."

In the autumn of 2010, Harry was given the opportunity to write a first-person article in the *Irish Independent*, the paper that had reacted so nastily to him two days after Denman won the 2008 Gold Cup. It was a remarkable piece, not a word of which was challenged.

In it, Harry said: "The day I was banned, Guy Sangster was told: 'Harry Findlay's not allowed in the yard, he's not allowed in the driveway of the yard. If he meets you in the pub, you can't talk about horses. You can't even talk about the bills.'

"No one was allowed to talk to me when I was banned. I wasn't allowed prize money for the horses; I wasn't allowed to pay any bills. But more than all that, it was known in racing circles that I had gone to the sales, and with my last few quid I bought 16 two-year-olds. Every penny I had was tied up in those two-year-olds I had the balls to buy.

"The ban would have been just as the horses were coming to fruition. If it had been any other person – without the financial muscle of Manton and the Sangster family – they'd have had to sell all the horses immediately, because they wouldn't have had the finances to keep them going. The Sangsters paid for my half. Otherwise they'd have had to sell £600,000 worth of horses, none of which had run, and take what they could get for them. If the ban had stood, the BHA may as well have hung me up and left me out to dry.

"The past months personally have been very difficult and very frustrating. My approach to Nic Coward – the BHA chief executive – at Doncaster last month to challenge him on the BHA's motives and conduct towards me resulted in a warning letter from Paul Scotney [the BHA Director of Security] telling me that, because of my behaviour, 'you are on notice that you may be removed from racecourse property or subsequently refused entry to racecourses.'

"I've had a lot of support within horse racing, and lots of people knew what had been going on here. Mark Davies, the former Betfair Head of Communications, wrote in his blog on September 27: "The gossip was that Findlay was being encouraged to attend the [Doncaster] racecourse on St Leger day. Apparently, someone who shall remain nameless was trying to persuade Harry not to spend his Saturday at home watching sport on the box, while not only tabloid journalists but plain-clothed policemen were being set up to witness – and act upon – the fact that he 'wouldn't be able to control himself' if he were indeed to attend.

"The brief, apparently, was: 'Wait before ejecting him, 'til he has his hands on the lapels, so that the photographers can get a decent shot.'"

***

The eight horses jointly owned by Margaret Findlay and Paul Barber were dispersed at the Doncaster sales in August 2010. Harry attended with Barber, and though they ended up bidding against each other for a horse called That'll Do (Barber won that challenge), there was not a hint of rancour when the former odd couple shook hands and departed. Indeed, they enjoyed a meal together fit for kings.

"The ending was classic Harry," Paul Barber said. "We had about seven horses to sell – I bought one or two back in and I think he bought one. As we finished lunch, we went to leave the dining room, opened the door, and in fell a heap of the press. Harry said: 'Welcome to the Last Supper.' It was just the way he said it. It brought the house down.

"He was a huge character and whatever you did or said, you couldn't put him down. He trusted me implicitly. For instance, if a horse cost £100,000, I would pay half of it; if there was something wrong, I'd put an extra £1k in rather than the other way around. Harry never questioned anything I did.

"Maybe there was a jealousy from others about what he did in the sport. He came from the bottom up, so to speak, but he introduced a hell of a lot of interest into National Hunt racing.

"He never discussed his betting with us. He paid all his bills, he was never a worry, never. We never judged him nor criticised him. He was honest and straight. He knew I wouldn't do him out of a shilling and I knew he wouldn't do me out of a shilling. We went really well together. With some things latterly, he got a bit hot under the collar, and that was difficult. But that's life. If he was here now, he could walk straight through the door. I still love him."

14

THE TRYING GAME

"It took Richard Dawkins until his mid-teens to work out what religion was all about – he was at least two years behind me," Harry Findlay said. "We moved into a nurse's home next to a church when I was 11 years old, and for a few months I would go to Sunday evening service, not as a believer, but with an open, inquisitive mind.

"You were always invited to speak to the preacher after the service, and every week we'd end up having a mini theology debate, normally started by something I'd found fault with in his homily. I drove the poor guy mad, but the bottom line was that before I went to senior school, I knew it was a trick to keep the masses in their place and give people who were scared of dying, a ray of hope.

"Our Gods are the sporting legends, like the Ancient Greeks. They were light years ahead of their time. If heaven exists, it has to be on earth, all you have to do is find it."

It was Paul Webster, one of Harry's Australian mates, who introduced him to the delights of Coogee Bay in Sydney. Harry had found his place. "For years I'd been staying down by the Rocks in the city centre and even tried Double Bay one year," he said. "But thanks to 'Pop-Up' Webster, I discovered that for serious sports fans, Sydney's eastern suburbs was the only place to be in the summer time.

"At Coogee, there's a great Thai massage or the freshest sushi available on nearly every street corner. You could go and see a serious movie at the Randwick Ritz at 10am, only a stone's throw from the famous racecourse. There's nowhere better for a pre-breakfast swim than Coogee beach, and when you're done, there's the choice of a dozen different styles of Eggs Benedict within 150 yards. The Coogee Bay Hotel is busy all weekend showing live sport from across the world, practically round the clock.

"Go to the Clovelly Hotel pub on a Monday afternoon and there's sure to be a great group of guys sharing an ice-cold beer and debating the weekend's sport, the unlucky losers and the next week's handicaps. In the background, there's a live betting service second to none, with racing, trots and greyhounds from every corner of Australia."

At the Clovelly, multi-millionaire Sydney bookmakers, small-staking out-of-form punters, well known TV sports presenters, nursing auxiliaries, former National Rugby League superstars and binmen mix easily. Any outsider walking in for the first time wouldn't have a clue who was who. Everybody dressed in T-shirts, shorts and thongs – "Nobody gives a fuck," Harry said.

"And don't forget, at that time of year they would have just finished watching the big late Sunday night game from the American NFL on the large screen.

"It was almost impossible to pay for anything with these lads, and in the literal sense, I'm very rarely first to the bar, and so, on my last night in town every year, it's 'Harry's Shout.'"

In January 2014, he selected Bombay Bloomers, a cracking Sikh-owned Indian restaurant at The Spot in Randwick.

Harry had always had a soft spot for the NRL's South Sydney Rabbitohs. It had a lot to do with their colours – red, green and white (occasionally black). "When I was a youngster, I was obsessed with football kits and loved the Chelsea reserve kit in the early '70s, which was red shirts, white shorts and green socks with a red and white top," he said. Harry sent Manchester City FC mad a few years ago ringing incessantly to insist they should bring back their purple socks. The club did so for a while, until new manager Roberto Mancini decided he didn't like them for the same reason as Don Cuddy hated Harry and Margaret Findlay's purple racing colours (because of its religious connotations. It is the colour associated with penitence and mourning, as in Lent).

"The NRL is king in Coogee, and it's the same in my house in Devon," Harry said. "Pop-Up is an out-and-out [Sydney] Rooster fan, a season-ticket holder for over 25 years. He's tried his hardest to persuade me to conform, even getting my younger daughter, Ella, to meet the team mascot at her first game when she was seven years old. But I just wasn't having it."

At the end of the meal at Bombay Bloomers, Brad Stevens – son of Gary, the Rabbitohs' pre-eminent captain, who made 163 appearances for the club and represented Australia five times – had something he wanted to say. After a few words, Brad presented Harry with a team shirt signed by the entire squad.

"We were the only two Rabbitohs fans at the table and got some serious abuse, especially from Shane Filipek, AKA 'the Punters' Pal', a Sydney bookmaker and Manly Sea Eagles fan," Harry said.

"'They're pure shite,' Shane shouted as I held up my shirt. I said: 'If they're so bad, give me a price on them to win the Premiership next season.' On the Australian TAB [the official Aussie Tote price] the Rabbitohs were 7.5 [equivalent of 13/2 in the UK].

"Shane offered me $A8 [7/1] and I said: 'No, but if you give me $A8.5 [15/2], I'll have a $30,000 to $4,000.' He deliberated and said: 'Yes.'"

"It was the bet that saved my life."

***

The moment Harry jumped onto his regular tea chest at Clonmel straight after landing back from Australia, he had a sense that things weren't right. He had returned to Tipperary for the National Coursing Meeting and John Boyle, the owner of betting company BoyleSports, was on his own box a few feet away.

In 2013, Boyle had been the only industry figure to openly support Harry's attempt to secure Coventry's status as the centre of the British greyhound-racing universe. The day after Clonmel, the pair met at the company's main office in Dundalk, and Harry's initial fears were confirmed.

"John Boyle and JP McManus had spent millions trying, without success, to win the coursing Derby or the Oaks at Clonmel," said Harry. "And I'd won both and only bought a dozen dogs trying to do it.

"But as I sat talking to John, I was sure it was only a matter of time before he asked me to make the tea. When he said he knew a good psychiatrist near Southampton, I knew I was fucked. I thought his behaviour was strange and I got the distinct impression he was trying to warn me of worse news to come."

That evening, Harry received a call from the owner of the Coventry track, Avtar Sandhu, a rarity in itself. He was told 'all the money in the world can't save greyhound racing at Coventry.' It took Bob Webb, the general manager of Coventry dogs, nine hours to drive Harry to Sandhu's offices in Birmingham the following day. The roads in the south west of England had been particularly badly flooded. It was a treacherous, fraught trip.

Webb said: "Nobody but Harry, myself and the racing manager knew that, for the last few months of trading at Coventry, we had effectively run out of money. Every month, without fail, Harry managed to win over £60k-£70k on Betfair to cover the costs. The only month he didn't win, he and Glen Gill picked up £200k from the Scoop6 to keep us afloat. But when Sandhu, who always promised that there would be no premium on the lease, asked for half a million up front to extend it, the die was cast."

The original deal had been that Harry would cover all the expenses and there would never be a charge on the stadium's lease. If and when the venture started to show a profit, Sandhu would receive a 50% share of everything. Harry said: "On numerous occasions over the two years, he gave me his word, and the last time I mentioned it was when he invited Kay and I to his son's sumptuous wedding reception in Birmingham, where he confirmed to both of us that there would never be a price on the lease. That was only a couple of months before he stiffed me."

HARRY FINDLAY

***

Harry fell head over heels with greyhound racing that first night at Slough in 1977 and, for many years, went to the dogs six nights a week. He had been to every track in Britain and Ireland and most of the independents. He travelled to over a dozen of the top tracks in America and all of the best venues in Australia. Thanks to his friendship with the legendary trainer Don Cuddy, he had met many of the top people in the industry in both countries.

Harry left school to work as a kennel lad, and over a 35-year period, he not only owned many of the country's top dogs, but spent plenty of time with leading trainers, the likes of Charlie Lister, John McGee, Geoff De Mulder, Tony Meek, Barrie Draper and Chris Lund. As a trainer himself for a couple of years, Harry had a winning strike rate of over 60% after his first 12 months, but as he said at the time: "I had good dogs in the kennels but in reality it was Don Cuddy who trained them or, at the very least, told me everything I should be doing, so it was no big surprise.

"Because of these experiences, I knew two things: Coventry was the best and safest track in the world, and greyhound racing in Britain had been abused and ripped off to an extent that was hard to believe. And leading this was the cannibalistic Greyhound Racing Association (GRA).

"In my time they devoured and closed down Catford, Harringay, both the London and Manchester White Citys, Oxford Hall Green, Slough, Portsmouth, Wembley, Wimbledon and Watford. They were ably supported by a select group of promoters allowed a feeding frenzy from the industry's funding system that brought the sport to its knees.

"On the same day Wimbledon closed, Nottingham was handed £10,000 by the British Greyhound Racing Fund to improve the air-conditioning in the restaurant – the same restaurant they'd already been given £200,000 to enhance a couple of years before. In the 2013/14 season, you can understand Monmore receiving a £25,386 grant for the grandstand roof, but why did Nottingham get £175,000 for the downstairs bar? Were they installing solid gold hand pumps? To be fair, the following year they only copped £86,309 – over £43,000 for a disabled lift, £22,000 for a canopy and £20,000 for betting hall and other works.

"When Clive Feltham took over the GRA, they had eight tracks left, and by the middle of 2017, they had two! Even worse for greyhound racing is the news that Feltham has been selected as the top man among the group of promoters chosen to run the sport in an advisory capacity. You've guessed it – they're the very same people who've been given carte blanche to ransack the sport's remaining coffers. Feltham has even been made a trustee of the Retired Greyhound Trust. What's that for – trying to wipe out the entire breed as quickly as possible?"

The closing down of Wimbledon in March 2017 signalled the end of greyhound racing in London, tumbleweed where once there was such vibrancy and life. Within two months, Hall Green – the most popular track in Birmingham – went the same way, deprived of its BAGS [Bookmakers Afternoon Greyhound Service] contract and at the mercy of developers. The contract and the dogs went to nearby Perry Barr.

Harry said: "In my opinion, everyone knew what had been going on in the Hall Green racing office for the past 20 years. Perhaps the fact that someone wanted to have £8,000 on

Moynevilla West in Trap 6 off scratch in a four-bend handicap race at 2/5 [1.4] when 11/10 [2.1] was freely available in every betting shop in the country was the straw that broke the camel's back. But, in truth, it was going on all the time.

"For a two-year period, I ploughed over £1.6 million of my own funds into the venture without getting a BAGS contract, even though one of their top people, Gordon Bissett, came to visit me at the track a fortnight after we opened. I knew he was putting me away. At no stage while I was at Coventry did I ever think there was a chance we'd get a contract.

"I was happy to work with Turf TV to offer a different kind of service and take BAGS on. But all they did was string me along. Nine months before we closed, they asked us to take a feasibility test, which we obviously passed with flying colours, but despite their chief Adrian Ford's man-to-man promise that whatever happened afterwards, I'd get a definite 'Yes' or 'No' answer, all I got was more of the same waiting-room bullshit. I knew Adrian was a top man – he now works for the Premier League – but in business, his word meant nothing, and that killed me. If I couldn't trust Adrian Ford, I knew I couldn't trust anyone.

"Tony Bloom always told me I was far too gullible to be a businessman, and he was right; but I'm not a complete fucking idiot, and before I left to go to Australia at the end of the year, the CEO of Racing UK [now RMG], Richard FitzGerald, was jumping up and down in his box at Cheltenham declaring: 'We want Coventry, we want Coventry' in front of top National Hunt trainers Nicky Henderson and Venetia Williams.

"On numerous occasions, I begged David Craven, the CEO of Timeweave, who owned half of Racing UK, to come and look at our product. All to no avail. I knew David from his days running the Tote and even he rang me when I was in the bank at Leamington Spa before I left for Australia and told me: 'We need Coventry.'

"I couldn't have got the green light from two people higher in the company that they wanted to do business, but it was all bollocks."

BoyleSports had come on board with Harry in autumn 2013, investing £20,000 a month for the Coventry track to become a display unit for their wares. Their logo was prominent on the traps, the trainer's jackets, the racecards, everywhere. In harness with the company's head trader, John Wright, Harry priced up every race 36 hours in advance. "In a matter of months, we'd built a betting platform second to none in the history of the sport," Harry said. "I had the best seven-man algorithm [below] of all time to make sure we got the prices right.

Race 4 Leg 1

GD	CB	NF	RD	JM	TJ	DM
4	7/2	9/2	4	4	11/4	9/2
9/4	5/2	3	9/4	9/4	9/4	5/2
7/2	5	4	9/2	4	7/2	5
6	3	7/2	5	5	11/2	9/2
5	8	7	6	11/2	9	7/2
5	5	4	9/2	5	7	9/2

Race 8 Leg 5

GD	CB	NF	RD	JM	TJ	DM
6	13/2	8	7	10	4	6
5	5	9/2	9/2	3	4	7
11/4	5/2	2	9/4	5/2	4	5/2
9/2	5	9/2	5	5	11/2	9/2
3	3	7/2	3	3	5/2	7/2
9/2	4	9/2	9/2	5	6	7/2

Race 5 Leg 2

GD	CB	NF	RD	JM	TJ	DM
3	5/2	5/2	7/2	5	5/2	3
3	3	5/2	4	5	7/2	7/2
6	8	12	10	10	10	8
7/2	7/2	5/2	5/2	2	3	5/2
13/2	5	7	6	9/2	7	5
5	5	9/2	5	3	5	9/2

Race 9 Leg 6

GD	CB	NF	RD	JM	TJ	DM
5	4	9/2	6	10	6	4
9/2	6	13/2	9/2	11/2	11/2	4
5	9/2	11/2	9/2	5	5	5
9/2	7/2	11/4	7/2	4	4	4
3	7/2	5/2	11/4	5/2	3	9/4
3	3	6	5	3	3	7

Race 6 Leg 3

GD	CB	NF	RD	JM	TJ	DM
5/2	5	7/2	7/2	3	5/2	7/2
4	5/2	5/2	7/2	4	11/4	7/2
7	9/2	9/2	5	11/2	11/2	9/2
3	7/2	9/2	9/2	5	9/2	9/2
9/2	7/2	13/2	5	7/2	11/2	7/2
6	6	7/2	7/2	7/2	7	9/2

Race 10 Leg 7

GD	CB	NF	RD	JM	TJ	DM
9/2	7/2	11/4	7/2	4	3	7/2
7/2	4	4	4	5	5	4
7/2	4	9/2	4	7/2	5	6
3	9/2	9/2	4	4	5	7/2
5	4	7/2	9/2	4	3	4
5	4	9/2	5	4	5	4

Race 7 Leg 4

GD	CB	NF	RD	JM	TJ	DM
4	9/2	11/2	4	9/2	4	3
5	9/2	4	11/2	5	6	4
9/2	9/2	11/2	6	11/2	6	6
7/2	4	9/4	11/4	7/2	7/2	3
3	9/4	9/2	11/4	9/4	3	5
9/2	5	9/2	11/2	9/2	7/2	4

Race 11 Leg 8

GD	CB	NF	RD	JM	TJ	DM
7/2	4	9/2	4	7/2	7/2	7/2
9/2	11/4	5/2	3	3	7/2	3
6	9/2	9/2	6	6	6	4
5	5	6	5	6	6	9/2
5/2	7/2	9/2	3	3	3	7/2
4	5	9/2	9/2	9/2	11/2	9/2

Wright agreed. "What Harry had at Coventry was not only unique, but totally bombproof," he said. "It took him less than nine months to set it all up, and for the next six months we traded the model without getting a single race wrong or having any integrity issues. It was perfect, but even at that stage, nobody in the industry wanted to know."

That wasn't quite the case on the other side of the world. Harry said: "TABcorp and SportingBet in Australia work on a revenue share system, and after seeing my Coventry product, they both said they would take it straight away. I was trying to show TABCorp's top bloke our races on the internet, but after seeing my algorithm, he said he didn't care what the track was like, it [the algorithm] was sensational, whereas anyone I dealt with in the UK wanted to string me along or tell me a pack of lies.

"Don't forget, I was the man with the experience and knowledge of how straight and honest greyhound trainers in Britain are. Every trainer who walked through the door of Coventry knew they would be respected and well paid. They weren't allowed to cheat.

"Our ability to price up every race so well meant we knew immediately if anyone stepped out of line. And, of course, I'd always known that in terms of speed, reliability and consistency, greyhounds were the perfect animals."

Bob Webb, the general manager, worked side-by-side with Harry on the venture. "All he wanted was to save greyhound racing," Webb said. "From the outset, the Greyhound Board of Great Britain was obstructive and non-supportive. For an organisation purporting to promote this great sport, it was disappointing, but, to be fair, they did warn Harry not to get involved with Sandhu.

"Harry knew the future wouldn't depend on footfall through the gates. He foresaw the need for Saturday morning racing, live streaming to the Asian market as well as to UK betting shops, and live evening TV. He knew that the integrity of the sport had been badly damaged over the previous decades, and that it was of paramount importance to regain the trust of the public and of the bookmaking industry.

"Trainers and owners at Coventry were getting more prize money than elsewhere, an excellent running track and a fair deal all round.

"Harry knew Wimbledon and Hall Green would close, despite the efforts and promises of those involved, and that the ideal venue for the Greyhound Derby and other major races would be Coventry, because of the quality of the track and the geographical location. Almost every owner and trainer agreed with this view, including the Irish trainers who had virtually deserted the event at Wimbledon.

"Harry wanted the best dogs and the top trainers at Coventry, and was prepared to put his hand in his pocket to offer significantly improved prize money. He also reduced the Tote retention from the industry norm of 30% to 10-13%, giving punters a fair chance of taking home a profit from their evening out.

"We had a top-quality product and along came Racing Post TV. With them paying £5,000 a meeting, we were on our way towards becoming self-sufficient. Harry's integrity could not be bought, so when RPTV, funded by bookmakers, started demanding how we set up our races, Harry told them that if they didn't like our product, they could fuck off – so they fucked off.

"We were advised that, with carefully worded requests, we might possibly claim grants from GBGB for equipment. But with rumours of corruption and misuse of the fund, Harry wanted no part of it and told them to stick it up their arse.

"We were reliant on Harry to fund the project, and with promises and half promises from prominent people in the sport, we were confident a deal was just around the corner, but nothing came to fruition. We may never know why."

What was clear was that Harry's pockets could sustain Coventry no longer. The project folded in 2014.

Harry said: "Thirty years ago, Ladbrokes knocked down the big old peat dog track at Crayford and went for a completely new model. The architect must have been told to make it look and feel like a prison, but the biggest mistake was in the maths, because they obviously built it for Italian greyhounds or, at a push, whippets, and if the sport is to survive, it should be closed down as quickly as possible before the antis work out just how bad it is!

"It's a billion-to-one that another track is ever built in the UK. But what if Betfair, instead of trying to turn itself into Paddy Power, decided to give something back and reopened Coventry and Oxford? I'm sure Coventry can still be bought, and at the same time they'd also be doing a great job for the city's Speedway team. The GRA can't do anything with Oxford – legally they can't even sell it – and it was actually making money when they closed it down. It wouldn't cost them more than £5 million to take over both venues, and very quickly they would have a major say in the sport. They could have the same trainers at both venues, with the bigger, stronger running dogs at Coventry and the smaller, early-paced types at Oxford. The Derby, St Leger and Oaks could be run at Coventry with Oxford hosting big events like the Gold Collar, Pall Mall and Scurry Gold Cup – both tracks would be able to price up every race with confidence

24 hours or more in advance and provide a solid betting platform that horse racing couldn't even compete with.

"For almost £10k a meeting, BAGS should be guaranteed integrity on every betting show, but currently that's just impossible, and they know it. Towcester's running track was built with eight-dog races in mind, and that's what they should stick to, because if greyhound racing does fight back, they certainly will have a purpose, and because other tracks just aren't wide enough to accommodate the two extra runners, although I'm surprised Ladbrokes haven't tried it out at Crayford."

***

"I can clearly remember the tie and shoes the famed Jewish bookmaker Tony Morris was wearing the first night I walked into London's White City Stadium, the best dog track in the world, in 1977," Harry said. "Twenty years later, in my weekly dogs column in the *Racing Post*, I called him Doctor Death," Harry said. "He screamed at first until he realised everybody loved it.

"I knew Tony a lot more than he knew me. I found the way he treated punters shocking, primarily because if there was a remote chance of you knowing more than him, you couldn't have a tanner on. If it was the other way around, he'd cleverly let you hang yourself, smiling while you worked it out.

"On Derby final nights at White City, the whole place was packed to the rafters and millions would be wagered on the 12-race card. The betting percentages for all races week in and week out at White City were between 116% and 122% [1], and

---

[1] *Bookmakers' percentage over-round [i.e. profit margin]*

purely because of the amount of money bet on the big night, he mercilessly jacked it up to over 150% for every race – sheer, unadulterated greed.

"All the bookmakers at the track did the same thing, but he was very much in charge of the orchestra. Tony was an intelligent man, immaculate, funny, a perfectionist, and like Jonathan Sparke of City Index, a regular at Zen Central in Mayfair.

"Bookmaker Ben Keith of Star Sports described Tony as his hero and mentor, and after sponsoring the 2017 Greyhound Derby at Towcester – its new venue – he declared that Tony would be very proud of him. What a load of bollocks. The Lizard introduced me to Keith in Marbella when he was 18 years old. I'd never met a bigger tosser in my life. After less than five minutes, I wanted to strangle him. The only thing Keith and Tony Morris have in common is the way they do business. I'd happily bet my last £1,000 to win a tenner that Tony Morris wouldn't have pissed on him if he was on fire."

***

Coventry had barely been up and running for two months when Chris Page, former racing manager at Walthamstow and then acting as an advisor for a group beginning to tout Towcester as a potential greyhound venue, prompted a meeting between Harry and Turf TV.

"The Towcester mob set me up with Turf TV, and with the sole exception of spending £1.6 million on the track instead of £2.6 million and buying it outright, it was my biggest mistake," he said. "I spent 15 months' time, money and effort chasing a deal that was never there."

It was not long after the stumps were pulled on Coventry that building work began at Towcester. Within six months of its opening as a greyhound venue, people in the dog world were extolling its virtues as a potential Derby venue, and once the course threw its hat in the ring, it was the odds-on certainty because there was nowhere else for the race to go.

"I guarantee that if Coventry had kept going, there would never have been a spade in the ground at Towcester," Harry said. "Even now, if you asked the top 50 trainers, kennel lads and owners in the country what's the best track for the Derby and the dogs themselves, at least 48 would say Coventry. Everybody knows it. But I had to be stopped.

***

Harry Findlay was eating, sleeping and breathing Coventry dogs. He was on a mission. "For the first time in my life I was actually working hard, the algorithm had to be spot-on for every meeting and I was always on the go," he said. "The Wednesday mornings, when we received the entries for our big races on the Sunday night, was my favourite part of the week.

"On race days, I'd often end up doing the commentaries and wrote two columns a week for the local paper. As usual, I was doing three things at once when I received a bizarre phone call."

The woman's voice on the other end of the phone was from Warwick County Court telling Harry he had been declared bankrupt. Harry told her she was mad, to leave him alone and it couldn't be him because he'd never had a debt in his life. "All the bills were in Kay's name, I'd never been on the electoral roll, never had a national insurance number, I couldn't have credit even if I wanted it. I thought I was going completely mad when she said: 'It's all about one bill – a debt to the Paragon School in Bath for £3,400.'"

Two years earlier, in the wake of the BHA warning off that scarred him so badly, Paragon's headmaster, Titus Mills, had allowed Harry to take his younger daughter, Ella, out of the school. Mills explained that without sufficient notice, Harry would have to pay for the winter term, even though Ella wouldn't be attending. The money was in the school's account the following day.

A year on – "I was still like a caged tiger," Harry said – the family decided they would up sticks and move to the other side of the world. "Getting a work permit for Australia wasn't easy, but we were more than happy to travel around and spend a lot of time in Fiji – Kay and Ella's favourite place," Harry said. "Titus fully understood, and we left with his blessing. But once again, I hadn't given the school enough notice, so paid for the winter term.

"We were away for nearly five months, but Ella wanted to come back and go to a British school. I knew Coventry was the best track in the world and that the sport was being raped and pillaged by a notorious gang of promoters, and I wanted to show how it could and should be done."

When he shook hands with Sandhu and secured the lease on the track, Harry moved the family to Leamington Spa to be near the stadium. "We found a nice school for Ella straight away and all settled in quickly," he said.

"A couple of months later, I was astonished to get a letter from Paragon saying I owed them for the summer term, though Ella hadn't been there and they knew I'd left the country. I rang the school and spoke to the bursar, explaining that I'd paid two terms for nothing and we were never going to be there in the summer.

"He said: 'Yes, but you didn't send us a letter saying she wouldn't be there for the summer term. Technically, you've got to write us a letter.' I said: 'Are you telling me the sole reason for this bill is a technicality, even though you knew I was emigrating and had already paid for a term in lieu?' He said: 'Yes.'"

Harry was walking his dogs a few weeks later when his phone rang. The call was from a firm of debt collectors. Harry explained the situation to them and was told they would ring the school and call him back. Within ten minutes, his phone rang again. Harry said he was told the school would accept half the summer term's fee, around £1,750. "I told them that there was more chance of me sticking an oak tree up my arse than paying 17p, let alone £1,750."

Subsequently, a letter arrived from Warwick County Court summoning Harry to appear. He was more than ready with his defence but mislaid the letter, forgot the date and missed his appointment. His bankruptcy was formally announced. He had to go to a firm of solicitors and lodge £18,000 with them before they would even talk to him about having the bankruptcy annulled at the first opportunity.

"Even then, they spoke to me as if I was a peasant. I had to go to two excruciating meetings [insolvency hearings] in Birmingham where a young girl asked me a barrage of personal questions without even looking at me. I told her: 'Let me pay you the cash now.' I couldn't remember the last time I had a losing week and I was being made bankrupt over £3,000. The whole thing was fucking insane.

"I ended up screaming at her and the supervisor had to come and calm me down. I felt exactly like the character in *I Daniel Blake*, Ken Loach's brilliant 2016 film about the treatment of the unemployed. Critics like Camilla Long of *The Times*, who said the film wasn't realistic enough, should be ashamed of themselves."

Julian Snow, barrister-at-law and longtime betting associate of Harry's, was unequivocal in his belief that the bankruptcy was unfair and unwarranted. "The purpose of bankruptcy laws is to provide for the equitable treatment of all the creditors of an insolvent person," he said. "Harry was not insolvent – far from it. At the time, he was winning plenty [£112,000 on Betfair that week], as he needed to in order to keep Coventry dog track going, and had no creditors other than, arguably, his daughter's previous school, who merely alleged a disputed debt."

***

The South Sydney Rabbitohs bet with Shane Filipek on a happy night at Bombay Bloomers had disappeared into the deep, dark recesses of Harry's mind. Almost five months had gone by before he went onto the Australian NRL website to check where the team was on the ladder, but – such was the mess his head was in – he scoured the Holden under-20 placings instead of the Premiership, and immediately wrote off their chances.

It was only when he noticed a small piece in the paper a couple of weeks later that he realised the Rabbitohs were in the hunt for one of the crucial spots in the top four.

"For over 30 years, I genuinely believed I was the happiest man in the world," Harry said. "Even being Billy No Mates and getting a good hiding in prison wasn't enough to get me down. I didn't even know how to spell the word depression. But when I returned to Devon, I just wanted to die. I left with family with next to nothing after following a dream, and was a broken man.

"As a gambler, if I'd lost everything as I had in the past on a sporting outcome and fallen on my own sword, I'd have been okay – but not what happened to me at Coventry. I didn't go out of the house for months with the exception of walking the dogs.

"It felt like I was walking uphill, even when I wasn't. The wind and the rain was unrelenting in Devon at that time. I wouldn't get out of bed before 2pm most of the time. I just wished the house would be sucked up like Dorothy's in the *Wizard of Oz* and taken us all away. Thanks to Guy Sangster, I had the best doctor in London, but I knew the tablets wouldn't work.

"Fortunately, it was a World Cup year and I had a family to feed, so I had to do something to get myself right. With the Rabbitohs in with a squeak, I started to watch the NRL again, and that made a massive difference because the mornings really were a fucking nightmare.

"Thanks to Premier Sports' blanket coverage, you could watch all eight NRL games live every week in Britain. I'm often asked what's my favourite sport to bet on and then watch live, and my answer is always Australian Rugby League.

"I let the Sydney boys take the piss out of me all the time for not knowing about their game, but I served my Rugby League apprenticeship in the very best company. When I first met Kay, I lived in or around Sheffield for over 20 years, and most Sundays, Kay's father, Ramon, drove us to places like Dewsbury, Batley and Featherstone to take in the matches.

"We'd meet up with the late, great John Speed, and Shaun Edwards' father, Jackie. We were Wigan fanatics, they were the great team of that generation." Shaun became a rugby league superstar in his own right, but it was in the company of his dad that Harry learned so much about the intricacies of the game.

Harry had always considered Benni McCarthy's equaliser for South Africa against Denmark in the 1998 World Cup as the most critical turning point in his punting life. But something clicked in his head watching the Rabbitohs play Newcastle Knights at Barlow Park, Cairns, on August 3, 2014. Tony Bloom told Harry more than once he had a sixth sense about a sportsman's mindset, and Harry was convinced after that game that the Rabbitohs would win the Premiership.

"It wasn't because they beat a moderate Knights team 50-10 without Sam Burgess and John Sutton, it was the reaction when full-back Alex Johnston scored a length-of-the-pitch try in the second half," Harry said. "You can't believe how humid it is there, but every single one of the Bunnies ran from wherever they were on the pitch to join in the celebration. It looked like they were playing under-16 football and were all the best of pals.

"I knew they had six genuine world-class players in the team, and although Chris McQueen probably wouldn't be considered one of them, he epitomised everything that was great about them that day. I honestly can't remember him dropping the ball once for the rest of the season.

"I started pressing up on the Rabbitohs the day after the Newcastle match, and any time I backed a winner, I had a bit more on them and sellotaped the betting slips to the fridge. I was still on a massive downer, but every time I made a cup of tea, I got some kind of buzz knowing the Bunnies could get me back into the game."

Finishing in the top four in the regular season was vital in the NRL, because if a team reached the preliminary final (the NRL equivalent of a semi-final) via a top-four place, they had a week off, whereas their opponent could be involved in back-to-back wars in a week. That was true of the opposition that year, who just happened to be their arch rivals, the Sydney Roosters. The Roosters had barely survived an intense 31-30 victory over North Queensland Cowboys. Seven days later they had to face the more relaxed Rabbitohs.

"I had everything on the Rabbitohs," Harry said. "It's hard to believe, but when they were 11/4, I made them evens; and when they were evens, I made them 4/11, so everything had to go on – what was left of Kay's jewellery, paintings, sculptures, anything with a decent selling value was dumped, with the proceeds going straight on the Rabbitohs.

"The NRL is the only sport Kay really enjoys watching nowadays. She went to plenty of games in Yorkshire and then fell in love with the Cowboy's Johnathan Thurston watching the NRL. For the final eliminator against their local rivals, the Roosters, Kay and I were pugged up in our tiny barn in Chardstock. South Sydney's quest for the Holy Grail that year was the only thing that mattered.

"I loved a frontrunner more than anyone else on earth, but because of the week off, the Roosters caught them flat-footed at the start and took a 12-0 lead, but I was still convinced they would fight back. And it didn't take long for the Rabbitohs to get back on level terms and then take control of what became a very one-sided contest, going on to win 32-22.

"I was under massive pressure and wouldn't have been able to afford a decent breakfast if they'd got beat. But it wasn't just about the money, I needed something to hold on to. Supporting the Rabbitohs in 2014 felt just like when I travelled the country as a young boy watching Wycombe Wanderers back in the 1970s.

"Since the beginning of July, I'd been ringing my NRL team newsman, Matt Proctor in Melbourne, five times a week. He was a good judge of both the NRL and the AFL. Nobody got the injuries and off-pitch information better than he did."

"Harry sounded like a different man on the phone in 2014," Matt said. "The confidence, humour and piss-taking was all gone, but he was on some mission with the Rabbitohs. He even wanted to know what the players were having for breakfast. There wasn't a single man in Australia who fancied them half as much as he did."

In the days leading up to the Grand Final, the central story was if Rabbitohs' New Zealand hooker Isaac Luke would be available for selection after picking up a one-match ban in the preliminary final for a dangerous tackle on the Roosters' Sonny Bill Williams. He appealed the sentence, but to no avail. It did not lessen Harry's belief.

"I can't remember the last time I fancied or backed their opponents in the final, the Canterbury Bulldogs, and I was convinced the Rabbitohs could win by 50 points or more," he said. "Whatever spare money I could scrape together was on them at -11.5 points. At the kick-off, I was like a raging bull, stomping around our living room that was no bigger than the size of an average stable."

Less than ten seconds into the final, and in the first tackle, the Rabbitohs captain and No.1 battering ram Sam Burgess suffered a fractured cheekbone and fractured eye socket. He just shrugged off the inconvenience and played on. "It was inspirational," Harry said. "The only reason I hadn't backed him to win the Churchill Medal [for the Man of the Match] before the game was that his brother, George, was playing almost as well and had to be the value bet at 14/1. I had £350 on him, but it was Sam who deservedly took it."

THE TRYING GAME

The Rabbitohs scored the first try in the sixth minute, and though they failed to convert it, a penalty gave them a 6-0 lead they held at half-time. They should have at least doubled that lead but the Bulldogs were living up to their name – aggressive, snapping and snarling. When Tony Williams crashed over for them ten minutes into the second half, they had levelled at 6-6.

"I was wobbling for five minutes, but then George Burgess thundered under the posts and, from that moment, it was purely a matter of how many," Harry said. "When GI [Greg Inglis] broke away in the last minute to wrap the match up 30-6, he wasn't the only one doing his famous goanna crawl. Kay and I were also bounding around like kangaroos."

Back in Sydney, straight after the game, ex-Rabbitoh and player's manager, Mark Ellison, bumped into one of Australia's most respected Grand Final-winning coaches, Warren Ryan. "If they'd have played for another ten minutes, the score would have been 100-6," Ryan said. "That alone tells how well the Bunnies were playing at the time," Harry said. "I've watched every NRL match since that final and I'm convinced that, for whatever reason, they all played at the peak of their powers that year.

"I knew I still had a long way to go after they'd won and how badly I'd miss the NRL in the weeks ahead. But I knew I couldn't have faced defeat that day."

15

YOU COULDN'T MAKE IT UP

In the reception area of Brixton prison in 1918, one of the world's most renowned philosophers stood in front of his prison warder and was asked: "What's your religion?" Bertrand Russell replied: "Agnostic," and spoke of having a buzz for his first week of custody because the officer didn't know how to spell it and just thought it was another form of religion.

Sixty-five years later, on exactly the same spot, Harry Findlay's answer to the same question was: "I am an anti-theist," and as he said it, he was thinking of the words of the great man – 'We must attach some meaning to the words we use if we are to speak significantly and not utter mere noise, and the meaning we attach to our words must be something with which we are acquainted.'

YOU COULDN'T MAKE IT UP

"I've neither heard a Katy Perry song nor read a single page of *Harry Potter* in my life," said Harry. "But with nearly 200 million Twitter followers between them, for the sake of the planet, will somebody please tell JK Rowling and Miss Perry about Bertrand Russell."

***

On December 1, 2008, Paul Barber and Margaret Findlay were jointly named as Owner of the Year at the Horserace Writers and Photographers Association awards in London. Denman's victory in the Cheltenham Gold Cup had been the sport's emblematic moment, so the judges' choice hardly came as a shock.

Someone had to get up to say a few words, and Harry was nominated. Whenever he had won prizes in the greyhound world, the celebrations tended to be relatively low-key affairs, with a premium on speeches, and he was entirely relaxed. The contrast was a well-filled function room at the Royal Lancaster Hotel, best bib and tucker to the fore. Harry needed a little Dutch courage.

Before the awards were due to be presented, he stepped out to the hotel forecourt and reached for the tiny pre-rolled spliff in his trouser pocket. But he had nothing to light it with.

Half a dozen fellow patrons wanted to take advantage of a lull in the festivities and go outside for a cigarette. One asked Harry how he was feeling. "A bit nervous," he said. "Got a light?" The guest proffered Harry the flame from his lighter.

The second Harry ignited his Smokey Joe and took a single puff, two men burst forward from the hotel entrance 'like a couple of SAS storm troopers and the guy in the light grey suit who'd offered me the light almost shit himself.' They shoved their ID at Harry. They were two Metropolitan Police officers.

"One of the coppers said: 'You're smoking cannabis,' and I said: 'Yes, sir. I was.' I'd already tossed it over my shoulder. They were so heavy-handed and I knew it was a set-up. I was spontaneously on my best behaviour.

"The older of the Old Bill shouted: 'We'll have him.' I looked the younger guy in the eye. He wasn't quite so confident. 'You're not allowed to do this, officer. I haven't done anything wrong – feel free to search me. I'm about to make a big speech and I'm having a puff for my nerves, you can search me up and down.' They had to back down, but I knew what the plan was.

"If I'd have bought a lighter at Bath station that morning, I would have been gonzo, and the papers the next day would have been full of it. I'd have walked around the corner on my own so no one could smell the cannabis, and when they jumped me, I wouldn't have worked it out so quickly. I'd have definitely told them to fuck off. I'd have been in the van and back to the station for a couple of hours before they just let me go. But the damage would have been more than done."

After his close shave with the law, Harry made his way towards the function room to deliver his speech, and Charlie Sale, the *Daily Mail's* noted sports columnist, approached him.

Charlie had been tipped off (he couldn't remember who by) that Harry was going outside for a joint, and if he was caught in the act, it would be a rather seismic story. "I didn't see Harry smoking anything, but as he came back in, he looked a bit rattled," Charlie said. Harry recalled that Sale asked him something about 'being arrested for smoking cannabis.' I said to him: "You must be fucking telepathic, Charlie!"

John Gosden – who trained the winner of that year's Breeders' Cup Classic, Raven's Pass, to add to past successes in the Derby, 1,000 Guineas and St Leger – won the International Trainer of the Year award, and at the end of his speech, it was Harry's turn to step up to the plate.

"I began by eulogising the French PMU [Pari-Mutuel Urbain] Tote system, their really high turnover figures and blowing hot air up the arse of Louis Romanet, their boss. Then I told the truth. It's all bollocks. I explained why, with the Government's help, it was so easy for the PMU to give it the big one. In France, for example, there was nowhere in the country you could have a bet on racing or any other sport, other than with them, and the biggest sporting jackpot bet in the country was ultimately decided by a random ball machine.

"I went on to explain how we should do it in Britain – not only taking on the likes of the PMU, but showing them how it really can be done. What UK Racing really needed was a competitive, well-managed Tote, able not only to provide an alternative product to bookmakers' fixed-odds betting, but also to return good money to the industry. To do this it needed to make itself attractive to serious and regular punters, rather than only to uninitiated occasional racegoers. The Tote also needed to reduce its percentage takeouts on all its markets. The way to increase turnover was first to devise a system that made sure it was a level playing field for all and gave every punter a chance to win. Then, the Tote should immediately cease offering rebates to their biggest players.

"Australia started the craze, and after giving their biggest and cleverest punters enormous rebates, earning them millions, they sent the taxman to try to get the money back and chased them out of the country.

"I explained how 'co-mingling' was the buzzword among PMU, Phumelela [the South African Tote] and other Tote bodies. But the bottom line is that everybody wants a decent slice of the pie, which inevitably leads to a rise in percentage takeouts for the operator, leaving a betting model that is only any use to mugs and part-time gamblers who don't know what they're doing.

"To say I got a standing ovation would be a slight exaggeration, but I got a great reception, and as I finished the speech, the late great Peter O'Sullevan put his arms around my mum's neck and said: 'That was a good night's work, Margaret.'"

***

In 2011, the billionaire Fred Done of Betfred won the licence to manage the UK's pool-betting operation (the Tote) until 2018. It was not much of a contest as the opposition consisted of a conglomerate of Martin Broughton, Paul Roy and Andy Stewart.

"Broughton appeared on the *Jeff Randall Show* on Sky Business Report and tried to explain their manifesto," Harry said. "Jeff did a great job keeping a straight face. It was an embarrassment. Between the three of them, they obviously knew as much about pool betting as I did about repairing washing machines. Betfred duly romped to victory."

Since then, Betfred have increased the takeout from the Tote win pool markets by more than 40% – from 13.5% when they took over to 16.5% in October 2012 to an eye-watering 19.25% by June 2017.

"With such obscene takeout margins, anybody who now has a win or place Tote bet in Britain is a bloody idiot," Harry said. "Greyhound racing in the UK has been taking out 30% for decades. When I was at Coventry, I went down to 13% and was widely ridiculed – though not by anyone with an IQ over 10. History will prove I was right. The sport is going to die very quickly in Britain if it doesn't change the people running it and start doing business along the same lines they use in Australia – without the rebates.

"We've been reading about these great co-mingling deals for years from Phil Siers [Totepool's MD], but where is the proof? Where is the action? It's all fresh air and bullshit and to combat the lack of interest from punters because of the far too greedy takeouts.

"How does the Tote rapidly increase their turnover to make their business look more attractive than it really is? As the meerkats would say: 'Simples!' Just give massive – around 20% – rebates to its very biggest players. For example, when laying out over £200,000 on the Scoop6 when there's a big rollover, they know that, over a period of time, they can't lose. When laying out such high stakes, it's impossible to miss out on a place dividend [around 20-25%] as well as their guaranteed 20% kickback [rebate]. The ordinary punter has no chance.

"If that's too technical, think of Fred Done looking out across the biggest saltwater swimming pool in the world, ten times the size of an Olympic pool. On a Saturday, the water is teeming with plankton, from the totally invisible £2 single-ticket variety to the biggest you can find in the sea, the £320 permutation plankton. Then along comes the Glaswegian Phil Siers, fresh from his Hebridean holiday, and slings two of the fattest basking sharks he could find off the island, into the middle of the pool.

"In effect, the Tote's regular punters are just the krill being gobbled up by Siers' sharks with their built-in edge. Make no mistake, the Tote is eating itself alive.

***

Eamonn Willmottt, whose playground bravado with poker dice ignited Harry's love of gambling, became horse racing establishment in December 2014 when he was appointed as a director of the BHA, the body that chased his schoolboy pal over the edge four years earlier.

Eamonn thought it wise to check with potential fellow colleagues that his longtime association with Harry would not conflict his nomination. It was made very clear that the BHA executive bore no ill will towards Harry at all. As usual, Willmott's admiration for his old friend never wavered.

"Even as a kid, Harry possessed a formidable intellect and mathematical processing power," he said. "He'd look at something and immediately calculate the odds – and in gambling, the margins were bloody fine. Was a horse a bet at 11/8? – Yes; was it a bet at evens? – No.

"He had two gifts that were incredibly crucial for his ability to win – not just his assessment of a horse or an athlete, but an ability to take that assessment in. If you were a good judge of talent, you might be okay, but you wouldn't be successful to the extent he was, because you wouldn't be able to quantify it and know when it was wrong [to bet]. Look at his trading records – you would think it couldn't be done.

"To spread those talents across five or six sports, when each individual sport had a myriad of elements he had to calculate in, was amazing. He took these strengths to a freakish level.

"He stood out, not just because he worked so much out for himself, but he was prepared to share that good fortune with others less skilled. You'd walk into the races with Harry, a horse was running he was betting £50k on, and someone would ask him: 'How is X, Y, Z going to go today?' and he'd say: 'Yeah, I fancy it,' and then go on to explain why, which was incredible. Other racehorse owners or professional punters just aren't like that. He had this unbelievable man-of-the-people view, but it was genuine.

"Harry had a massive affinity with gamblers. When Betfair started, they charged 5% commission to everybody, and the more you bet, you could reduce it to 2%. Harry was paying 2% as one of their biggest gamblers, and he said to Betfair it was wrong that he was paying 2% and betting against people who didn't know what they were doing and were paying 5%. He even went to the press and explained how it would be fairer if everybody just paid 2.5% – anything to make it a more level playing field.

"Yes, he's a dinosaur, but the billionaires with all their resources couldn't kill him off. It was never just about the money for him. The money was keeping score – the game was winning. He is perhaps the last of the swashbuckling gamblers who would bet fortunes on an opinion and then, against received wisdom, he would be far more likely to go in again, than hedge.

"There have been so many massive changes in his life, but nine times out of ten, he was beating whatever came at him. On the Asian Handicap, he went from being skint to making millions. That was every gambler's dream."

***

Kay Duggan has not only remained loyal to Harry for the best part of three decades – a frankly astonishing and surely unmatched commitment to a gambler – she learned to hold her tongue and accept the successes and losses, large or small.

"It's all I've known since I was 19," she said. "You'd be mad to go into a relationship like this thinking he was going to win all the time, because that didn't happen, even to the best.

"They'd have a good run for a while and then it would be shit again, but as long as you were prepared to take the good with the bad, you could ride out any situation. You don't say: 'What the bloody hell did you do that for?' while lying on a private yacht in the middle of the Med, so why say it when he was bang under pressure?

"I didn't go out to work after I met Harry, and I practically brought the kids up on my own, Ella [16 years old in 2017] especially. Harry takes a lot of looking after as well!

"I accepted some people would find our kind of life weird. When I meet somebody new, I tend not to get on to: 'What does your husband do for a living?' because I can tell it is hard to appreciate when I say what Harry does. I understand most people need to know what they need to do with their money, how much for electricity, food, the phone bill, all their outgoings. It's hard to explain to you why, with me, it wasn't – and isn't – a massive thing.

"I never found material things too important. Even in the recent terrible spell after Coventry, it never bothered me having to sell jewellery or cars. It was a privilege to live in a house like Rowas Lodge in Bath, and to drive an Aston Martin was lovely, but I had a proper grounding before Harry really made it big.

"I grew up in a two-up, two-down terraced house. There was no bathroom, just a toilet outside, so I tended to like smaller houses. When we moved to Bath, I was a little intimidated by it. I didn't really know how to be. We lived there for five years and the first year felt as if I was on holiday. I used to go to Sheffield to see my mum and Jade, and when I came back it was like returning to a hotel. I got used to it, but I can't say I ever found it a home. Harry didn't really give a shit when we lost the big house, he always considered it to be the 'Big Fella's' house. When the dog died and we buried him there, the house didn't mean anything to Harry.

"We left at Christmas in 2010, spent a couple of months in Australia, and then moved into an old chapel that had been converted into small block of a two-bedroom flats. Harry was right that the BHA had been after him, and he needed to feel safe and secure somewhere. He actually enjoyed being locked up in the top-floor flat whereas I, after spending most of the time in Bath out in the garden or in the countryside, was like a caged animal."

Kay's devotion to Harry is undiminished. "In a lot of ways, he's misunderstood," she said. "When he had a box at the racing, everyone was welcome in, he never expected people to pay for anything. All Harry wanted is for people to have a good time. Don Cuddy used to call him the memory man because he gave people so many wonderful memories. If he can't do that, he feels inadequate. If he doesn't make people laugh or have a great time, he hasn't done his job."

And so what of Kay's own betting career? "Dad once let us

have 50p on the Grand National. We got a hat and put all the bits of paper in and I pulled out Corbiere. I didn't like the name and put it back in. Corbiere won. That simple mistake ruined the Grand National for me for life.

"When Harry and I first got together, I loved watching Chris Eubank box. He was fighting Nigel Benn one time. I put £20 on Eubank at 7/4 and went home with £55, while Harry had four-and-a-half grand on Nigel Benn. Harry lost so much, I felt that bad I couldn't do it any more."

***

On May 21, 1994, Kay got to see her boxing hero close up. She and Harry were in Belfast for what she thought was a greyhound awards dinner. She donned her best dress and Harry had on his black tie, but when they climbed from the limousine, it was outside the Kings Hall, where Harry had persuaded Barry Hearn, the boxing promoter, to get them ringside seats for Eubank against the local boy, Ray Close.

"I won't forget how excited Kay was when she was eight months pregnant and thought she was going to see Stephen Hendry play Steve Davis at the NEC in Birmingham, and Jimmy White had got us front row seats for George Michael's concert at the same venue," Harry said. "But when she arrived for the fight and found out where we were sitting, she was blown away by it all."

The fight was a rematch for the WBO Super Middleweight title, after the first contest between the pair had ended in a draw. The Kings Hall was packed, the atmosphere thick with partisan Irish. A leprechaun danced into the ring before the first bell and sprinkled some dust over Eubank.

At the end of 12 gruelling rounds, there was little to choose between the fighters, though Eubank had, as usual, finished strongly. Then Harry saw Don King – the American co-promoter, who had been sitting within touching distance of him – pick up a scorecard from the desk of one of the judges. There was a long delay before Eubank was announced the winner on points on a split decision.

"I'd had my bollocks on Eubank, and King's behaviour all night was disgraceful. He was shouting: 'Ray Close this and Ray Close that,'" Harry said. "He was screaming after every round, but after the decision, he just went crazy."

Harry Mullan, in *The Independent* described the aftermath: "The fans accepted the verdict with a degree of decorum that would have graced Henley Regatta. The only unsavoury scene was provided by King who – in an impromptu press conference-cum-public-meeting, conducted, bizarrely, in a crammed exit corridor – ranted loudly about substituted scorecards and a WBO supervisor's tally sheet, which he claimed had mysteriously gone missing before it could be inspected and checked."

What Mullan did not mention was a toe-to-toe confrontation between King and Harry in said corridor. "The only person who went anywhere near the scorecards was fucking you," Harry shouted at the American. "You've been talking shit all night."

By the time Harry extricated himself from the melee and reached Eubank's trailer, Kay had already had five minutes chatting and her picture taken with him. "I only got to say hello and I was back out of the door," Harry said.

Sat next to Harry at ringside had been English coursing legend Freddie Worrall and his respected Irish pal Archie McGeehan, who, having heard the fracas between Harry and King, puffed on his cigar and said: "Bloody hell, Harry. You're some man – it's your first night in Belfast and you're going to get yourself killed by the biggest gangster in America."

***

By the age of 10, Jade Findlay knew that she liked her fish raw, her eggs runny and her steak blue. "Our lifestyle at that time was absolutely insane," Jade, now a pastry cook living and working in Sheffield, said. "I didn't understand much about what Dad was doing, but I thought he had the coolest job in the world, and wherever we went, there was this incredible atmosphere. People loved Dad so much.

"Wherever we lived, he took the local kids out to the dogs, got them all a takeaway, had them all round the house, and that helped me so much because even though we moved around a lot, the way we lived our lives helped me find friends.

"When we lived on an estate in Sheffield, every Bonfire Night he'd go to the Chinese firework store in the city and buy out the whole shop, spending a fortune, even though sometimes he didn't have it, to make sure the kids had a great bonfire."

"He's into so many different things, and that says so much about his personality. He's massively into his classical music. Wherever he travels, he always knows if there are any good concerts on, he's a freak about old trains and an expert on Salvador Dali. In my mid-teens, I struggled the most with my relationship with him. I thought we didn't have much in common, he was so much into the horses and I was going down the art route; it got a bit difficult. But it's a part of growing up and our relationship has become stronger through things he's not necessarily built his life around.

"I was nine the day Big Fella Thanks won the Irish Derby, and I know I'll never feel like that again in my life. There were hundreds of people lifting my dad up – he was like a king. Dad was so much about other people and making them feel great.

"You might be worrying about something, but as soon as you were with him, as soon as you were talking, things changed. He had this way of making you feel everything was going to be fine. I don't think I know anyone who speaks to people and makes them feel as good in a situation where they may be unsure or nervous. So, when things were tough for him [as the greyhound venture failed], it was really hard.

"I wouldn't sugarcoat it, but I knew before he did that it would be all right. I just knew he was too strong a person – he's got way too much in him for it to have been bad for a long time. We spoke about him taking medication and I said: 'You don't need that.' I told him: 'This is not the end, it's just not.'"

***

Copnor North End under-11s from Portsmouth were competing in a five-a-side tournament in Trowbridge in 2007, and Harry's mate, 'Fat' Barry Pennery's son, Ryan, was in the team. When he found out they were playing so close to home, Harry said that Kay might like to spend a weekend with her mum in Sheffield and promptly invited the whole squad over to Rowas Lodge. A dozen pizzas and bottles of coke were ordered.

Harry went to watch their three group matches on Saturday morning, and after the second game, he was on the phone to

Frank Harvey in Derry asking him to work on an entry for Copnor into the prestigious Foyle Cup junior international tournament, which was only a couple of weeks away.

Copnor duly won in Trowbridge, and by the time they paraded the trophy on Sunday afternoon, they were already in the draw for the Northern Ireland event, and Cliftonville C – awaiting their moment of glory – couldn't be found on the radar.

Copnor were coached by both Barry and the former Swindon and England youth defender John McLaughlin, who was astounded that within ten minutes of watching the team play for the first time, Harry knew the names of every player, was helping with the tactics and completely engaged.

Barry said: "The difference with Harry was that by half-time he'd worked out the weaknesses in the opposition and knew which of our boys would benefit most from a boost to their confidence – typical of him.

"After taking care of Shepton Beauchamp and Semington Mapgies in the Trowbridge event, the next thing we knew, thanks to Harry, we were in a group with Werder Bremen and Anderlecht."

McLaughlin – who had seen a few things in the game – was gobsmacked by the whole experience. "Our kids were 11 and most of the other teams played a year up, but we did well, won one, drew one and lost one. Harry was the most excited bloke in the party and loved being involved. I'd give the half-time team talks and then say to him: 'Anything you want to add, Harry?' He knew his football all right. It was important for us that our boys played a certain way – we were a passing team.

"With the boys being so young, they all travelled with their parents, but nobody was allowed to part with a dollar. Then

Harry treated everyone to a night at the Brandywell dogs and gave the lads a tenner each to bet with. They'd never experienced anything like it."

***

Clare Balding recalls a simple text from Harry when she was at one of the more stressful times of a luminous broadcasting career. At Newmarket in 2013, she was keen to press Sheikh Mohammed – whose horse Dawn Approach had won the 2,000 Guineas – on allegations circulating about his Goldolphin operation and the use of anabolic steroids. Clare asked the Sheikh if he was happy with the BHA's decision to ban one of his trainers, Mahmood al-Zarooni, for eight years. The Sheikh muttered something, turned his back and disappeared into his entourage.

"I received a lot of stick from the racing press for my line of questioning," Clare said. "The next day, Harry sent me a message saying that everyone else was too petrified to ask the right question, to keep up the good work and that he might see me on a racecourse one day when Paul Roy left the sport. There weren't many people who stood up for me, and what he did was very sweet. When you've been kicked, you need to know there are people who say: 'I'm still with you.'"

***

Andrew 'Chubby' Chandler rang City Index to place a bet one Friday afternoon in December 1987. Harry answered the phone. Chubby was nearing the end of his career as a professional golfer and their paths had briefly crossed over the years, and not only at the golf. "Chubby was taking the piss out of me for answering the phone and that I had to be a bit of a boring bastard," Harry said.

But the next thing Chubby said was that if Harry caught the 10.30pm flight from Heathrow to Cape Town that night, he'd meet him and his pal Davy Crockett at the airport the next morning, have a convertible waiting for Crockett to drive and five grand in readies for Harry to have on the first favourite at Kenilworth, the city's famed racetrack.

Harry's next call was to book himself and Crockett onto the flight. It would be the last time Harry spent the winter months in England.

At the racecourse, Harry's 5,000 rand was placed 'with that rarest of breeds, a genuine good guy bookmaker, Sedley Barr,' and his selection romped home by a length and a half. But it was at his next visit to Kenilworth where Harry landed the Hawkins' touch.

Chubby introduced Harry to Pip James, another bookmaker, who drove a Porsche, had long blond hair and was a member at top gentlemen's clubs around the world – the ultimate Jack the Lad, but one with a real touch of class about him. Harry said: "The end of the first night I met Pip, he gave me his card and said: 'If you're ever in Cape Town again, let me know where you're staying and what time you arrive, and within an hour, you'll have a Miss World knocking on your door.'"

The next day on the beach in Chubby and Harry's company, Pip wanted to discuss equine matters – specifically the only hurdle race staged in South Africa each year. It was at Kenilworth the following day. Pip said that one of his mates was connected with the red-hot favourite, Hawkins, who had won the race the previous three years. He was sure to go off as a long odds-on shot, but as nobody had seen him run for a year, any punters taking the short odds were doing so in the hope that he was still on his A game.

Pip rightly worked out that it wouldn't be hard to get the betting ring in a right panic simply by having a few rand on the only two dangers to Hawkins in the market. There were five runners, two of which had no chance. Pip's plan worked to perfection. His floor men and the sharp faces he knew the bookmakers would respect, kept chipping away on the same two runners, and when the big, fat, loudmouth punter from England, who apparently wouldn't know anything about Hawkins, walked into the ring, the horse was 1.6 on nearly every board from an opening show of 1.2. But by the time Harry had finished his business, the horse had returned to 1.2. Any bets Harry struck were 50/50 with Pip (apart from Chubby's slice of the action).

Hawkins won by about 150 yards and Harry flew back to Heathrow with an adidas bag in his hand luggage that was crammed full of red South African rand. It was five-and-a-half rand to the pound at the time, but when Harry went to exchange a lump, no one wanted to know and he ended up having to pay one for one. "I thought I was on Hawkins at an incredible average of 2/5, but it ended up being more like 1/6 when I cashed up."

***

When Harry first met Kay in Sheffield in April 1989, there were a few local lads still thinking they had a chance with her, and

Harry decided a trip to idyllic Mauritius in the Indian Ocean would get them both away from it all. He was seven years older than Kay, and after her first big night out at Wembley dogs, she was apprehensive that he might know too many people and was too much of a 'lad' for her taste.

In one of the more remote spots on the planet, Harry assured Kay it wasn't always like that – "It's only at the dogs where everybody knows me, it's not the same everywhere I go," he said. After a few days of secluded beach life, Kay had been somewhat reassured. Then the hotel concierge told Harry about a race meeting at Champs de Mars in Port Louis, and there was no chance of him missing that. He was told he'd have to be smartly dressed to get into the members' enclosure.

"It must have been the hottest day of all time," Harry recalled. "I couldn't have been turned out any better in a shirt and tie, but I hadn't brought a jacket. Kay looked great, but they wouldn't let us in. The general admission area was mobbed and there was no shade, the bookies had pitches lined up next to the trees, it was a great atmosphere, but we couldn't have lasted longer than half an hour in the sun, so in desperation to get into the owners' area, we went to where the horses were led onto the course.

"I implored the gateman to let us in. There was nobody else around, so I even offered him a nice few quid, but he wasn't budging. Suddenly he realised he had to open the gate to let the horses through for the second race, and when he did, the South African 'Lester Piggott', Karl Neisius, bellowed in the broadest Afrikaan accent: 'Harry The Dog, what the fuck are you doing here?' The gate was immediately thrown open for us. Kay nearly fainted.

"It only got worse. As we walked into the members' bar, I was

recognised from at least 30 yards away by none other than Pip
James, who shouted: 'Harry, just the man. I'm supposed to be
going to London to meet a film-star bird at the Piccadilly Club
this week but I can't be there, do me a favour and sort it out for
me when you get home.'"

Over a bottle of the finest champagne you could find in
Mauritius, Pip explained to Harry and Kay that he was flying
around the neighbouring islands with a pal in a private jet
looking to feed off weak-link, big-money mug players at poker.

Harry said: "When Pip asked if we wanted to come with him,
I knew that was more than enough for Kay, and was sure if the
Star Trek button had been in front of her, she'd have bust her
finger trying to beam herself back to Addy Street in Sheffield."

***

Harry and Chubby Chandler kept in touch down the years.
"I'd give him little pointers before the majors," Chubby said.
"He was on a roll with Tiger Woods, and if they keep on the
roll and they're the best, you're going to do all right. For seven
years, Tiger was almost unbeatable, and nobody got more out
of Tiger than Big H.

"Harry's life is remarkable. It's an interesting concept because
you start with nothing, might end up with nothing and you've
still had a fantastic time in between. That's what he's done. He's
a huge character that people don't usually forget. 90% will love
him and 10% will absolutely hate him.

"The buzz for Harry is that he flies by the seat of his pants –
that's where he wants to be rather than have loads in the bank.
What would Harry do if he had loads in the bank?"

For the 2000 Open Championship at St Andrews, Harry and a bunch of mates had rented a house not far from the course when Chubby rang with an offer. "I've played a blinder," he said. "It's the house Colin Montgomerie had rented and he's decided to go somewhere else, so you can have it for the week. And it's the same deal he had."

The owner of the house was present lady captain of St Andrews. "She knew Monty wasn't coming and obviously presumed it was a golfer and his entourage taking his place," Harry said. "She walked us round the house – 'this is bedroom one, this is bedroom two,' living room, kitchen, beautiful.

"We'd been there ten minutes and she asked when we'd like breakfast – 'I'll do bacon and eggs for you every morning.' I said: 'Listen Doreen or Maureen, whatever your name is, I'm not being funny, but some of us won't be home until late at night, there are many nice places in the town, we won't be doing a lot of cooking,' and she said: 'Oh no, I'll do one every morning for you. I'm staying in a little room under the stairs.'

"I said: 'No you're not mate, lady captain or no lady captain.' I was straight on the phone to the rental people. Half an hour later she was gone, but as she was walking down the path with steam rising from her ears, she said: 'Do you mind if I come in on Saturday morning and spend half an hour tidying up?' No problem at all.

"She came round on Saturday and was heartbroken. There were pizza boxes all over the place, we made sure we had plenty of takeaways late on Friday night and had extra people staying over. She was hooting. She had pictures of her kids on dressers and sideboards, and as she cleaned up, she turned most of them round. She didn't want them to see the carnage."

The day after the Championship, Harry walked into the town to buy the breakfast rolls, and when he returned, Finbar Giltinen, one of his group, was sitting on his suitcase in the front drive. "Finbar said: 'She's kicked me out.' I couldn't believe it," said Harry. "I said to the lady captain: 'Let me explain one thing – when you sold your house for £12,000 for a week, you sold your soul. You should have had your friends here for summer nights out, steaks on the barbecue, whatever you wanted, but you took the 12 bags of sand. We will be leaving at 2pm as agreed.' She had to back down."

The lady captain may not have fallen for Harry's charms, but one neighbour was smitten. "Even if I'm under pressure and losing, when I walk down the street, I've got manners," Harry said. "I like to look people in the eye and say hello. It's the way I've always been and the way everybody is when the Open is at St Andrews. If you haven't been, it's hard to explain what the atmosphere is like for seven days every time the biggest golf tournament in the world returns to its most famous venue. It's as if everybody is living in a separate bubble from the rest of the world and nobody cares about anything other than the golf.

"A lady neighbour was especially friendly. She obviously hadn't heard that Colin Montgomerie wasn't staying next door, and she'd clearly never seen me play golf. On Saturday, I was in the back garden stressed, under pressure – was I going to stick or hedge on Tiger for the title?

"I was planning to hedge some of my position with the Lizard, but on a Saturday he was far too busy to worry about the golf and I had to sit it out with what, for me at the time, was a massive position.

"I had a wedge in my hand, swinging away at an imaginary ball and deep in thought while Grant Devonish was puffing away on a cigarette on the patio. He decided to use the fine brickwork as his personal ashtray and I just lost it, screaming: 'You bastard, what the fuck do you think you're doing?' Then we saw the neighbour walking along the side of the house in full view of the garden. It was as loud and severe a volley as I've ever served and I thought: 'Oh my God, she must heard every word.'

"She just looked across, waved and shouted: 'Good morning, have a good round.' Grant collapsed on the floor in hysterics. It took us both two minutes to get over it before Grant said: 'Fuck me, she really does think you're Colin Montgomerie.'"

***

Inevitably, Harry is often asked how much he misses owning horses. The answer is usually: "Only Marianne Barber's breakfasts. I really do miss spending time with my old partner Paul Barber, especially when we were away from the racecourse. I even enjoyed visiting his pigs on a stinking hot summer's day."

And then there were his weekly visits to Mick Channon's stables in West Ilsley where, after a 5.30am start (bacon sarnies at 7.30am), the day's work and gallops would finish just in time for a fine lunch with three pints of Ruddles County and a bottle of wine to wash it down. Mick would have a sleep before the evening stables and Harry would have one on the way home.

Mick related perfectly to the trouble Harry had coming to terms with the way he was treated by a lot of the racing establishment. "I had the same when I came into racing," Channon, the former England footballer, said. "People think you're something other than you are, and you can develop a complex about it. Harry wanted to have a chat and a laugh. He had an opinion and voiced it. He lit the racing world up. He certainly shook it up. We don't have enough Harrys in the sport now. All he wanted was the best for his horses and everyone else.

"He was Mr Denman. We're his mates and we all wanted Denman to win the Gold Cup, and at that time you couldn't stop him, he was like a runaway fucking train, in the nicest possible way.

"He knew the characters in other sports, and he came into a sport where you didn't have a character – you had a fucking horse. He got it right with Denman, but in football and tennis, he knew the players, he knew their temperaments, and then it came down to his judgment. And look how good that was.

"You can't do that with our four-legged friends, a horse; they can't tell you when they're not right, there's a million different things that could be going on you don't know about."

On the wall of Mick's office hangs a photograph from his Southampton playing days alongside Alan Ball, one of his dearest friends. A few weeks before he died of a heart attack at the age of 61 in 2007, Ball was a guest of Channon at the Sydney Cricket Ground to watch the final test of the Ashes Series that secured the Aussies a 5-0 whitewash. Harry was sharing the box with Mick and was introduced to Ball.

"They were like kids in a sweet shop – they never stopped talking," Mick said. "Harry told Bally that his dad used to hate him because he always played well against Scotland [Harry's father, Alf, was a proud Scot]. The talk inevitably got on to the 1966 World Cup final. Harry's dad hated Bally even more that day. They were having a right laugh."

The previous day's play had finished early because of a rain shower and the first session was two-and-a-half hours instead of two. "I had Alan all to myself for every ball," Harry said. "And when the umpire took off the bails for lunch, I couldn't believe it. I didn't even realise they'd had drinks. What I'll never forget is Bally telling me what it was like in the 1970 World Cup in Mexico, when England played Brazil in Guadalajara at altitude.

"The players were convinced they couldn't have been better prepared, but after five minutes, Alan said he could barely breath and wondered how he could possibly get through 90 minutes. He described it as hell.

"That certainly wasn't what he thought of West Ilsley. He was going to move from his house to a smaller cottage near Mick's yard to be closer to the action full-time when he died of a heart attack trying to put out a fire in his back garden, burning the stuff he didn't need for the move."

It was 16 months after the tragic loss of Ball that another of Mick's best friends, Tim Corby, was killed in an accident on the M1 on the way back from the Doncaster sales. Mick and Harry had bought a horse there the previous day they would name Mr Corby, in honour of Tim. It was a miracle that Mick survived the crash, and his then 15-year-old son, Jack, was also in the vehicle and taken to hospital.

Knowing Mick was in intensive care and couldn't have visitors, Harry and Glen Gill went to see Jack. "I was in the children's ward in a neck brace when they came in," Jack said. "Glen had four or five Playboy-type magazines and banged them on the desk next to the bed. 'These'll keep you busy, boy.' Harry and Glen chatted for about an hour. I was their perfect audience because I couldn't move."

Like anyone who meets him, Jack Channon had a favourite Harry story. In July 2007, he was at Newbury racecourse when his phone rang. "We had a horse called Atlantic Sport running for the first time that season in a seven-furlong race," Jack said. "Harry's number flashed up, he said he couldn't get hold of Dad and asked if the horse was going to win. I said: 'Yeah, we really like him.'"

It had become a standing joke between Harry and Mick as to how much they would have on the horse when it next got to the racecourse. For the previous few weeks, Atlantic Sport had been working like a Rolls-Royce and appeared to have plenty in hand. On the day of the race, all Harry needed was the green light that everything was as planned and there were no last-minute hitches, but he couldn't get hold of Mick all morning.

With less than an hour to go before the race, he decided to call Jack. "I heard Harry say: 'Okay, we'll have 200 on that.' I thought it was 200 quid and I found out later it was £200k, on the word of a 14-year-old! The horse was nearly 2/1 when Harry called, and ended up winning by a head at 11/10."

***

Harry appeared before a Football Association disciplinary committee on February 19, 1987, a case brought against the chairman of Southwick FC, the Brighton bookmaker Terry Harrison. Harry was the only witness on Terry's behalf.

Maidstone United made the complaint after an almighty FA Cup fourth-qualifying-round struggle with their West Sussex opponents. The first match at Southwick ended 1-1, before which the Maidstone chairman had marched into one of Terry's betting shops and asked what price his team was to win 6-0. "He was giving it the big shot treatment, but when I offered him 100/1, all he had on was a tenner," Terry said.

The replay also finished 1-1, which meant a toss of the coin was required to determine home advantage for the second replay. Terry refused to take part in the coin toss unless his side was afforded the same hospitality as the home team, referee and linesmen. "I ain't tossing no coin until you blokes get some decent tea and sandwiches for my boys right now," he said. Maidstone raged. They won the toss for ground advantage and the atmosphere for the second replay was more than heated. Harry sat next to Terry in the directors' box and could feel the vitriol directed at his mate. It wasn't long before the pair gave as good as they got.

Southwick held Maidstone to a feisty 2-2 draw and Harry was on the bus with the team as they drove home. It stopped at a first-class fish and chip shop. Terry Harrison paid for all the suppers, collected them in a big box and handed them out to the players as he walked down the bus. Harry couldn't help thinking he was back on the Wycombe supporters' coach on its way to Evenwood as an 11-year-old kid.

"For so many reasons, it was one of the best fish and chip suppers I ever had," he said. Southwick lost the third replay 5-1 at home, and the FA subsequently charged Harrison with bringing the game into disrepute because of his behavior at the second replay. He asked if Harry would speak up for him.

Maidstone brought 12 people to the hearing, held at the FA offices at Lancaster Gate the morning after England beat Spain 4-2 in Madrid where Gary Lineker scored all four goals. A few members of the disciplinary committee had been part of the England entourage and were giddy with excitement.

Harry was called to speak up for his friend and explained what had really happened in the director's box during the game. "Harry reminded me of Henry Fonda in *Twelve Angry Men*, he was pure class," Terry said. "I got off with a fine of £25."

***

Before Christmas 2016, Harry didn't know where the next decent winner was coming from. He badly needed the airfare for his annual trip to Australia but could barely afford the train fare from Axminster to Exeter. Throughout the year, Harry was travelling once a week from the West Country to visit his mum in hospital, and after seeing her on December 14, he stopped off for lunch with old golfing mucker Paul Way who, in turn, introduced Harry to a mate of his.

Knowing Harry's racing background, Paul's mate said he had a marquee at every Boxing Day meeting at Kempton Park and would Harry mind texting him what bets to have on the day. That was no problem for Harry, who gave him his mobile number. During the lunchtime conversation, Harry learned that the bloke was a next-door neighbour of Len Goodman, the chief judge on *Strictly Come Dancing*.

Three nights later, Harry's saw a text message from a number he didn't recognise suggesting he might have a few bob on Ore to win the final. Harry had no idea what the message meant and genuinely thought 'Ore' was a biscuit. It was only when he checked who the text was from and asked Kay: 'Who the fuck is Ore?' that the penny dropped. Len Goodman's neighbour was telling Harry to back a 14/1 chance in a three-runner dance-off. "The geezer certainly knew all about Len because he told us about his split from the BBC and why he'd gone to work in America," Harry said. "I had to have a few quid on."

But Harry wasted valuable time and the 14/1 disappeared in front of his eyes. He scrambled £200 at 11/1, but he wasn't the only one trying to get on, and when the odds shortened to 6/1, he had another £100 at that price. Somebody else he'd never heard of, Danny Mac, was a red-hot 4/7 to win it, and before they all did their final dance, Ore (Oduba) had drifted back out to 8/1.

"Ore was the first to dance, and to my naïve eye, he was sensational. I thought: 'Aye, aye, I've got a chance here,' and then 'Fred Astaire' walked on! Danny Mac was out of this world, and anybody who bet the odds-on must have been on great terms with themselves. To be honest, I'd practically given up hope when, all of a sudden, Ore was holding up a great big crystal ball and everybody was going mad. I booked my flight to Australia 15 minutes later."

***

After a very quiet Cheltenham Festival in 2017, Harry has finally hit a bit of form. His only football ante-post bets in the 2016/17 season were Hibernian at 11/10 to win the Scottish Championship and Glasgow Celtic at 11/8 for the Scottish FA Cup. Since Aintree, Glen Gill has been in consistent form with the horses, although for the first time in years, he and Harry did their bollocks at Royal Ascot. Harry came out of tennis retirement to lump on Rafael Nadal to win Roland Garros in June – just like the good old days – and went for a real touch on Marin Cilic each-way at 40/1 to win Wimbledon *before* he played at Queen's, where he reached the final.

Harry's penchant for the big bet had not diminished. When you have finished reading this book, he could be flying high or have touched the bottom again. For the first time since his Rabbitohs bet in January 2014, he had gone all-in on Floyd Mayweather to beat Conor McGregor at 1/5 (1.2).

"In 49 fights, nobody laid a finger on Mayweather," Harry said. "So how the fuck can someone change sports and beat him? I always said that best ten-on chance I ever bet was Steve Davis to beat American pool champion Jim Rempe at snooker. I felt this was just as good, and I got 1/5. Surely, Mayweather was a fucking certainty."

But now you – and he – will know if he was right or not. And that whatever the result, today he will be back on the game again.

***

Harry always had a passion for the philosophies of Dostoyevsky. His novels may have been too dark and heavy for Harry, but in his literary masterpiece *The Gambler*, printed in 1867, the Russian discussed the psychology of desperate gambling, a compulsion that brought him to the brink of ruin.

In a dramatic finale, Dostoyevsky wrote: "Can I fail to understand that I am a lost man, but – can I not rise again! Yes! I have only for once in my life to be prudent and patient and – that is all! I have only for once to show willpower and in one hour I can transform my destiny! The great thing is the willpower.

"I was going to the casino, I looked, there was still one guilder in my waistcoat pocket. 'Then I shall have something for dinner,' I thought. But after I had gone one hundred paces, I changed my mind and went back. I staked that guilder on *manque*, and there really is something peculiar in the feeling when, alone in a strange land, far from home and from friends, not knowing whether you will have anything to eat that day – you stake your last guilder, your very last!

"I won, and twenty minutes later I went out of the casino, having one hundred and seventy guilders in my pocket. That's a fact! That's what the last guilder can sometimes do! And what if I had lost heart then? What if I had dared not to risk it? Tomorrow, tomorrow, it will all be over!"

Harry's Reflections

'To enjoy sport, both live and televised, for over 40 years is indeed an immense privilege. To all those mums, dads, guardians, tutors and coaches who nurtured, moulded and fine-tuned these gladiators, I doff my cap. I've been lucky enough to attend so many memorable sporting events and have met many good people along the way. Here are a few that have enriched my life...'

ROGER FEDERER

For nearly ten years, I went to every Grand Slam tennis event, but only for the first week, and nearly always on the outside courts looking for clues. Every now and again, you'd come across a jackpot. The best one ever was Xavier Malisse versus Roger Federer in the second round at Wimbledon in 2001. I'd never seen a better standard five-set, grass-court match.

Nowadays, it'd be on the BBC Red Button with 200 odds compilers across the country watching every point, and thus it'd be worthless. But not back then. I recall looking around and realised there were no warm journalists or professional punters – just Muggles everywhere. It's impossible to say how good the Belgian could have been on grass. He made it to the semi-final the following year but his career was blighted by a heart problem.

Federer – who saw off Malisse – put in another fine performance in the next round against Jonas Bjorkman, and although 'Pistol' Pete Sampras had won me plenty over the years, I couldn't resist backing Federer at 5/1 and 9/2 ,with £400 on at both prices. The only reason I didn't back him at flashy prices outright after beating Xavier, was because he had a horrendous draw.

To this day, I know if Tim Henman hadn't beaten Federer in the quarter-finals, I can't imagine a situation where it would have been possible to get telephone numbers out of the man who was to become my very own Cash Federation Society!

The following year, Federer drew big-serving Croatian Mario Ancic in the first round, and lost in straight sets. Ancic barely missed a first serve. Two months later, Roger's best friend and coach, Australian Peter Carter, died in a car accident in South Africa. The Swede Peter Lundgren was one of the tour's real good guys; he stood out, was more than just amiable, and loved a beer and a good laugh. He knew Roger well, and after Peter's death, became his full-time coach.

It was a real tough time for The Fed, and in such circumstances, Lundgren was the ideal choice. But I knew Roger would be inconsolable after losing to Luis Horna in the first round of the French Open in 2003. He said he didn't know how long it would take him to get over it: "A day, a week, or perhaps my entire career."

When I heard that, I tried to get on a flight to Halle in Germany for the tournament there because I wanted to tell him to his face that the best thing that could have happened to him was that Paris defeat. He could concentrate solely on the grass and be fresh for Wimbledon. In the years that followed, I often told Roger he shouldn't even bother with the European clay court season at all.

To be fair, I was only (half) joking, but when I caught a 19-year-old Sam Querrey checking out of the Crown Towers after losing in the third round of his first Australian Open to Tommy Robredo of Spain, I was deadly serious when I told him exactly the same thing – "All you're going to do is get your socks dirty." I explained how hard it would be to beat Robredo on the European red dirt, but also how Sam would smash him to bits on grass at Nottingham. He looked at me like I was mad, but he might have taken some of it on board. He's since won Queen's, and I got a nice few quid out of him when he turned over Novak Djokovic at Wimbledon in 2016.

It would have been easier to get to the moon than to Halle – door to door in 36 hours – so my only chance of speaking to Roger was at the practice courts at Wimbledon. The betting at the time had defending champion Lleyton Hewitt as 3/1 favourite and Federer at 10/1. I didn't get a chance to speak to Roger for very long but I did explain that Hewitt was the clear favourite with the bookies and that he and I both knew that, on grass, Roger had to be the jolly if ever they met, reminding him that the early defeat in Paris was a help and not a hindrance. I told him: "You're a fucking certainty." He just laughed.

I averaged out at about 17/2 and went for the biggest touch of my life, because I made him less than half that price. The only heart attack moment was when he was lying on the ground having treatment for a sore back during the warm-up before his fourth-round match against Feliciano Lopez of Spain. His body language was terrible, and I think he lost six of the first seven points when they started, before normal service resumed and he won in straight sets.

Jim O'Rourke was on Peter Lundgren duty for the rest of the tournament to make sure that everything was okay with our man. Federer made it to the final (without dropping another set) where he was the 8/15 favourite (I made him 1/4) to beat Mark Philippoussis. He duly obliged in straight sets to leave Lundgren and him hugging in the players' box and me raking in the readies.

I won half as much again on Roger the following year. We were in Lisbon for the European Championship final between Greece and Portugal, but all I was worried about was getting a good TV spot to see Federer beat Andy Roddick. In a high quality match, Federer won in four sets.

It was at Kooyong – the old home of the Australian Open in Melbourne – where Roddick and Federer were playing an exhibition match a few months later. I had a decent seat behind the server and when Federer flushed three returns from first serves on the trot, Andy turned towards the crowd and handed his racket to the girl sitting next to me. The following night, I bumped into Roger outside the Japanese restaurant in the Crown and said I thought it was strange of Roddick to let down his guard like that. Roger just smiled and said: "Oh yes, he knows I can read his serve, he knows he can't beat me."

I wonder how much money that saved me in the 2009 final between the two when Federer won 16-14 in the fifth set? I didn't think Roger was on his real A game throughout the fortnight and all the value was with Roddick at the prices. Three or four times in-running, I was almost desperate to back the American, but I just couldn't get away from what Roger had said outside Koko.

FRANKIE DETTORI

Frankie is the best thing that's happened to the sport of Flat racing in my almost 40 years as an observer. His enthusiasm, personality and passion for what he does, makes him a PR man's dream.

I was in Baden-Baden, Germany, one Sunday afternoon when one of Godolphin's top handicappers pissed up in a Group 3. With no one there to represent them, Frankie went up to collect the awards for jockey, owner and trainer. Looking on was a rowdy but good-humoured gang of guys on a weekend stag do. The next thing, they were up on the stage with Frankie and the trophies having a great time, even the press photographers were getting involved. You'd have thought they were all best mates. Only Frankie could have done it.

I once followed Frankie and Catherine, his wife, out of a restaurant in Dubai. Kay and I were 80 yards behind them on a beachside path that ran parallel with the sea. Suddenly, further ahead, their five kids, who were with their nanny at a playground, spotted Mum and Dad. Straight away they sprinted towards them like crazy Jack Russells. I was working out the odds in my head, making Mum a genuine 1/8 shot, but all five of them jumped on their Dad. Frankie looked like a tree, one kid on each arm and leg and the other around his neck. I don't know much about what he does in his spare time, apart from going to watch Arsenal, but he certainly spends plenty of it with his family.

My favourite Frankie sporting moment is a given – Dubai Millennium winning the World Cup in Dubai in 2000. Dubai Millennium was sired by Seeking The Gold, out of Colorado

Dancer. I've watched all the big live races around the world as a punter, I know how it feels to own a Gold Cup winner, and have a winner at Royal Ascot, but in all my time, I've only once experienced an almost ethereal spirit on a racecourse. That was on this warm, hazy night in the UAE.

There's no gambling allowed in that country, but I had done my business back home. I had £200,000 to win £165,000 on a horse that not only looked a certainty, but very much on home territory in every sense. No stone would have been unturned, everything was in his favour and all I hoped was that Frankie would keep it simple.

The atmosphere was building pre-race, mainly because of one unique situation – almost every single person on the racecourse wanted the same horse to win! I sensed what might happen and cleverly made sure to get a really good position at the back of the main grandstand. I've never backed an easier winner in my life. Dubai Millennium not only set the pace, but did so in his own comfortable cadence and settled like a dream. After 300 yards, everybody knew he was going to win – the waitresses, the peanut sellers, the Dubai royalty.

Even before he came to the first bend, a rhythmical four-clap applause rang around the course. By the time he turned into the home straight, he was a mile clear, this great big, black, shiny monster on the bridle in the brilliant Godolphin blue. It was fantastic. Never have the hairs on the back of my neck risen like they did that night – not even watching Denman, or Desert Orchid beating Yahoo (I did my bollocks on that), or even Dawn Run catching Wayward Lad on the Gold Cup run-in when the late Sir Peter O'Sullevan delivered the greatest horse racing commentary ever.

Sheikh Mohammed was certain that Dubai Millennium would

be the sire to take him to the top. But sadly he never got the chance. In 2001, the horse picked up an infection that turned out to be the dreaded grass sickness, and he was gone in hours. Being one of the richest men on the planet was no consolation. He was desolate, and I've no doubt it was the worst moment of Sheikh Mohammed's life. I'm a dog person and wouldn't know how it's possible to get that close to a racehorse, but the Sheikh certainly does. Being around people who've been with him when he's with his horses, you quickly realise that he's very much at one with a thoroughbred and, take it from me, there aren't many people you can say that about. I'm sure Dubai Millennium will always be the best and most important thing in his life.

JIMMY BARRY-MURPHY

When Harry Carpenter interviewed world heavyweight champion Larry Holmes and said boxing was a dangerous sport, Holmes put on a video of a hurling match – "This is what you call dangerous, Harry," he said.

Dublin bookmaker Jim Brown took me to my first game, the All-Ireland semi-final between Tipperary and Galway in 1989. The whole thing took my breath away, and when the whistle went at half-time, I thought it was a trick and they'd been playing no more than 15 minutes.

The speed, skill and occasional violent clash was intoxicating in front of a packed crowd of over 64,000 at Croke Park in Dublin. After the game, I was raving about Tipperary's Nicky English and Galway's Gerry McInerney.

I'd been coursing in Ireland for a few years and met many

great people. One of these was Jimmy Barry-Murphy. I knew him as a punter, owner of coursing dogs and an all-round good guy, and for many weeks, I didn't have a clue he was one of the finest hurlers of all time, such was the modesty of the man. He was just as well known for his talents as a Gaelic footballer, and drew the attention of scouts from Manchester United for his soccer ability. He's widely acclaimed as the best hurler from Cork since the great Christy Ring, but you'd never have known it sharing four or five pints of stout in his local pub, Moks.

Incredibly, I went on to win the Oaks at Clonmel as an owner myself in 2006 with Mountain Guest, but I clearly recall a few years earlier when Jimmy's Telematic Touch was beaten in the quarter-finals. He was on a tea chest three rows in front of me. I wondered before the course what it would be like to own a dog in the last eight of such a prestigious event. After watching her get beat and how Jimmy took his medicine, I hoped I'd do the same if I was ever in that position.

Abbeyfeale is the biggest coursing meeting that takes place just before Christmas, and in 1998, it was like being in the Antarctic and a miracle that the coursing took place on the first day, and when it finished, all the roads were covered in ice. Only Jimmy Barry-Murphy was daft enough to make the hazardous journey back to Cork, and I was his passenger.

Ten minutes after getting on the N20, we both knew we'd made a stupid mistake. On a journey that took over three hours, we only saw two others cars. I was sure it was only a matter of time before we slid off the road and into a ditch, and that looked all the more likely when every three or four minutes Jimmy took his hands off the steering wheel to bless himself each time he passed a memorial or gravestone at the top of either side of the road.

HARRY'S REFLECTIONS

I was pleading with him: "Please, Jimmy. For fuck sake, leave me out of this religious shit, at least until you get us home."

Jimmy Barry-Murphy had his own fond memory of Harry bursting into the dressing room after Cork [JBM was the manager] beat Offaly 19-16 in a see-saw 1999 All-Ireland hurling semi-final. As you'd expect, security at Croke Park was tight for such an occasion, but despite this, Jimmy didn't seem at all surprised to see Harry.

"Timmy McCarthy hadn't even taken his helmet off and Harry – head to toe in full Rebel regalia – was telling him how well he'd played," said Barry-Murphy. "Most of the lads couldn't understand a word Harry was saying, but we all had a great laugh. His enthusiasm for live sport and having a bet is relentless. Curley O'Driscoll rang me after Harry won 1,400 euros at a road-bowling match at Rosscarbery. As Eddie Donnelly said at the time: 'There's more chance of Aiden O'Brien never training another winner than a foreigner ever doing that again.'"

LESTER PIGGOTT

My brother, Gordon, was nine years old and I was ten. The label on the bottle of Bell's clearly read: 'Eight Years Old.' That was good enough for us and we both had our first swig of whisky. The second the taste hit me, I immediately knew that in 50 year's time, I'd still hate it. I was spot-on.

But considering I'd only been going horse racing for a couple of months in 1979, and even now I've such a limited opinion on how good or bad any jockeys are, how on earth did I know that when

Lester Piggott won by a head on a horse called Known Fact (first time out at Newbury), that I'd never see a jockey like him if I live to be 1,000 years old?

I was in the old wooden stand at Windsor the following season when Lester was riding a 1/16 chance. In the betting ring was Willie Thorne's fat friend, bookmaker 'Racing Raymond', and he was betting on whether the horse would win by under or over two-and-a-half lengths, because the horse was such a red-hot favourite.

I watched the finish of the race in sheer incredulity as Lester got up to win hard held by a short head. I looked over at Racing Raymond who was delirious, he reminded me of the Jolly Fat Sailor you used to see at fairgrounds. He obviously correctly worked out how he'd ride the horse, and duly got the lot, but I was just stunned by the audacity and danger of what Lester had done and I knew for sure it would never happen again. But Lester never batted an eyelid. In so many sports, it's contentious to offer an opinion as to who is the greatest of all time, but Flat racing doesn't have that problem. Everybody who knows anything about horse racing, knows he's the finest jockey ever to sit on a thoroughbred.

I was lucky enough to be in the Sports Book in the Mirage in Vegas when he came out of retirement at the age of 54 and won the Breeders' Cup Mile in 1990 on Royal Academy. I've already mentioned earlier in the book what the atmosphere was like in there on the big day, but when Lester came with one of his withering runs on the outside to get up on the line to win, the whole place erupted. Every single punter threw a racing paper high in the sky and cheered. And to think that we were over in the States, and here they were, going mad for a British grandfather. It was a magical moment (shame I wasn't on!).

JIMMY WHITE

There's only one person or team that I still check the results for if I haven't had a bet, and that's Mr James White. I first met Jimmy in Zan's Snooker Club in Tooting when we were 18, and I'd see him now and again at the odd tournament exhibition or holiday camp Pro-Am.

As a person, I just can't speak highly enough about him. He often mentioned that his truancy from school left him somewhat lacking in terms of his reading and writing skills. But boy did he make up for it in so many other ways.

In all my life, I've never met anyone half as socially clever and overwhelmingly cool as Jimmy. Over the years, I'd be lying if I said I was financially in front from backing him with hard cash, but he really has a genuine sixth sense I've not seen in anyone else. One time, half a dozen of us were in a busy bar in Belgium on a Friday night. There wasn't much room, but we were having a great laugh and I saw no reason to move anywhere else, when Jimmy suddenly said: "Let's go."

As we were getting to the exit, I started to moan about why he'd been in such a rush, when back where we'd been drinking, there was complete pandemonium. I'd never seen a fight like it. It was like one of those tear-ups you see in an old-fashioned Western. Jimmy always knew what was going on and what everyone was up to. I never questioned him again.

It's not only me who thinks so. You don't become best pals with the Rolling Stones because you're good with a snooker cue!

The fact that we didn't know each other that well in the early '80s made what he did for me stick in my mind even more. On more than one occasion he got me accommodation and somewhere to lay my head when, to all intents and purposes, I was homeless. I was living on my wits and talked Jimmy, Tony Meo and Jimmy's right-hand man and good friend Alan Bell into going to the flapping dog track at Breen Sands, right next to the holiday camp where the lads were playing in a competition.

Like all flapping tracks (independent with no governing body), there was no form or racecard to go on, and unless you're connected, it's pretty much guesswork and at very much under the odds. I wiped us all out. The next morning we had to use tokens in order to get any breakfast, and that was the only time Jimmy gave me half a bollocking, but afterwards he had sorted it for me to go and stay with his manager, Geoff Lomas, for the weekend in Manchester, which I really appreciated, and the following year, back in London, he asked a hard-working pal of his, Roger, to put me up for a few days that ended up becoming nearly three weeks. He had a great knack of getting things sorted without a lot of fuss, and I've never forgotten it.

How Jimmy has never won the World Championship remains one of the sport's great mysteries. He might have won it as an 18-year-old if he hadn't had the misfortune to draw the Nugget in the first round. He was in six finals without getting his hands on the Holy Grail. It was during the last of those I spent the most time with him.

Jimmy was playing Stephen Hendry and held a big lead early in the match, I watched every frame in a different place before taking the perfect seat in the arena for the final frame. As always in close defeat, many are far too quick to use the word 'bottle'. Jimmy was on a break of 29 with five easy reds remaining before many thought he twitched on the black. Straight after the game he told me he knew as he played the shot he'd got it wrong but it was too late to pull out of it. Even after missing the black, for some reason I felt confident that Hendry wouldn't clear up this time.

I still don't know why, but I was sure it was Jimmy's year. I was wrong. An hour later, backstage, and under the venue seating, one at a time I watched four of his five daughters come up and give their dad a hug. There was no one else around. I was crying my eyes out.

I've always been a movies man and now and again I talked Jimmy into coming to watch a film in the afternoon – our tastes weren't always the same, but the most amazing thing was that even in total darkness, people would still come up during the film and ask him for an autograph.

I can't forget the first time I went into a snooker club in China with Jimmy. It was like a massive aeroplane hangar, there must have been well over a hundred snooker tables in there. The first thing that hit me was the cacophony of the snooker balls and then, in a split second, total silence followed by spontaneous applause from everyone inside. No disrespect to Hendry or the Nugget, but I'm sure it wouldn't have been the same if you'd walked in with them, but Jimmy, as usual, took it all in his stride.

He was great to be around whenever you were travelling, because he always had a real top man waiting to look after us. Jimmy is now doing a superb job on Eurosport with my old mate Neal Foulds, and showed his class once again when Anthony Hamilton won his first tournament at the age of 45 in 2017. He was in the booth after the match and was clearly emotional from a sporting point of view that he had finally got over the line.

Jimmy's flat in Epsom was destroyed by fire in January 2017. He lost nearly all his snooker memorabilia but, most importantly, his favourite cue was safely in the boot of his car. Make no mistake, he still thinks he can win the world title and is practising more than ever.

COURAGE UNDER FIRE

Courage Under Fire was the greatest-ever two or three-year-old champion pacer from New Zealand. As well as being well named and looking like *Black Beauty*, he was a flying machine who won six derbies and his first 24 races. He was going for win number 25 at Moonee Valley (they no longer have trotting racing there, but I did make sure Jade and I were at the final night in Melbourne and also the fantastic Harold Park's last night in Sydney).

The son of In The Pocket looked an absolute moral and I was more than happy to bet the 1/10. It proved to be an expensive mistake, but to say the horse owed me nothing was an understatement, and what I will always remember about the race itself is the commentary. It was the best call from the sport's best-ever caller, Dan Mylocki. Turning for home, Courage Under Fire moved into second place – he had plenty on to pick up the leader, but he was still the favourite – when he suddenly missed half a stride and the front runner shot clear. It was more than obvious that Dan was funking for his hero and there was that split half a second of silence before he screamed in agony: "THE WORLD HAS ENDED."

STEVE DAVIS

You only have to look at the current state of the sport of darts to see what Barry Hearn is like in business. He has turned a pub game into a global phenomenon. Don't worry about the World Championships, he's selling out massive venues for league matches on Thursday nights.

He was also a major factor in why snooker was so big in the late 1970s and 1980s. Back then, he had the time of his life. He had his own creation, his own form of currency – a personal friend of his I called 'the Golden Nugget'.

Steve Davis' father, Bill, was a quiet gentleman who only ever wanted to watch his son play snooker (he never missed a match) and smoke a good cigar. He had an enormous influence on Steve's career from well before he arrived at Hearn's Locano club in Romford, remaining so throughout his career. Hearn was a very different character. He was the perfect manager, confident with tons of street-wise nous. Together, the three of them were deadly.

When the young Nugget beat Terry Griffiths 9-0 in the semi-final – and Alex Higgins 16-6 in the final – of the 1980 Coral UK, he was mesmerising. I was working for a fiver a day as a board man at the betting shop in Hughenden, High Wycombe, that would become, for a very short period, Findlay & Bowler, but I couldn't take my eyes off Davis on the bookies' small black and white TV. It was like watching a metronome for four days. On the Monday morning, I had my first bet on him to win the World Championships six months later – £30 with Corals at 8/1. I kept chipping away for small stakes whenever I backed a winner.

By the New Year, Steve was a 9/2 chance and went to as short as 11/4 to take the world title before he got the worst draw possible for the famous Crucible event and duly went back out to 7/2. In the first round, he had to play the 18-year-old everyone was desperate to avoid – Jimmy White. I had to have a saver on Jimmy at 100/1 but, in truth, neither of them were great value at that stage because whoever won the match still had plenty to do to make it to the final. Davis won 10-8 in a real classy affair, but everyone knew that both players were destined for greatness. The Nugget went on to beat Alex Higgins, Terry Griffiths, and Cliff Thorburn just to make it to the final, where he came up against Doug Mountjoy, who was playing the best snooker of his life.

The Welshman couldn't hold on to the Nugget in the early stages and the Plumstead potting machine quickly established a 6-0 lead. Barry Hearn has now got bundles and still looks as fit as a triathlete, but if he had all the money in the world and half a dozen of the top world championship boxers under his umbrella, he will never be as happy or as excited as when the brilliant Steve Davis finally went over the winning line in 1981.

When the Nugget – 22 points in front and leading 17-12 – potted a tricky brown down the cushion, his driver and right-hand man, Robbo, let out a guttural roar and Hearn had his 'Big Fella Thanks' moment.

Davis himself recalled: "Harry was one of my biggest fans in the early days, but it was a few years later when he paid me the ultimate compliment. I'd gone through the first lean spell of my career but felt I'd finally put it behind me and was returning to form. I was coming out of the lift at a hotel in Preston before the first round of the UK Championships, just as Harry was getting in. He bellowed: 'Hello, Nugget. Welcome back to the accumulators.'"

In terms of the winning mentality stakes, Davis, Eric Bristow and Phil 'The Power' Taylor (thanks to Bristow teaching him everything he knew) were light years ahead of anybody else. Stephen Hendry was soon to join the exclusive club before the freakish Tiger Woods arrived on the scene, taking the bar even higher. But it's a very different world we live in now and, in general, it's a much more level playing field.

MARTINA NAVRATILOVA

After my tool shop antics over Martina Navratilova at Wimbledon in 1979, I wasn't totally wiped out when she lost to Chris Evert in the semis the following year (although I thought she was a certainty in-running when a set and a break up) because of her form against Billie Jean King in the quarters. I had a very small bet on Evonne Goolagong at 11/2 in the final, so I won some back.

In 1981, it wasn't Navratilova's defeat to Hana Mandlikova that did the damage, but the final itself. I gave Mandlikova a squeak in the semis, and after beating Martina, I declared her a good thing to beat Evert in the final at 11/10 (I borrowed £200 off Den – the landlord at the Bricklayer's pub – for the bet and made him have £50 on himself) only for her not to take part and lose 6-2, 6-2.

It wasn't long after that when Martina teamed up with Nancy Lieberman, the basketball player, and turned herself into the ultimate, ruthless, crushing machine – the greatest human cash cow of the generation.

Where she came from and who she was, made her very hard to beat in the first place, but at that stage, she was operating on a completely different level. Already the best, she took fitness, mental strength and diet to another dimension. In that white Puma outfit with the sky blue V, matching headband and glasses, I thought she looked like a predator walking on the court, and with her brilliant serve-and-volley game and in decent conditions, I really believed she was unplayable on grass.

From 1982 through to 1987, she was unbeaten at Wimbledon, winning the title six years on the trot, and there wasn't one of them where my chips weren't all-in, including when she beat Steffi Graf in the last of them.

I was potless and living in Brighton before the French Open that year and desperate for a clue on the event when Corals went 10/11 Mats Wilander to beat Boris Becker in the men's semi-final. On clay, I made the Swede more like a 4/11 shot, so this was an emergency (i.e. my mum had to get a loan to fund a major punt). I had £660 on Wilander at 10/11 and a £330 double – Wilander 10/11 and Steffi Graf at evens to win the singles events outright. I travelled to Paris to watch the Becker match and as I arrived on court, Boris had break points for a 5-2 lead in the first set and I nearly shit myself.

Over an hour later, Wilander had won 6-4, 6-2, 6-1, and I was on to my then long-suffering girlfriend Carole telling her to come over for the weekend because I'd managed to get two cheap tickets for the women's final.

I'd managed to blag a press pass for the Pretty Polly women's event at Brighton the previous year and saw for myself Steffi's outrageous forehand that definitely gave her the edge against Martina on clay. What a battle it turned out to be, Graf won 8-6 in the final set. The windy conditions didn't help either player, but on the most crucial points at the end of the match, Martina copped some terrible bad luck with severe gusts in the middle of vital rallies.

She so easily could have won the tournament. As she made her speech after the final in English, and took defeat so well, I was in tears, feeling like Judas Iscariot, as it was the first time I'd ever bet against her and it didn't feel right. As Carol and I walked out of the grounds, and passed Auteuil racecourse, I said to her: "Martina's a fucking certainty for Wimbledon!"

Getting into the Wimbledon grounds wasn't hard in the early '80s, but I can't say I got to see much of Martina on the show courts. I probably watched more of her live when playing doubles with Pam Shriver on the outside courts. I do remember being very impressed with young Zina Garrison in 1982 despite her losing 6-3, 6-2, to Martina in the fourth round. (Wimbledon played so much faster in the old days and I was always on the lookout for solid, aggressive grass-court players). I made all my early money in tennis on players like David Wheaton and Tim Mayotte. Throughout the '80s, I was betting on women's tennis much more than the men's, and that trend certainly continued when Steffi Graf arrived on the scene.

Twenty-five years later, and after a fine lunch, I was heading towards the steam bath at Crown Towers in Melbourne, and coming in the opposite direction, with nobody else in sight or earshot, was none other than the great Martina herself. She was in a businesslike mood, pretty serious, and she was past me in a flash. Even I couldn't work out quickly enough what to say, but I realised this would almost certainly be my one and only chance to get to meet her. She was 30 yards past me when I turned and shouted: "Martina!"

Her face started to turn a darker colour and I'm sure, given half the chance, she'd have hurled me into the adjacent swimming pool. I had about three seconds to work out what to say. "I'm sure you've heard it all before, and it's the last thing you need to hear right now, but I really am your No.1 fan," I told her. I've been with Kay for 20 years and Carole for six before that, neither of them have a jealous bone in their body, but both independently declared that I really do love Martina Navratilova, and they were spot-on.

Martina smiled and was more than gracious with her time and company. I even got to talk to her about the '87 final in Paris. At the end of our conversation, I asked if it would be all right to have a photo taken with her – telling the truth that I'd never asked anyone else the same question. She told me she'd be practising the next day and said: "No problem."

There were no selfies in those days and this was the GOAT of GOATs. I got a proper photographer to take this shot. Martina introduced me to her team. She was at the end of her career (only playing doubles) and they explained that if she spent one hour practising, she needed two hours warming up beforehand and two hours to warm down afterwards. Later in the week, I spent two of those warming down hours with her coach and hitting partner, talking of nothing else other than women's tennis.

Her friend asked me: "What, then, is the best bet you've ever had on women's tennis?" I replied spontaneously: "Andrea Jaeger to beat Billie Jean King, Wimbledon semi-finals 1983 – match odds and straight sets." I couldn't believe how funny she found the answer. She roared with laughter and said: "You're absolutely right, it was the biggest certainty of all time." And Martina beat Jaeger 6-0, 6-3, in the final!

TIGER WOODS

It was Angus Loughran, Statto of TV fame, who first marked my card about Tiger Woods' affection for the Old Course at St Andrews. Tiger made the cut before finishing seven over par in 1995 as the US Amateur Champion, and Angus had followed him around each day and backed him to make the cut, finish top amateur, finish in the top 20, top 50, all kinds of bets, some at real big prices. But at the end of the week, Angus told us all that Tiger was a mortgage job when we all come back in 2000.

I'd had a few quid on him in 1998 at Royal Birkdale, when he finished third without ever threatening to win. His mentor and best pal, Mark O'Meara, was the champion that year. We had a bit more on Tiger at Carnoustie the following year.

HARRY'S REFLECTIONS

Tiger had played there in the Scottish Open in '95 before going on to St Andrews, but I still kept the stakes at a sensible level because I'd spent a lot of time in that area as my mum's family were all from Perth and I was fully aware it was the trickiest course on the Open rota.

For 69 holes, Tiger was tortured. Many golfers leaving Carnoustie that week would have been screaming about the rub of the green, but I can assure you nobody got it worse than Woods. When a chip shot from the back of the green at the 15th went wrong, he bent the club over his knee and had clearly had enough.

It was more than understandable and, like me, he'd already started thinking about St Andrews. The following morning, I had my first lumpy bet on him to win there in 2000.

The fridge freezer at home was covered in Woods tickets, and he warmed up for the millennium bash at the Old Course by winning the US Open at Pebble Beach the previous month by a record 15 shots that effectively made my investment at St Andrews a free bet, so we decided to make a proper week of it.

We hired a lovely big house next to the course and, just like Tiger, we were on the first tee at 5am every morning for his practice round. The only other person I recognised who was always there at each break of dawn was Sir Bruce Forsyth. He was mesmerised by everything Tiger did. I've never met him but I'd bet he is Tiger's biggest fan.

One morning, I was with my old coursing pal from Ireland, Finbar Giltinen, when Tiger's mum, Kultida, was giving out little Tiger badges to loads of kids on the way around. She found Finbar charming and it gave me the perfect opportunity to graft away for a hole and a half. I asked her what was so different about Tiger when he was small. Straight away she said to me: "Pressure, not just in sport, but in everything he does. He revels under pressure. He just loves it."

Everything was going to plan and Tiger went off as the hottest Open favourite ever at between 2/1 and 9/4. I'd been backing him for almost 12 months and, in total, averaged roughly £65,000 at just over 3/1 to win £200,000. Ten minutes before his tee-off time, I was two-thirds of the way down the first hole with my racing binoculars, and from 300 yards, as he was warming up, I could see he was nervous. It's hard to explain but I felt his hesitancy in my bones and it never left me for at least an hour and a half.

I followed him over the first five holes and it was like watching Tommy Bradley play, however Tiger's razor-sharp scrambling ability kept him afloat on all those important opening holes. He played the fourth like a 25-handicap golfer, but still didn't yield to par. I've never seen anything like it, and the scary thing was that even if the hole had been an inch and a half wide, he'd have made every single one.

He teed off on the ninth, the easiest hole in the world of golf, but even there, a poorish drive and an average chip left him with a tricky, slightly downhill, 15-foot putt for birdie. Once again, he made it.

If I ever get the chance to meet Tiger Woods, the first thing I'd say is: "How did you feel when you drove off on the 10th in that first round at St Andrews in 2000?" I already knew what he was thinking: 'Oh my fucking God, I've just walked into the biggest and best jewellers in the world, nicked the finest diamonds from the display case right under their noses, and got away with it scot-free.' I think both of us knew he was going to win.

This was the first year phones weren't allowed on the course, but I had mine and had another £10,000 on (to win £25,000) before he played his second shot to the 10th. He finished five under par and was 11/8 to win the championship.

Anybody who knows the Old Course accepts you have to shoot under par around the loop and, incredibly, when the second and third favourites – Sergio Garcia and Ernie Els – failed to do that in the second round, Tiger's price remained the same. The conditions were perfect. It was bizarre. Even if Tiger shot level par, he still wouldn't be much bigger than 11/8, so this was a once-in-a-lifetime opportunity. I already made him an odds-on shot when I had another £80,000 at 11/8 thinking that, whatever happened, I'd lay some back before he teed off for the third round.

It was a clever and calculated risk, but it paid off in big style when he shot a wonderful 66.

I'd stuck Tony Bloom into the 11/8 on the Friday and told him to get me on as well. I had every intention of hedging some of my position at around 2/9 with him before Tiger teed off in the third round. But when I couldn't get hold of him, I had to stick with my position, which was a total of £155,000 to win nearly £335,000. It was the first time I can ever remember not being able to get hold of Tony on a Saturday.

If Tiger had shot an 80 on the Saturday, I'd have been inconsolable, but like everything else that week, it went my way and he shot another 67. He went into the final round six shots clear, he was 1/25 or 1/20 best price with all the bookies. I rang Tony and offered him £160,000 at 1/16 (£160,000 to win £10,000). He said: 'Yes.' So my position went from risking £155,000 to win £335,000, to winning £5,000 if he lost or £325,000 if he won. It was a pressure-free final round. Tiger shot 69 to win by eight shots and Finbar and I got to see him lift the Claret Jug from a private house patio by the side of the 18th, having also seen Jack Nicklaus say goodbye to St Andrews on the Swilcan Burn a couple of hours before. Happy days.

The following month, Tiger went to the US PGA where he got into a final-round dogfight with his old mate from Orlando, Bob May. I'm sure Mr May has never got over it, and his records since seem to prove it. He torched Tiger from tee to green all day and I still don't know how Tiger managed to force himself into the three-hole play-off he ended up winning by a single stroke. Tiger simply refused to bend the knee and it was another Woods payout for me.

He was in the process of changing my life forever, and it was more of the same only a week later at the NEC Invitational at Firestone Country Club. He played his final shot to the 18th in pitch darkness and hit it to two foot from the cup.

When he arrived at the green, everyone who had a lighter was using them to offer as much brightness as possible, which only added to the atmosphere. The famous US all-sports commentator Jim Nantz was blown away by it all and was almost in tears. I was watching it on my own in the house crying my eyes out and once more counting the cash. Thanks for the memories, Tiger. We all miss you.

AYRTON SENNA

"We don't need myths, we need examples to be followed, examples of courage, determination and hope. We need to believe it is possible to win and it is our duty to pursue it."

I think everybody at some stage of their very young life thinks they might live forever or perhaps the whole world is built around them. Maybe that's why, even in today's so-called technically-savvy world, we still have so many people relying on religion as some kind of emotional crutch, basing the very meaning of life around fairy stories.

For me, immortality was revealed as an absolute myth when Ayrton Senna crashed into the Tamburello at Imola in May 1994. The fact that he did it while holding off a young Michael Schumacher, who was driving a far superior car, made his death even more tragic.

HARRY'S REFLECTIONS

When they towed away his broken Williams car, they found a tightly-folded Austrian flag in the foot recess of the cockpit that he would have unfolded, upon victory, to remember Roland Ratzenberger, who had died on the same circuit two days before.

He told his girlfriend, Adrianne, on the morning of the Grand Prix that he didn't want to race. She'd stayed behind in Portugal and begged him to return, but she was talking to the wrong man. If he'd have withdrawn, or indeed the crash was avoided, both myself and his team boss, Frank Williams, firmly believe, by now, he would have become not only the greatest Formula 1 driver of all time (arguably he is anyway), but ultimately, the President of Brazil.

It's hard to know what made Ayrton so special. I had the advantage through meeting the two lads in Pentonville prison to find out all about him before he hit the big time. There was the first time he sat behind the wheel of a rally car. He was warned to be careful of the first banked bend and twice put the car into the ditch, much to the mirth of onlookers. On his third attempt, he got the bend just right, and a few minutes later had obliterated the course record.

A real beach boy from Sao Paulo, Ayrton hated it when he first came to England, especially because of the relentless cold weather. He had absolutely no experience of racing in the wet and was useless whenever the clouds opened, but he was obsessive about conquering it. Whenever it rained, he was straight out onto the track, and long before he sat in a Formula 1 car, all the faces knew he was impossible to beat when it pissed down.

I loved hearing about when he was caught with a torch in the middle of the night checking on his tyre degradation before a race the next day. Everything he did was underpinned by a ruthlessness I've never seen in another sportsman. Only Tiger Woods comes close, but Senna had something else.

HARRY FINDLAY

My favourite quote regarding who is the best driver in F1 history was by Senna's fellow Brazilian, former housemate and team-mate at Van Diemen, Mauricio Gugelmin. "What I can tell you is that, if you managed to get the 12 greatest drivers of all time to the starting line at Silverstone and gave them each an identical London double-decker bus to drive over a 10-lap race, Ayrton would win every time."

Senna was well-known for his religious beliefs, but they would hardly be considered orthodox. He didn't go to church on Sunday mornings as part of a congregation, only when nobody was there, not even the priest. Just him and God. He really believed that God was with him all the time when he was truly inspired.

All his sensational laps were done when God was right there beside him, guiding him through every twist and turn. I never met Senna but I would have loved the chance to explain to him that, in my opinion, it was all just him all along who really was the God. Physically, mentally, it was all him.

It's patently obvious God had fuck all to do with 40 billion year-old fossils or the thousands of blind deep-sea creatures we didn't even know existed that archaeologists and scientists are currently finding, and I'm just as certain nothing to do with Ayrton's record 65 pole positions and 41 Grand Prix wins.

When former Renault technical director Pat Symonds accused the young Senna of solipsism, I didn't even know what it meant, but after looking it up, I thought he was spot-on. Furthermore, as long as he was driving a racing car, I don't think he ever changed (Alain Prost once quite rightly said Senna had an unfair advantage because his unique relationship with God gave him immunity from danger), but when out of the car, he was a world champion philanthropist and mighty philosopher.

As he said: "I believe we start to see our true personalities when we go through the most difficult moments – this is why we get stronger."